THE JOY OF CRUISING

Passionate Cruisers, Fascinating Stories

PAUL C. THORNTON

The Joy of Cruising: Passionate Cruisers, Fascinating Stories

Paul C. Thornton

ISBN (Print Edition): 978-1-54395-923-9

ISBN (eBook Edition): 978-1-54395-924-6

TABLE OF CONTENTS

DEDICATION

For my wife Cheryl, and my grandchildren Kalen and LaKi.

Any day at sea is better than a day in the office.

—*John Honeywell, aka Captain Greybeard*

ACKNOWLEDGEMENTS

Writing *The Joy of Cruising* was a labor of love. I enjoyed interviewing, reading and writing about, and sharing the stories of passionate cruisers from all over the world. Thank you for enabling me to tell the readers of *The Joy of Cruising* about you: Marcus Adams, Winchester, United Kingdom; Karen Ahr, Fort Myers, Florida; Alonzo Bodden, Los Angeles, California; Danny Bradley, Poole, United Kingdom; Tim Cabral, Fort Lauderdale, Florida; Joe Church, Dover, Pennsylvania; Thomas Eastwood, Estero, Florida; Bronwyn Elsmore, Auckland, New Zealand; Danielle Fear, Newcastle upon Tyne, United Kingdom; Dana Freeman, Burlington, Vermont; Flavia Gray, Surrey, United Kingdom; Sheri Griffiths, Southern California; Elizabeth Hill, Chesterfield, United Kingdom; Matt Hochberg, Orlando, Florida; AJ Jamal, Rancho Cucamonga, California; Mike Jason, Washington, DC; Linda Johnson, Las Vegas, Nevada; Manny Kellough, Washington, DC; Emma Le Teace, West Sussex, United Kingdom; Jason Leppert, San Diego, California; Carole Morgan-Slater and Paul Morgan, Gloucester, United Kingdom; Matt Mramer, Miami, Florida; Bill Raffel, Milwaukee,

Wisconsin; Scott Sanders, Celebration, Florida; Joan and Jim Sloan, Wilmington, Delaware; Barbara Stewart, Fort Myers, Florida; Steve Wallach, Nashville, Tennessee; Mark Weston, Queensland, Australia; Cindy Williams, Augusta, Georgia; Lucy Williams, United Kingdom; Patricia Nicholson Yarbrough, San Francisco, California; and, Jim Zimmerlin, Grover Beach, California.

Thank you to James Abraham, publisher of my first book, who taught me how to be an author; Carolyn Howard-Johnson whose motivating pre-*The Joy of Cruising* writing consultation with me was among my awards for winning the North Street Book Prize for my first book; Jodi Kohn and Alonzo Davis, who are responsible for the gorgeous cover photo taken in Venice, Italy; Dr. Toni Shoemaker, copy editor of *The Joy of Cruising* (punctuation goes inside the quotation mark!); and, Kina Thornton Frazier and Shornay Thornton, my millennial daughters and social media-savvy muses.

The Joy of Cruising

THE JOY OF CRUISING

The Joy of Cruising is about passion. Virtually every traveler who tries cruising for the first time gets hooked on the experience, or at least develops a fervent desire to cruise again as soon as is feasible. After that first cruise or two, a passion often is inflamed and individuals choose to manifest that passion by, of course, cruising more. Sometimes a lot more: like five or ten or fifteen cruises a year; or hundreds of cruises in a lifetime; or cruising to exotic locations; or world cruises for months at a time with stops in dozens of countries. Others live out their passion by starting entrepreneurial ventures related to cruising: creating a cruise blog or YouTube channel; writing cruise-related books; even using cruising to minister to others. *The Joy of Cruising* examines passionate cruisers and the fascinating ways people pursue their passion.

* * * * *

I traveled on my first cruise vacation thirty years ago. I was intrigued by the idea of a cruise for a somewhat superficial reason: I had done a fair amount of vacation traveling to Bermuda, the

Bahamas and the Caribbean, and had become enamored of the concept of "all-inclusive" vacation resorts, where for a fixed price vacationers' lodging, meals, alcoholic drinks, entertainment, activities, and even cigarettes (hey, it was the eighties) were included. My first visit to an all-inclusive was to a resort in Jamaica that was called, aptly, "Hedonism". With youthful exuberance, less maturity, and lack of self-control that comes with being in my twenties, I approached that first all-inclusive stay with the same rationale I approached all-you-can-eat buffets back at home: "they're going to lose money on me!" I partook in it all, indulging to excess in everything that was available, especially liquor (screwdrivers with my eggs and bacon at breakfast). It was on that first all-inclusive vacation that I cultivated my taste for cognac—even if it was not exactly top shelf. Up to then, the concept of an after dinner cordial was foreign to me. My rationalization of getting my money's worth veered into stupidity. For instance, even though I had kicked the smoking habit several years prior to that vacation, I could not resist the saucer of complimentary cigarettes that adorned each of the bars at Hedonism. Convinced that I could indulge for just the week I was there, I ended up re-starting the smoking habit again for another several years.

Cruise ships promised many of the same amenities of all-inclusive vacations, at least the food, activities and entertainment part, with the added benefit of being able to visit more than one destination. Despite cruises having obvious appeal, I had demurred. For one thing, I just was not a "water person." In my boyhood in Brooklyn, NY, the closest I got to the ocean was occasional visits to iconic Coney Island. I never learned how to swim; my only opportunities to visit a swimming pool in my youth were when my summer day camp occasionally took field trips to the Department of Parks and Recreation McCarren Pool. Furthermore, I was apprehensive about an unknown: the possibility that me or my companion would experience seasickness that would ruin our vacation. Nevertheless, I was intrigued by these floating all-inclusive resorts.

In 1988, Royal Caribbean launched *Sovereign of the Seas*, then the world's largest cruise ship at over 73,000 gross tons. It was 12% larger than the then cruise ship size champ, the *Queen Elizabeth 2*, and almost 60% larger than the *Titanic*. Its scale was so unimaginable that a May 1987 article in the Chicago Tribune exclaimed that "it is doubtful any larger cruise ship will be built in the near future." The article was sort of correct; depends on how "near future" is defined. In 1995 Princess Cruises launched the larger *Sun Princess,* the setting for *The Love Boat: The Next Wave,* a revival of the iconic *The Love Boat* television series that ran from 1977-1986.

Sovereign of the Seas promised as many, or more than, the amenities of the most luxurious all-inclusive resorts. The floating city boasted 14 decks traversed by glass-encased elevators, a high-end shopping mall, the largest casino at sea, night clubs and lounges, spa, and numerous photo-friendly vantage points. A stunning atrium soared five stories and surrounded tropical plants, a splashing fountain, more glass-enclosed elevators and a sweeping staircase.

My cruise on *Sovereign of the Seas* was my first "real" date, well, the first time traveling together, with my then girlfriend Cheryl. Besides the obvious sentimental value I hold for that cruise—Cheryl is now my wife of 26 years—my recollection of that voyage is that it was magical. Amazing, grandiose midnight buffets with ornate ice and butter carvings, formal nights where everyone dressed to impress (both now forgone cruising traditions), a grand atrium unlike any cruise venue seen before according to veteran cruise mates on that voyage with us, and all the other amenities and trappings of a new, state-of-the-art vessel easily convinced me that cruising was something that I wanted to do more of.

In 1988, the first time traveling with my future wife Cheryl, on the revolutionary new mega-ship, *Sovereign of the Seas.*

In the ensuing years, Cheryl and I cruised on Carnival, Disney, Norwegian, and Celebrity Cruise Lines. Christmas 2018 we returned to Royal Caribbean after almost 30 years, taking our two daughters, son-in-law, and two grandchildren on a cruise on the *Anthem of the Seas.* At 170,000 gross tons, *Anthem* was a ship that the one-time world's largest cruise ship *Sovereign of the Seas* could fit inside of with plenty room to spare.

There was not much in the way of consumer-oriented internet sites in the eighties where you could do extensive research on a major consumer purchase such as a cruise. Brick-and-mortar travel agencies were the primary means for potential cruisers to get informed about destinations, cruise-lines and individual ships, and then book the cruise. In the years that followed, each time my family cruised, I was able to take advantage of a plethora of ever-increasing online resources for researching and booking it online. For an information junkie like myself this was much more convenient, efficient, and satisfying than collecting brochures from a travel agency, taking them home to look over, returning to the agency to ask questions of the agent, then going home and summarizing the discussion with my wife, and then finally going back to the agent to book the cruise.

When online travel websites started to proliferate, initially they were one-way information sources; then gradually along came discussion forums, blogs, podcasts, YouTube, Facebook, and Twitter. As these information sources became increasingly social and interactive, it became clear to me just how passionate a sizable and growing segment of travelers were about cruising. The more I browsed discussion forums, watched videos, and listened to podcasts, the more I realized that I was not just satisfying my own information needs as a prospective consumer of cruise travel; I was becoming intrigued about the passion that I sensed many cruisers possessed about their avocation.

There are passionate fans of many other pastimes and hobbies. I just don't notice or pay any attention to them because they are not front and center in my consciousness. Cruising is. It is not unusual to hear words like "addictive" to describe cruising, even after just one cruise. I thoroughly enjoy cruising. While I am nowhere near what would be considered an avid cruiser—although I'd like to be—I do cruise with my grandkids on a fairly regular basis (once or twice a year for the past several years), which means I conduct a lot of consumer research on cruising. The more I browse, the more I find myself living vicariously through the more seasoned cruisers I read about. The passion portrayed through the words of many of these seasoned cruisers fascinates me. I envy these cruisers and wish that I could live their life. Like the couple I read about that has averaged sixteen cruises per year for the last several years. Or cruisers who sail on months-long cruises with as many as fifty ports of call. Consequently, I want to learn more about the cruisers through whom I live vicariously.

I found that as I visited various discussion forums and blogs, I was motivated as much by learning about other cruisers as I was about gleaning insights about what ever cruise ship I had booked or was considering booking. The most highly trafficked cruise site on the web, Cruise Critic, became for me a multiple-times-daily destination, and the time I was spending on the discussion board gradually became focused as much on reading about the exploits of other cruisers and their passion for cruising. I recall a discussion pertaining to a question regarding the frequency with which individuals cruise. I found some of the comments to be simply amazing. Sure, I expected to read about people who were retired and thus able to cruise regularly over a sustained period of time. However, I did not anticipate reading about just how prolific cruisers were. They would make comments like they "went on four, or five, or six cruises in the past year," and that they planned to cruise more "after they retire!"

At the same time, I noticed a different phenomenon, particularly on Facebook cruise groups and in comments accompanying YouTube videos; there was a relatively high number of group participants and commenters who admitted to having never been on a cruise. Yet, they participated vigorously, inquisitive about the particulars of cruising and awe-struck and appreciative of informative and fun videos on YouTube, especially those with high production values, which offered information without having something to sell, like the fun, informative videos offered by Jim Zimmerlin, a leading YouTube vlogger profiled in Chapter 3. That suggests to me that cruising is viewed as aspirational. Just as I viewed cruising vicariously through those passionate cruisers alluded to earlier, I suspect many of those who had never cruised before viewed cruising vicariously through the eyes of those who had.

* * * * *

I once worked in the corporate world for a boss who often repeated a refrain in meetings: "What would a person have to think and believe to do the things they do?" Out of earshot the staff wondered if the saying was from the military—he was a US Naval Academy graduate and tended to act and see things in ways heavily influenced by his background. He was very stern and did not suffer fools. None of us on his staff knew precisely what the phrase meant, and all were too intimidated to ask. I interpreted it as he was saying to understand behavior it is important to consider motivation. Or something like that. Though a long time ago, that phrase stuck with me over the years. When someone does something I find perplexing, intriguing, curious, or fascinating, I find myself asking, "What would someone have to think and believe to do that?" Not in a disparaging way; just an inquisitive way.

The more I learned about how others pursued their passion for cruising, I kept thinking about "What would a person have to think and believe to do the things they do." What motivates someone to average a cruise per month. Or cruise on a voyage lasting 180 days. Or cruise for the first time on their 18th birthday, and then despite working in a modest position, cruise another dozen times by their mid–twenties. Or sail on a *Star Trek* themed cruise. Maybe it's just because they can. I would like to think it is more than that, especially given that individuals act on their passion for cruising in so many diverse ways, and not all require substantial resources. What motivates cruisers? Obviously there is no single answer to that question. Whatever it is that motivates them, travelers are becoming increasingly motivated according to numerous metrics and indicators. Cruising is up across the board. The race for cruise lines to introduce bigger and more technically advanced ships continues unabated. More cruise lines are offering extended sailings. Theme and specialty cruises are available to cater to every taste, hobby, lifestyle, and affinity group, and regularly sell out.

The Joy of Cruising is for those current and prospective cruisers who are interested in reading about the fascinating stories that illustrate the passion of other cruisers. *The Joy of Cruising* is not just about individuals who cruise far more than the typical cruiser. Sure, there is some of that; a woman with several hundred cruises; a 34-year old who has cruised 138 times; a couple who cruised 21 times last year. However, a couple of passionate cruisers profiled in *The Joy of Cruising* had neither cruised, nor even considered it when the story behind their first cruise made them worthy of fascination. One of those stories, chronicled in Chapter 4, The Godmother: Elizabeth Hill, is a modern day fairy tale. *The Joy of Cruising* is not cruise-line specific, nor an industry overview, cruising guide or how-to, exposé, or behind-the-scenes look at cruising. *The Joy of Cruising* is a positive examination of why cruisers do the wonderful things they do in the pursuit of their passion.

MARATHONER OF THE SEAS: JOE CHURCH

This sounds like a profile of one of those prolific cruise travelers that many look at with a blend of awe, intrigue, and wonderment. Those cruise travelers I have read about on internet discussion forums who sail multiple cruises every year, or on itineraries that keep them away from home for as much as over 100 days at a time. Or even more prolific cruisers, like Mario Salcedo, the financial executive who walked away from the corporate milieu in his forties and has sailed on a series of back-to-back-to-back seven-day cruises ever since. Super Mario, as he is affectionately known by cruise line staff, is now in his sixties and rarely returns to the home he maintains in Miami. Or "Mama Lee" Wachtstetter, who sold her home after her husband died—with whom she had cruised almost 90 times—and took up permanent residence on Crystal Cruise Line's luxurious ship *Serenity* and has been cruising nonstop for the past 12 years.

Yes, you could say Joe Church is a marathon cruiser. Not in the same sense as Super Mario or Mama Lee though. Joe Church is literally a marathon cruiser; he runs marathon distances, 26.2 miles, on the running track that is a fixture on virtually every large cruise ship. In fact, Joe Church has run a marathon distance on each one of the 28 ships in the Royal Caribbean fleet, most recently the June 3 sailing from Barcelona, Spain on Royal Caribbean's newest ship, *Symphony of the Seas*, launched April 2018 as the world's largest cruise ship.

Joe running the marathon distance on *Symphony of the Seas*

Joe has been a passionate runner for a long time. His passion for cruising, on the other hand, developed much later, and initially quite reluctantly. Before running or cruising became significant to Joe's life, he was passionate about a pastime altogether different and far-removed from either the track or the ocean. Joe was an avid bird watcher. To pursue his birding passion Joe traveled on a number of bird-watching excursions not far from his home in Harrisburg, PA.

In 2001, having recently become empty nesters after their son left home for college, Joe and his late wife Eileen decided to do some of the traveling they had often mused about. Joe embarked on a birding foray to the Andes Mountains in Ecuador for the breathtaking landscapes offered by Cotopaxi Volcano. Joe did this particular trip solo as Eileen did not share his passion for bird watching. When he returned, he confided a confession to Eileen. Joe noted that during the trip he found that he was so out of shape and overweight that in the thin air at 14,000 feet elevation on the side of Cotopaxi, he could barely participate with the rest of his tour group in the search for birds. Upon sharing that story with Eileen, Joe resolved to get in shape and stop leading a sedentary lifestyle. The six foot, 205-pound Joe joined a gym and took up exercising. Not too long after Joe took up exercising, Eileen was diagnosed with breast cancer. She joined Joe exercising, and they both began eating healthier.

In the ensuing years Joe became bored with just exercising and started running. By 2005, now down to 160 pounds, Joe ran his first marathon and a new passion for long distance running was born. Just as he traveled to pursue his bird watching passion, Joe traveled as part of his new passion, first visiting different states to run marathons and then establishing a goal to run a marathon in all fifty states. Eileen had also started running and sometimes traveled with Joe on his running trips; other times Eileen would leave Joe at home and join her siblings who liked to travel on cruise ships. Eileen sailed on three cruises without Joe, and of course she would rave to Joe about the wonders of cruising after each one. Eileen pointed out to Joe that each ship she had cruised on had a running track, so he would not have to miss his running if he joined her on a cruise. Joe reluctantly agreed to accompany Eileen if she acquiesced to one condition: on the first night of the sailing, he would get out of bed shortly after midnight and run the 26.2-mile marathon distance before the deck became populated with sunbathers, lounge chairs were moved into positions that can obstruct runners, and the running track became congested with casual walkers and joggers. Eileen was elated, and in January 2008, Eileen, Joe and some family members embarked on Joe's first cruise, sailing Royal Caribbean *Liberty of the Seas* from Miami for a Western Caribbean cruise.

Late on the night of embarkation, Joe changed into his running gear, quietly so as to not disturb a sleeping Eileen, and at around 1:30 in the morning he went up to Deck 12 to the running track. Not that long prior the sports deck had been busy with first night cruisers milling about or lounging and enjoying the views of the ocean. Now chairs were strewn about with empty glasses and bottles sitting beside them, and the deck was stained where drinks had been spilled. The reddish-brown tinted, lightly padded, almost one-quarter mile running track circled the perimeter of the deck and offered exquisite ocean views—when the sun came up. Joe was not up there for the view.

Although the track consisted of two lanes, one for walking and one for running, for the first couple of hours of his run Joe had the entire 6-foot wide track to himself. There were plenty of revelers still partying in the wee hours of the morning elsewhere on *Liberty of the Seas* but the sports deck was deserted. However, well before sunrise Joe found that he no longer was the sole presence on the deck. Some of the 8-10 interlopers flashed a thumbs up sign to Joe as he continuously circled the track in the darkness. They were Royal Caribbean staff who had arrived to wash down the deck and prepare it for the swarm of sunbathers, mini golf players, and walkers and joggers who would overrun the sports deck once the sun came up. Joe kept running laps and the crew fastidiously went about their business. During the course of his runs, on *Liberty* and subsequent ships, it became apparent to Joe that most cruisers never see the deck crew that keeps the outside of the ship in good order. They hosed down the deck, cleaned the glass surfaces, and removed the evidence of the previous hours' revelry. For the most part they put up with Joe running around in circles, hopping over their hoses. Joe and the deck-swabbing crews sort of co-existed, with the crews ensuring that they aimed their hoses away from Joe's direction. Most of the time....

Before dawn Eileen came up to Deck 12 and joined Joe for a few laps around the track. When Eileen knew Joe was approaching the end of the 26.2 miles, she decided to leave the track to go find some coffee for them to celebrate. Exactly four-and-a-half hours after stepping foot on the track in the darkness, Joe had finished his first cruise ship marathon-distance run. Joe had circled the track for 118 laps, and the "marathoner of the seas" legend was born. The sun had not yet risen.

For the remainder of the cruise Joe experienced all of the other aspects of cruising that had caused Eileen to rave following each of her previous cruises. In addition, Joe got in some bird-watching both at sea and especially in the ports where the *Liberty* stopped: Labadee, Haiti; Montego Bay, Jamaica; George Town, Grand Cayman; and Cozumel, Mexico. The cruise enabled Joe to spot several new birds to add to his list of sightings.

Reflecting on that first experience on *Liberty of the Seas*—running, bird-watching and cruising—it was an easy call when Eileen tried to convince Joe to accompany her on subsequent cruises. As with most after their first cruise, Joe was hooked. Consequently, Eileen didn't really have to do much convincing at all to get Joe to sign up as long as it was with the understanding that at some point on the cruise Joe would run the marathon distance.

Typically, Joe ran around the same time as he did on that first marathon length run on the *Liberty*, starting around one in the morning. Joe was able to enjoy the solitude of each ship's sports deck for a couple of hours until the deck swabbing crew arrived. At least most of the time; there were occasionally exceptions. On one ship, the sports deck running track overlooked the pool deck and the hot tubs, and when Joe started his run several couples were sitting in one of the hot tubs. At first the group in the hot tub ignored Joe and for over an hour he ran in the dark with the solitude he was used to from previous cruises. When Joe passed above the hot tub after about the twentieth time, the folks in the hot tub yelled up to Joe and asked how much farther he intended to go. Joe yelled back that he had about 60 laps to go. For the next three hours Joe had a cheering section; the group remained in the hot tub and counted down the laps left each time Joe passed above them. When he finished the last lap they all jumped up and down and cheered as if he had won the New York City Marathon! After conveying their congratulations, the cheering section wandered off presumably to bed as the sun was starting to peak through and early-rising cruisers were starting to amble on to the sports deck. For the rest of the cruise, whenever they saw him, they treated Joe like a celebrity athlete, offering him high fives and fist bumps. At this point in his cruising career, Joe was only three cruises towards his accomplishment of a marathon-length run on the entire Royal Caribbean fleet; little did they know that Joe would become an actual celebrity athlete.

That wasn't the only time Joe garnered his own personal cheering section. On one cruise, when Joe arrived on the sports deck early one morning to start his marathon–length run he was surprised to find there were still many guests milling around. They were mostly young girls—on a high school trip from Colombia—all in formal wear. Immediately after stepping foot on the sports deck Joe turned around; he decided to return to his stateroom with the intention to conduct his run on another night. But before he could get away, one of the students was curious as to why Joe was in running clothes at one-something in the morning. She laughed when Joe told her he had intended to run until sunrise. Joe assured her he was not joking. The young lady told some of her friends and quickly the word spread. Then one of the group yelled out to Joe, "Well then you better get started." So Joe stuck to his original plan and did his run, even though the track was overrun with young partiers. Each time Joe would come around to where the crowd was congregated they would be sure to part ways so that he could run unabated. As the hours wound down, the crowd thinned out, but a few were still present when the sun came out and they got to see Joe finish.

After several cruises, Joe began to entertain the notion of running a marathon-distance on all of the Royal Caribbean ships. Such an audacious goal was not uncharacteristic for Joe. After all, before he caught the cruise bug, he was on his way to running a marathon in every state. So, he and Eileen began planning Royal Caribbean cruises, especially paying attention to ship locations and ports of call—as that would influence what birds might be in the area that Joe could add to his sighting list. Joe lined up local bird guides in some of the ports; not only did he get his runs in, Joe saw many of the birds that are endemic to the Caribbean and Central America. How wonderful it must be to be able to meld multiple passions!

In the first four years of Joe joining Eileen to cruise on Royal Caribbean, they cruised eight times. Joe logged many more than the 210 miles resulting from running a marathon distance on those eight Royal Caribbean running tracks. He did not limit himself to only running the 26.2 miles on each cruise, usually choosing to run at least a few other mornings. Most of those eight cruises were in the Caribbean and the Bahamas. One of them, however, was an Alaskan cruise.

Joe, Eileen and their son Mike flew to Anchorage. Prior to embarking on the *Radiance of the Seas* they spent a week visiting Denali before taking the train to Seward to board the southbound cruise. During that pre-cruise week, they each ran in a local marathon, Joe the full 26.2-mile distance, while Eileen and Mike ran a half-marathon.

As opposed to Caribbean cruising, an Alaskan cruise definitely presented some physical challenges for Joe's cruise ship marathon-distance running. When Joe arrived in the middle of the night on the *Radiance* sports deck, the temperature was 38 degrees. There was a 25 knot headwind and the ship was moving at 19 knots; the apparent winds, that is, the wind speed given the moving ship that Joe had to run against was up to 50 miles per hour. And, analogous to when local television weather people used wind chill factor to inform viewers of what outside temperature feels like when the temperature is coupled with wind speed, it felt much, much colder to Joe than 38 degrees. So, despite the splendor of an Alaskan cruise, the running aspect of the *Radiance of the Seas* cruise was by far the most challenging of any of the cruises Joe had taken to-date, and would take subsequently. Joe was whipped around by the winds. As he headed to the bow, or front end of the ship, his paced slowed to almost a crawl on each lap; but as soon as he turned the corner at the bow, the wind whipped him back so fast he had to be careful to maintain his balance. To make matters worse, a couple of hours into the run, a stinging rain mixed with sleet began to pelt Joe. His long-sleeved running shirt and warm-up pants quickly became soaked, and he was freezing. He was undaunted though and the elements made him even more determined to finish this challenge. When Joe completed the run, most of his body looked like he had intense sunburn; Joe described his chest as looking similar to a piece of raw meat. Joe's marathon-distance run on *Radiance* took five-and-a-half hours, the slowest run of any of his 28 Royal Caribbean cruise ship runs.

In early 2012, not long before the Alaska cruise, Eileen, who had beaten breast cancer, was diagnosed with lung cancer. Joe and Eileen were able to go on two cruises that year, but by the end of 2012 Eileen's health began to rapidly deteriorate. Sadly, Eileen passed away in February 2013.

After Eileen passed away, Joe decided that he would participate in the local American Cancer Society's Relay for Life and run for either the full 24 hours or 100 miles, whichever came first. While in training for the Relay for Life run, Joe had a cruise scheduled for the *Jewel of the Seas*. As part of his training, he ran for 40 miles on Jewel. That is the longest single run Joe has done onboard a cruise ship.

Without Eileen, and Mike married and out on his own, Joe was what he described as "at loose ends." He had retired from his career as a financial executive at a Pennsylvania state agency when Eileen became ill. So, alone and unbound from the constraints of a career, there was nothing keeping Joe tied down. Joe plunged headlong into his avocations. He began planning trips to bird watch, run and cruise in rapid succession. Joe cruised twenty times in the ensuing three years. In 2016, he sailed and ran marathon distances on an amazing eight cruises. By the end of 2016, he had run 26.2 miles on nearly the entire Royal Caribbean fleet. Most were Caribbean cruises but there were some notable exceptions. As one of the largest cruise lines in the world, Royal Caribbean International itineraries cover much of the globe. Joe sailed on a transatlantic cruise on *Brilliance of the Seas* where he experienced a storm that included 30 foot waves breaking as high as deck five. Fortunately, he had run a couple of days prior to the storm, so it had no impact on his marathon-distance goal.

On another cruise, *Legend of the Seas* from Quebec to Florida, the winds and seas were such that the ship's Captain shut down the running track for the first couple of days, disrupting Joe's routine of doing his run on the first night of the cruise. One of the cruise ports of call was in Boston. The weather had calmed by the time *Legend of the Seas* docked in Boston. Instead of running in the middle of the night, while most of the passengers were touring Boston, Joe went up to the sports deck and ran his 26.2 miles. As best as can be determined, Joe is the only person who has run both the Boston Marathon and a Boston Harbor "marathon" on a cruise ship.

While the aforementioned *Radiance of the Seas* Alaska cruise may have been the most physically demanding one Joe encountered on the way to completing his amazing feat, it doesn't compare in terms of the most difficult cruises to arrange from a logistical standpoint. The trip that was the most complex for Joe to arrange to conduct his runs involved cruises on Royal Caribbean's *Mariner of the Seas*, and *Voyager of the Seas*. *Mariner* was sailing out of Singapore and *Voyager* out of Sydney. At the time, Joe was also trying to accomplish another goal—which he has now completed—of running an official marathon, that is, one with a race director, timer, etc., on all seven continents, and he needed to find a marathon in Australia, and in Asia. In addition, Joe wanted to combine this with some bird watching in Australia since they have so many endemic species. So the complex itinerary that Joe arranged involved first flying to Melbourne, Australia to run an official marathon there. Then Joe spent three weeks with a bird watching tour that covered pretty much all of the east coast of Australia. Then he flew to Singapore, where he boarded *Mariner* and completed his marathon-distance run on the cruise along the Malaysia Peninsula. In addition to his marathon-distance run, Joe also ran shorter distances most mornings on *Mariner*. On one early morning run, in the darkness, Joe observed a bird fluttering on deck. It was difficult to get a good look in the darkness so he returned to his stateroom and got his camera. Joe was able to get a few pictures of the bird before it flew off. It was a Gray-legged Rail. Rails in general are difficult to find because they skulk around in marshes, swamps and reed beds. This one happened to be migrating south and decided it would rather do it by cruising than by flying! After disembarking from *Mariner*, Joe flew from Singapore to Myanmar to run his official Asian marathon. He spent a week touring Myanmar and then flew back to Sydney and boarded *Voyager of the Seas*. *Voyager* was a 13-night cruise with ports of call in New Zealand, Vanuatu and New Caledonia. Joe's grand, multi-continent, multi-cruise ship, multi-marathon excursion took him away from home for two and a half months and got him that much closer to his dual goals of an official marathon on every continent and a marathon-length run on every Royal Caribbean ship. Passion!

This Gray-legged Rail decided to migrate south via cruise ship instead of flying!

Only on a couple of occasions did the deck-cleaning crew try to deter Joe and suggest that for safety reasons it would be better if he stopped while they cleaned. In those instances, Joe came up with a solution to the problem that was acceptable to the crew chief and allowed him to keep running. He negotiated with them—all while still running—that they clean the port side while Joe ran from stem to stern on the starboard side and turn around and run back, and when they finished the port side, reverse the process. On only one of Joe's 28 runs on Royal Caribbean ships was he directed by the crew to stop until they were finished. Joe obliged them, but stopping in the middle and then re-starting was not exactly an easy thing to do for a long distance runner. On most cruises Joe's interaction with the crew was uneventful, and they were oblivious to what Joe was doing and why. Often, later during the day as he walked about, crew members who had seen him running would come up to him and ask him how far and how long had he run. They knew that having seen Joe circling the deck for two hours or more that it wasn't a short run, but they weren't prepared to hear 26.2 miles!

Despite Joe's amazing feat and inspirational story, he for the most part maintained a low profile throughout the pursuit of his cruising goal. Joe didn't tell anybody other than family and a few running friends that he was attempting to run 26.2 miles on all the ships in Royal Caribbean's fleet. That included not sharing advance information with Royal Caribbean corporate administration nor the leadership staff of individual cruise ships. Early morning deck-swabbing staff who saw Joe running was Joe's only exposure to the ship's crew but they knew nothing about the background behind the lonely figure running in the dark. Joe always assumed no one from Royal Caribbean knew…until the *Quantum of the Seas*. *Quantum* was launched in 2014, and in November 2014, after *Quantum* was christened by ship Godmother, actress Kristin Chenoweth, Joe went on a two-night preview cruise principally for travel agents and media. Joe boarded and took a seat in the Two70 lounge, taking in a 270-degree view of the sights of the New York Harbor through the floor to ceiling windows while awaiting the muster drill. A man whom Joe did not recognize walked up to Joe and asked "Are you the guy who is running a marathon on all the Royal Caribbean ships?" Joe, taken aback stated that he was (and that included *Quantum*; even on this short cruise Joe was going to get his run in.) The man introduced himself and told Joe he had heard about him, and Joe's story had given him a brainstorm: the individual's name was Sean Tolkin, who after hearing about Joe decided he would run a marathon to raise funds for the Make-a-Wish-Foundation. Sean Tolkin raised $50,000 for Make-A-Wish by running a full marathon onboard the *Norwegian Breakaway*. It turns out that Sean Tolkin's family owned a large worldwide travel agency network and his family were friends with the top management of Royal Caribbean, and it was Royal Caribbean that had told him about Joe. Joe had no clue that Royal Caribbean leadership knew who he was.

Most of the time when Joe was finishing up one of his cruise ship runs it was around dawn and other cruisers were starting to make their way onto the sports deck to run, walk, do sunrise yoga or to just drink a cup of coffee and take in the majestic sight of the sun peaking out and then rising over the ocean. As Joe typically looked pretty worn by that time he was often asked by someone how long he had been running. When he replied all night, he was often met with a mix of awe, disbelief, and pity. But some of the inquirers or other cruisers who heard Joe's response were runners and would occasionally join Joe for a few laps and in some cases until he finished. In the ensuing days during the cruise when Joe would go for a run, his new "running buddies" would join him, wanting to hear more about his shipboard running story. On the other hand, there were times when Joe would go for a short run during the day when people were sunbathing or lounging near the running track and some would yell things like "hey man, you are on vacation, you should be having a good time!" Of course Joe's ready response was, "That is exactly what I'm doing!" One guy yelled "Stop that!" On the next lap he yelled again, "Stop that, you are making me look bad!" That evening he saw Joe in the cruise ship Promenade and bought him a beer.

After Eileen passed away, Joe mostly cruised by himself. For his last several cruises he was accompanied by a woman he had met who was a running friend of Eileen's, Marie Clark, to whom Joe is now engaged. Marie accompanied Joe on his next to the last Royal Caribbean cruise he took in December 2016 on *Rhapsody of the Seas*. Prior to the cruise, Joe posted on a Royal Caribbean Facebook page that he was going to run a marathon distance on his 27th Royal ship. A few people responded to the post that they were going to be onboard the same cruise, and some came to the running deck to watch him run his last several laps.

Joe and Marie on *Symphony of the Seas*

One couple, Samantha and Jesse Worthley, whom Marie and Joe did not previously know, and who watched Joe's last few laps, were renewing their wedding vows onboard *Rhapsody* and asked Marie and Joe to be their witnesses. Later, the Worthleys had dinner with the ship Captain and they told the Captain about Joe's running on the 27 Royal Caribbean ships. At the *Rhapsody's* Crown and Anchor Society reception (part of Royal Caribbean's customer loyalty program) the Captain called Joe out. The Captain stated, "As far as I know there are only two people on board who have sailed on all 27 Royal Caribbean ships." He noted that he was one of them, and that only one of the two had run a marathon on all of the 27 ships and that it wasn't him! Later, near the end of the cruise, in the grand Centrum, Joe was recognized by the Captain in front of hundreds of admiring fellow cruisers.

In April 2018, Royal Caribbean launched the largest ship in the world, an 18-deck, 19 restaurants, multiple pool, ice skating rink and water park floating city called the *Symphony of the Seas*. Joe had completed marathon-length runs on all the other 27 Royal Caribbean ships. *Symphony* was slightly larger than its sister ships—*Oasis of the Seas, Allure of the Seas,* and *Harmony of the Seas*—members of Royal's Oasis-class of ships. Joe particularly like running on the Oasis-class ships; they had a dedicated running track on the 5th deck separate from the higher sports deck. There aren't any sunbathers or cruisers walking aimlessly with food in their hands from the buffet, so Joe could run on those Oasis-class ships during daylight rather than just in the middle of the night. Furthermore, given the Oasis-class ships' gargantuan size, the running track was twice as long as on other ships. Joe could cover the marathon distance in 63 laps. (Conversely, despite being launched in 2006 as the then largest ship in the word, Royal Caribbean's *Freedom of the Seas* required 262 laps to reach 26.2 miles.)

Joe boarded *Symphony of the Seas* in Barcelona, Spain June 3, 2018 for a Mediterranean cruise. His marathon-distance run was scheduled for Friday, June 8. Shortly after walking into my house that morning still laboring from my approximately one-mile brisk morning walk through the neighborhood, my phone dinged with a message. It was Joe letting me know he had finished his own brisk 26.2-mile jaunt!

I asked Joe if he felt any special sentiments given that his run on *Symphony* completed his goal—for now, since he is out of Royal Caribbean ships. In his unassuming way Joe replied; "I think the one thing that was special was this was my first cruise since I had a series of heart attacks between my last cruise and this one." After I picked myself up off the floor, I thought to myself, you are kidding right? Of course, I knew that was not something to kid about, but Joe was so matter-of-fact about it, I was flabbergasted. It turns out that on December 21, 2017 Joe suffered four heart attacks. His doctors told him that because of the physical shape he was in he was able to revive himself twice prior to getting to the hospital where he had two more heart attacks. The following morning doctors performed triple bypass surgery on Joe. During convalescence Joe asked the surgeon and the cardiologist if he would be okay to run the Tokyo Marathon on Feb 25, 2018. Priorities! At his four-week check-up they gave Joe the go-ahead. So 66 days after surgery, and coincidently on Joe's 66th birthday, he ran/walked the Tokyo Marathon. (He is now up to having completed marathons in 33 countries.) 160 days post-surgery, Joe ran the marathon-distance on *Symphony of the Seas*.

In total Joe has logged over 1300 miles on the 28 ships…and counting. In 2019, Royal Caribbean will inaugurate the *Spectrum of the Seas,* and an as yet unnamed ship in 2020, both slightly smaller than *Symphony of the Seas,* and in 2021 will launch a ship that will surpass *Symphony* as the largest ship in the world. Joe and Marie Clark are already booked for *Spectrum's* inaugural voyage in December 2019 out of Shanghai. Joe intends to continue running on the Royal Caribbean ships as they come out as long as he is capable of running 26.2 miles.

I am a strong believer in the power of passion. I am convinced that it helped save my life and I have previously written a book about that. Joe Church has been able to incredibly combine the pursuit of three passions: birding, running, and cruising. I suspect passion contributed to saving his life as well. To say that I envy Joe is an understatement. Perhaps a more apropos title of this chapter, instead of Marathoner of the Seas, is "Joe Church: The Luckiest Man Alive".

JIM ZIM

My immediate reaction centered on the voice. Soothing, mellifluous. It brought to mind an eighties FM progressive rock, adult contemporary vibe. I was almost expecting Steely Dan or Boz Scaggs to start playing. In retrospect, my visceral reaction upon experiencing my first Jim Zimmerlin video pretty much nailed it. It turns out "Jim Zim," a journalism major from California Polytechnic University in San Luis Obispo, started working as an announcer at a radio station straight out of college, subsequently rising thru the ranks at several stations—yes, adult contemporary stations playing music such as James Taylor, Elton John, The Eagles, John Denver and the like—for a number of years and culminating in a radio station Program Director position.

Then came the disarming demeanor. Watching Jim Zim's YouTube channel on the big screen in my family room, it felt like he was sitting there in the room with me narrating what was on the screen. Listening to him was almost as if Jim was having a conversation with viewers rather than talking at them. I don't know much about stagecraft and production values in videography, but I know enough to recognize quality when I see it. What I do know is that—even though I initially searched only for a video by Jim pertaining to a particular cruise ship I had booked—I immediately subscribed to Jim's channel and proceeded to view every one of his cruise videos, despite the fact they included several ships that I am confident I will never board.

Jim Zim, as he is known to his legion of followers, is one of the top cruise video bloggers, or vloggers, on YouTube. Jim also has a slew of model train videos on his channel as well as videos about cocker spaniels from when he and his wife Kellyn spent 15 years breeding American Cocker Spaniels. Yes, he's another one of those fortunate individuals with several passions.

The voice, the easy going pace, great production values, and the thoughtful, in-depth, reflective commentary of Jim Zim's videos have contributed to Jim becoming one of the top cruise video channels on YouTube. His channel has over 205,000 subscribers, is comprised of almost 375 videos, and has garnered 200 million views including one—the Green Thunder waterslide onboard the *Carnival Spirit*—with nearly 100 million views.

I discovered Jim's YouTube channel somewhat by accident. Researching, or fantasizing, depending on how you look at it, in anticipation of my family's holiday 2018 cruise on Royal Caribbean *Anthem of the Seas*, I read dozens of reviews, articles, and blog posts from professional cruise writers as well as fellow cruisers. I admit it: I have no life! After awhile there was little new I could glean from my reading, but I just couldn't get enough. I'm sure that besides being an information junkie, I was sub-consciously looking to assuage the "cognitive dissonance" many of us feel after a major purchase. After reading *Anthem of the Seas* review number 100, or something like that, I came across Jim Zim's print review of *Anthem*. I say print review, however, there were so many great images and videos that it was more like a glossy brochure. I was captivated by the first two sentences of the review: "We did a 12-day Caribbean cruise on *Anthem of the Seas*, the latest ship in Royal Caribbean's Quantum-class. This is now my new favorite cruise ship!" Jim got my attention immediately because it was obvious from that beginning of the review that Jim was going to tell me what I wanted to hear. Remember, cognitive dissonance!

Before getting into the body of the review, Jim had an introductory paragraph where he shared some information about himself and his wife Kellyn. The disarming aspect about Jim I mentioned above came through right away. "I'm Jim Zimmerlin—everyone calls me Jim Zim—and I always cruise with my wife, Kellyn." The introduction went on to share some personal background information and summarize his fairly extensive cruise experience. Jim noted that though he has cruised quite a bit on Royal Caribbean, Princess, and Norwegian Cruise Line, especially lately, his first twenty cruises were on Carnival until Jim and Kellyn decided to branch out. Like Jim, I have cruised on various lines but mostly on Carnival. Wow, first Jim drew me in with that teaser opening line, then made me feel like I know him by providing some insight into his home and professional life, and then I found out I have a little bit in common with him with respect to cruising. I felt like he was writing this review for me personally.

Perhaps unsurprisingly given my first impression of Jim Zim, I thought the review was easily the best I had seen about *Anthem of the Seas*. The included photos and videos were amazing both in terms of quality—framing, lighting, resolution, and so on—and were very relevant to the accompanying text. When I came across

Jim's review, I was 335 days away from our family cruise. After reading it I was ready to depart "yesterday." Was this guy a plant from Royal Caribbean?

Since booking the *Anthem* cruise I had been putting together photos, highlights of fun things to do on the ship, kids activities, menus, descriptions of excursions, etc., to be inserted in a Christmas card, as the cruise was a surprise present to my 14- and 9-year old grandchildren, Kalen and LaKi. I have joked with their mom that what I have a put together for the card was so impressive that Royal Caribbean should publish it as a brochure and pay me royalties. Well, Jim's review was as nicely designed, well done and informative as anything on *Anthem of the Seas* I had seen by Royal Caribbean or otherwise, and actually could have been published by Royal as a brochure. If prospective customers were on the fence about booking *Anthem*, they would be converted after Jim's comprehensive review. Given the magnificent photos and videos, it came as little surprise to me when I got to the end of the review and Jim stated, "Whenever I post these cruise reviews, I always get questions about what camera I used to take the photos." So, he wrapped up the review with a small section on the equipment he uses.

I had already booked *Anthem*, so Jim's review had no influence on that. But this introduction to Jim Zim compelled me to do a couple of things—besides re-reading the review whenever the countdown days to embarkation seemed to drag on interminably. As soon as I was done "experiencing" the review, I subscribed to Jim's YouTube channel and proceeded to gorge on his cruise videos. Secondly, once I decided to write *The Joy of Cruising*, examining how passionate cruisers act on their passion in ways in which I think other cruisers and prospective cruisers would find fascinating, I knew I wanted to learn more about Jim and perhaps try to convince him to let me include him in the book, as I suspected that readers would find him fascinating as well.

Jim lives with his wife Kellyn in Grover Beach, California, a small beach town about half way between San Francisco and Los Angeles. The appeal to Jim and Kellyn of cruising probably is influenced somewhat by their living only a few miles from the Pacific Ocean. Despite Jim's successful YouTube channel and website, to my surprise vlogging and blogging about cruising is Jim's avocation, not vocation. Jim is employed as an administrator for Pacific Gas & Electric Company at the Diablo Canyon nuclear power plant in San Luis Obispo County, California where he has worked for 25 years, and is four years or so away from retirement.

Jim Zim with that giant mic in front of the *Carnival Freedom* in the foreground and *Carnival Liberty* behind that, in Galveston, Texas

Besides that voice, Jim Zim's background—the journalism education and experience in radio announcing—along with his hobbies of photography, videography, computers, video editing, and electronics serve him well in his YouTube career. I can imagine the hardware—audio/visual, photography, computers and more Jim must have at his house. He brings much of it on cruises with him—several cameras, including his primary shooter, a Canon EOS 80D Digital SLR, wide angle lens, and tripod among them. If you are ever on a cruise with Jim Zim, just look for the guy who carries around a giant professional-quality broadcast microphone so he can do voice-overs on his YouTube videos.

Jim's cruising passion was relatively late arriving. After a three-night cruise in 1996, he did not start cruising on a regular basis until 2008. Since then Jim has cruised close to fifty times. Early on Jim's cruising career was dominated by cruises on Carnival. He started his cruising life with twenty straight Carnival sailings, and there were a number of cruises having particular sentimental value. Jim and Kellyn renewed their wedding vows on *Carnival Spirit* in 2010. Today Jim is for the most part impartial with respect to cruise lines, having also experienced MSC, Norwegian, Princess, and Royal Caribbean cruise lines. He says a number of fans have suggested to him that given the content and style of his videos, Jim might like Celebrity Cruise Lines. Celebrity is known for gorgeous ships, upscale ambiance and amenities, and more personalized service. Jim has given Celebrity some thought. His interest is piqued by the just launched, stunning *Celebrity Edge* with a number of first-of-its-kind design touches and innovations like the Magic Carpet, a floating dining and entertainment space that rises and lowers up-and-down the side of the ship. Jim's videos tend to really highlight a cruise ship's "gee whiz" features such as Solarium on the *Anthem* and Observation Lounge on the *Norwegian Bliss*. Magic Carpet notwithstanding, Jim says he is a man of modest tastes when it comes to food, and Celebrity is known to appeal to foodies. Jim needs more convincing that there are buffets on *Edge* that serve food more to his liking than the gourmet cuisine in Celebrity dining rooms and restaurants. (I cruised on

Celebrity Equinox a few months ago. I am no foodie Jim, and I assure you that you would love their buffet.)

Although in recent years Jim has tried several different cruise lines, he has not walked away from Carnival. In late 2017, Jim Zim and Kellyn sailed *Vista*, at the time Carnival's newest, biggest, and most advanced ship, and they have already booked a 2020 cruise on *Panorama*, Carnival's newest ship which launches later this year.

Lately Jim has been spending a lot of time on Norwegian Cruise Lines including his last three cruises, on respectively, *Norwegian Bliss*—a "bucket list" cruise through the Panama Canal, *Getaway*, and *Breakaway*. Although in the review of *Anthem of the Seas* which first introduced me to Jim Zim he called *Anthem* the best cruise ship he has been on, Jim subsequently sailed *Norwegian Pearl* and stayed in the $1600 per night owner's suite and described that cruise as the most amazing experience he and Kellyn have had out of all of their cruises. If you want to fantasize a little, check out Jim's video of his experience on *Pearl* at his YouTube channel. For a preview, here are a couple of pictures from their suite which Jim and Kellyn rarely left— they did not even disembark at the ship's ports of call!

Jim and Kellyn in the Jacuzzi on the balcony of the Haven Deluxe Owner's Suite on *Norwegian Pearl*.

Jim and Kellyn's Haven Deluxe Owner's Suite on *Norwegian Pearl*

Norwegian Cruise Line unveiled *Bliss* April 2018, and on May 28 Jim and Kellyn sailed it as *Bliss* became by far the largest ship to ever transit the Panama Canal. I asked Jim for his reflections on that experience, as so many of the cruisers I interviewed for *The Joy of Cruising* listed a Panama Canal cruise as among their bucket list cruises. Jim told me it was a fantastic cruise, and he still enjoys thinking about how great it was. "We started with five days at a resort in Florida before the cruise, then 15 days of the cruise, so it was really a three-week vacation. I was totally impressed that there were zero learning curve issues for the crew. NCL must have cherry picked the best of their best crew members from the rest of the fleet for their new flagship. There were no issues at all that the crew had to get better at; they had every single thing down like pros. Going through the Panama Canal was certainly the highlight, and there were many things about the canal that surprised me and I had not expected even though going into this cruise I thought I was reasonably familiar with the Panama Canal. The food on the ship was a near-perfect match for my personal tastes in food, and I can't imagine a ship I'd rather be on for 15 days of meals! It was also really fun to have my sister along with us on this cruise." It would be impractical to address the technicalities and logistics of the Panama Canal passage here, but Jim covers it in-depth on his blog, and a Panama Canal cruise is now on my bucket list.

Jim embodies someone whose passion was inflamed by his experience cruising, and evinces that passion in a wonderful, interesting way. That is, by becoming a YouTube star. His involvement with YouTube began in 2008, although he did not think of himself as what today would be called a vlogger. Jim enjoyed doing video editing on his home computer and loved the idea of being able to share his experiences. As he was an infrequent cruiser, Jim would upload highlights from his occasional voyages for himself, family and friends. The very first upload to YouTube was not cruise-related and wasn't even shot by Jim: it was a video Kellyn recorded of Jim flying a remote controlled model airplane that she had given him for Christmas. Inauspicious start to their YouTube career—not because the video was poorly done, but rather because the plane flew for a few seconds, and then crashed into pieces! That first YouTube video is all of ten seconds long. The second YouTube video was a personal travelogue about one of their first cruises, showing some fun and memorable moments on a cruise to Mexico aboard *Carnival*

Spirit. Cruise videos were in the minority of Jim's early uploads to YouTube, interspersed with videos related to Jim and Kellyn's Cocker Spaniel breeding hobby. So it was, for the first few years of Jim Zim's YouTube foray.

Then, in 2012 things change dramatically when Jim uploaded a video about the first of its kind vertical-drop waterslide to be installed on a cruise ship. It was the Green Thunder waterslide, then the steepest and fastest waterslide at sea, with a 100 feet drop, through a trap door and entirely vertical for the first third of the way propelling thrill seekers at speeds of 20 feet per second. In 2012, Jim and Kellyn boarded *Carnival Spirit* for the fourth time in the past three years but this time it was like an entirely new ship as it had just undergone a multi million-dollar refurbishment, or dry dock in cruise parlance, and the Green Thunder was the featured upgrade.

Jim posted the video to YouTube much in the way he had posted his other cruise videos: he thought it was interesting. He had no illusions about the video becoming a hit on YouTube. In fact, he never even checked his YouTube channel metrics after posting his previous cruise videos, and it was months after uploading the slightly over one-minute long Green Thunder video before Jim visited his channel. To Jim's astonishment he discovered that his video on the *Carnival Spirit* had two million views! Jim was shocked! Of course there was that feeling of pride that comes with something you did being acknowledged and validated by others. But the popularity of the video spurred another thought in Jim. Being only vaguely aware of YouTube monetization—whereby video creators meeting certain benchmarks can earn money as a result of advertisements accompanying their videos—Jim conferred with his son who concurred regarding the monetization potential, and Jim researched the process.

Fairly soon Jim's *Carnival Spirit* Green Thunder video was generating advertising revenue for YouTube which they shared with Jim. Now the pride that came with discovering that he had a viral video had risen to yet another level as Jim Zim was now an official YouTube Partner. The promise of a new income source lay ahead, although Jim lamented the fact that he had not become a YouTube Partner prior to the Green Thunder video accumulating two million views. Jim was worried he was "too late to the party." Most of the people who wanted to see the video had probably already done so, and it would quickly cool off and stop getting views on YouTube. That worry turned out to be unfounded. The Green Thunder video is approaching 100 million views on YouTube!

The day Jim learned his little Green Thunder video had received two million views was the day he truly started to become a YouTube video blogger, or vlogger. Up to that point it had all just been for fun, but now that Jim realized there was the potential to make money off it, he set out to make a lot more videos.

The Green Thunder video is by far Jim's most-viewed video, but many other videos of his have gone on to get over a million views. Most of them have been about cruise ship waterslides, but Jim also does well with his model train videos. The model train videos are somewhat of an outgrowth of cruising. When the income started rolling in from that Green Thunder viral video, Jim spent a little bit of it on some model trains to just run around Jim and Kellyn's Christmas tree. Over time, Jim Zim accumulated more and more track and equipment, and eventually had a fairly substantial model train layout that he would set up temporarily to run throughout his entire house. Jim recorded some videos about the model trains display, and they started to catch on with YouTube. So these days Jim does cruise videos during the four or five times a year that he is able to cruise, and model train videos when "land bound" the rest of the year.

Jim with the Silver Pay Button plaque YouTube gives to content creators who have more than 100,000 subscribers.

What does the future hold for Jim Zim? Of course no one knows for sure, but it appears very bright. Things are pretty good for Jim now and he seems well-positioned for a happy, comfortable future. Currently he maintains his rewarding professional career at Pacific Gas & Electric Company, and YouTube stardom enables him to cruise the way he wants as much as his schedule permits. Besides the financial rewards of Jim's YouTube career, there are some collateral benefits as well. A cruise line recently offered Jim and Kellyn a free two-week cruise if he would just make some videos about the ship and the cruise experience while they were on board. Jim declined that particular offer, but will consider similar offers in the future.

And just think, Jim Zim is only a few years from retirement, which means more cruises, and checking off those bucket list items of traveling to the Galapagos islands and the South Pacific islands. Earlier in *The Joy of Cruising* I referred to a passionate cruiser as the "luckiest man in the world." On Jim Zim's website, he refers to himself as "luckiest man in the world." Each of these two "lucky men" manifests his passion for cruising in very different ways, yet have a common bond.

"At sixty years old, I am in a very comfortable stage in my life. Kellyn and I have been married for more than 35 years, I don't have to worry about money, and I spend a good deal of my energy planning the next cruise. In fact, to truly understand me, you have to know that these days, my life is all about the next cruise!"

THE GODMOTHER:
ELIZABETH HILL

Two queens, a convicted felon, and a schoolteacher board a cruise ship.... Sounds like the beginning of a bad joke. This is no joke however; these four individuals are, respectively, the Queen of England, Queen Latifa, Martha Stewart, and Elizabeth Hill, all Godmothers of cruise ships. Cruise ship Godmothers perform the task of christening a new cruise ship, ceremonially naming the ship marked by the smashing of a bottle of champagne against the ship hull. Cruise ship "Godparents" are usually women, even animated ones like Tinkerbell who was named Godmother to Disney Cruise Line's *Wonder*—although rapper Pitbull was selected as Godfather of *Norwegian Escape*. The notion of a ship godmother had its origins hundreds of years ago where ceremonial launching of seagoing vessels took place in various forms, either celebratory or religious, depending on local custom, but generally to bestow the ship and crew with well-wishes and safe travels.

Typically cruise lines select celebrities for the role of christening a new ship. Oprah Winfrey will serve as godmother of the just launched Holland American Line *Nieuw Statendam*. In addition to the aforementioned, Godmothers have included Helen Mirren, Dame Judi Dench, Sophia Loren, Whoopi Goldberg, Reba McEntire, Jennifer Hudson, Mariah Carey and many more that are well-known to most of us. Sometimes the choice of a Godmother is associated with a cause that the cruise line chooses to support. In 2001 following the terrorism of September 11, as a tribute to New York City first responders, Royal Caribbean selected four representatives of the New York City Fire and Police Departments as Godparents of *Adventure of the Seas*. In 2012 Celebrity Cruises named four employees, all of whom were either survivors of breast cancer or whose mothers had breast cancer, as the Godmothers of *Celebrity Reflection*. Elizabeth Hill, a retired teacher, was selected in 2008 by Royal Caribbean International as Godmother of *Independence of the Seas*, in recognition of her work with children and young people.

10 years after she was crowned Elizabeth Hill stands next to her portrait permanently displayed on *Independence of the Seas*.

Elizabeth Hill of Chesterfield, Derbyshire, UK is a 66-year old married mother of two and grandmother of three granddaughters, Josephine, Harriett, and Phillippa. Introduced above as a school-teacher, as she was often referred to by media when she was selected as Godmother, a more apt description of Elizabeth Hill is someone who inspired and tried to help individuals fulfill their potential, and who founded a charity in support of that cause. Elizabeth moved to Buxton, Derbyshire several years ago to be near her son Dorian and grandchildren, as her younger daughter Alicia had gone off to the University of Nottingham. Elizabeth spends her time in Buxton involved in local community matters, charitable causes, and volunteers as a befriender of young families who need a little extra support. She is president of the local Women's Institute, an advisor on the board of a local charity, runs an older person's club, and currently is in the process of setting up a community café. Most ship Godmothers' roles essentially end after the christening of their ship. Ten years later Elizabeth remains in demand by audiences eager to hear about her experience as a Godmother. Elizabeth gives interviews to press and national radio, and often gives talks at events or clubs. Elizabeth blogs—*Cruise Like a Godmother*—and tweets and continues to be an active participant with the UK cruising community.

Elizabeth's current busy life with social and charitable causes is very consistent with her earlier life which led ultimately to her being selected as Godmother by Royal Caribbean. Elizabeth spent most of her life in Derbyshire in the Midlands. She was born on a small farm in a beautiful rural area where her father had a plant nursery. As a child, along with her younger siblings, Elizabeth worked in the family business. Along with the nursery business, her father was passionate about horses, and the family always had several at any one time. Elizabeth's parents established a riding club to promote the well-being of horses and ponies by ensuring that young people knew how to properly care for them, handle them and ride them.

Although Elizabeth was expected to continue to work in the family business upon completing school, a headmistress regularly in assembly instilled in Elizabeth and her schoolmates that her girls were "the cream of the country." This motivated Elizabeth to strive for more. Elizabeth became a teacher; first rural science, and subsequently, Elizabeth focused on special education. After marrying and having her first child Elizabeth made a career change, retraining in beauty therapy, and even developing her own natural skin care products. Elizabeth also became an entrepreneur, and opened a clothing boutique.

Marital strife and then divorce derailed Elizabeth's entrepreneurial career, and she eventually returned to teaching. Through her second education career, Elizabeth met her current husband, Edward (actually reunited with Edward; they had attended grade school together). With Edward, Elizabeth had her second child Alicia. Though the birth of Alicia long predated Elizabeth being chosen as a ship Godmother, Alicia's birth was particularly relevant to the story of Elizabeth's selection by Royal Caribbean. Due to her age and some medical considerations, Elizabeth's pregnancy with Alicia was problematic and there was a high risk that Alicia would be born with disabilities. A healthy Alicia, who Elizabeth calls her blessing and bonus in life, was born April 30, 1995. (About herself, Elizabeth says "Yes, I am an older Mum.") Elizabeth's gratefulness for her good fortune given the circumstances of Alicia's birth inspired her to establish a charity for young people with learning disabilities.

The Gamelea Countryside Training Trust was established on Edward and Elizabeth's farm. The farm was an established commercial farm with cattle, sheep and pigs. The charity started as a small project, one day a week with a handful of young people coming to spend time out in the beautiful countryside, and help to feed and look after a few animals and tend to a few plants. Word spread, and the small project became more and more popular. More projects were added and more funding was received until the farm had workshops for inclement weather, a couple of rooms for arts and crafts, information and music technology, woodwork and engineering workshops, a commercial plant nursery, office space and a café. The farm added free-range egg laying hens and a collection of horses, dogs and small animals. Gamelea Countryside Training Trust employed twenty people and provided training and employability skills, and assisted the needs of over 130 students throughout each week with its mission expanded beyond people with learning disabilities to include at risk youth, people with mental health issues, and ex-service personnel finding it hard to cope with civilian life

In March 2007 Alicia, then aged 12, was watching a talk show when she saw Sir Steve Redgrave, British 5-time Olympic rowing gold medalist, announce that in conjunction with Royal Caribbean Cruise Lines he was looking for a woman who had done something good for the community. Royal Caribbean was about to launch the largest cruise ship in the world, and instead of having a celebrity christen the *Independence of the Seas*, they had decided to look for an "ordinary" woman who had done something extraordinary for the community. The Godmother selected had to be in UK, as *Independence* was intended to sail from Southampton on a regular basis. Enticed by the prize of a free cruise, Alicia nominated her mom, unbeknownst to Elizabeth.

It wasn't until Elizabeth received a call a few weeks later from a Royal Caribbean representative that she learned anything about the contest. The representative told Elizabeth that out of a couple of thousand entries Royal Caribbean had narrowed it down to six. Elizabeth thought the call was a hoax; perhaps she was being pranked and threatened to hang up. When the representative mentioned Alicia had entered her, Elizabeth assumed her daughter had entered her into some kind of reality television program competition.

Not long after answering a few questions and providing references, Elizabeth heard again from Royal Caribbean. The list of potential *Independence* Godmothers was down to four, and Elizabeth was asked to come to the airport with her passport and a ballroom gown in a couple of days. Then the four potential godmothers were flown in a private jet in the company of Richard Fain, Chairman and Chief Executive Officer of Royal Caribbean to the Aker ship yard in Turku, Finland where the finishing touches were being applied to the dry-docked *Independence*. Elizabeth had flown before—though certainly not in a Lear jet—and in any event she is not a happy flier.

The Godmother finalists toured the massive structure; already in a state of awe—the last several days since hearing from Royal Caribbean had been a whirlwind—Elizabeth was amazed taking in the sights of the massive, gorgeous structure, unlike anything she had ever seen before. After the tour the finalists then went to their suites to change into their formal outfits to attend the *Independence* "hand over ball," where the Finnish shipbuilders formally convey the ship to Royal Caribbean Cruise Lines. The ceremony was in the *Independence* main dining room, where the potential Godmothers and dignitaries dined at an enormous table in the center beneath a grand chandelier. After speeches and congratulatory applause, celebrations continued with music, dancing, and lots of champagne.

The following day the finalists returned to the UK and were interviewed by a panel lead by Sir Steve Redgrave, and the day after the panel interview Elizabeth got a call from Royal Caribbean informing her of the wonderful news that she had been chosen as the Godmother of *Independence of the Seas*! Elizabeth recalls the phone call, "Elizabeth, we had a lovely time interviewing the four of you, we think you all do wonderful things for the community, but we unanimously agreed that you should be the Godmother of the *Independence of the Seas*." Shortly thereafter, her phone rang incessantly as local press and radio and television stations all wanted to interview the first non-royal, non-celebrity British Godmother.

Besides her one-of-a-kind story of helping youth and others with challenges, there is another unique aspect to Elizabeth that sets her apart from the other subjects of *The Joy of Cruising*. Most of the cruisers discussed in this book have experienced dozens of cruises; one passionate cruiser as many as 350. When Royal Caribbean named Elizabeth Godmother of *Independence of the Seas*, she had never sailed on a cruise ship!

The christening day for *Independence of the Seas*, April 30, 2008 was special for Elizabeth in several ways. Besides Elizabeth having a starring role in a real life fairy tale, Alicia, who had set this day in motion with her email essay to Royal Caribbean, was celebrating her 13th birthday. What a birthday present; Alicia was going to receive that cruise she fantasized about when she nominated her mom! Elizabeth and close family members were put up in the *Independence* Presidential Suite, and extended family members in nearby suites. Champagne flowed copiously.

The actual ceremony was held in the ship's theater due to inclement weather. Both a priest and a rabbi blessed the proceedings, the British and American national anthems were performed, and a number of speeches were made by dignitaries (including Elizabeth, much to her surprise). Elizabeth was petrified to have to stand up and speak without any advance notice and preparation; she has no idea what she said, but apparently it was very moving, as media reported there "wasn't a dry eye in the house." As far as the actual christening, Elizabeth was terrified yet at the same time overcome with exhilaration as she pressed the button that activated the trigger to smash the bottle of champagne on the hull of the *Independence* while the audience watched on a huge screen the activity that was taking place outside. Elizabeth was presented with a diamond brooch, and the birthday girl, Alicia, was called up to the stage and given a lovely piece of heart shaped jewelry as well.

Alicia and Elizabeth back on "*Indy*" in 2018 for its re-launch after a multi-million refurbishment.

Oh, about Elizabeth being new to cruising? Well she has since surpassed many of us casual cruisers. Each year Elizabeth and guests are afforded a cruise in a suite on *Indy*, as it is affectionately called by Brits. Alicia, now a University of Nottingham graduate with honors in music and philosophy, even got to sing onboard *Indy* for her 16th birthday. In September Alicia was asked to sing for the Captain while Elizabeth and Alicia were dining with him in Chops Grille on the *Independence*. He then asked her to sing on the bridge tour for the *Independence* Pinnacle cruisers. It was arranged for Alicia to be recorded and a copy was sent to CEO Richard Fain at his request.

Elizabeth and her "bonus in life" will be forever intertwined in the Godmother of the *Independence of the Seas* story.

The Influencers

DANA FREEMAN TRAVELS: CRUISING WITH GRANDMA

*D*ana *Freeman Travels* is the brand of Dana Freeman, one of the foremost travel influencers in New England, specializing in both regional travel from her location in Vermont as well as global travel, where Dana visits about 30-40 destinations around the world each year. Dana started as a travel writer by creating the Find&GoSeek website in 2008. Find&GoSeek is Vermont's insider guide to kid-friendly fun, so it's all about finding things to do with or for your kids in the state of Vermont. Dana and her husband Andrew initially focused on creating a better way to find and compare the best summer camp programs for their children. Inspired by the economic crisis impacting the nation at that time, and the resultant *staycation* and *nearcation* trend, Find&GoSeek thrived as a source for locals to help discover and share in their family experiences in and around Vermont. Resorts and destinations sought Dana out to visit and review their properties. So, her travel writing career was born. "I had no idea of what it meant to be a travel journalist, but I did know how to be passionate about something and share it. Once I started to be asked to come to locales outside of Vermont and write about it, I decided I needed a separate brand." In 2010, *Dana Freeman Travels* was launched. Dana did not want to be pigeon-holed as a Vermont area only travel writer, or a family travel writer; she wanted the freedom to write about other segments of the travel industry. *Dana Freeman Travels* thrived; Dana is active in the travel writing community, writes columns and curates a travel radio program for local media, and is recognized by a number of organizations as a travel expert and ambassador. In 2018, Dana Freeman was named one of the "10 Travel Influencers Changing How We Vacation" by *Porthole Cruise Magazine*, and she was also selected as one the "30 Bloggers and Travelers to Follow for Summer Vacation Advice" by *Travel Pulse*.

Dana Freeman on a stop in Krems, Austria during her 2018 Viking River Cruise.

Dana has had a diverse career path to get to where she is today as a travel writer and influencer, but her passion for travel can be traced in a straight line back to her grandmother. Somewhat before her time, Dana's grandmother, Mildred, was an itinerant traveler dating back to the forties and fifties. After a divorce, her grandmother vowed to continue traveling, and cruising was particularly conducive to traveling solo; accordingly cruise travel developed into a passion for "Gram." It was not unusual, even in the fifties, for Mildred to save up her money, put her kids in summer camp, and go on a cruise. Mildred also frequently traveled professionally in her medical administration career. She introduced Dana to travel, first by having Dana accompany her on a business trip to Greece, and then shortly thereafter taking her on her first cruise—just the two of them. Consequently, Dana became addicted to travel as a young teen, and that passion for travel has morphed into a passion for travel writing, and Gram forever speaking through her as what Dana refers to as "her travel muse."

12-year old Dana on her first cruise with Gram on the *SS Veendam*.

In 1980, "Gram" decided to share her love of travel with her four grandchildren by inviting each one of them to accompany her on a trip of their choice. Each year Gram planned a trip with one grandchild to go anywhere in the world that they wanted to visit. Dana was the oldest of her grandchildren and got to travel with Gram first. 12-year old Dana knew Gram's true passion was cruising—and that was her pick to travel with her. "I wanted to see why she loved cruising so much," Dana said. In August 1980, Gram and Dana embarked on the Holland America Line *SS Veendam* on a cruise to the Caribbean.

In 2010, 91-year old Gram—known as Great Gram to Dana's two children, daughter Callahan, 8, and son Flynn, 11—expressed an interest in resurrecting the tradition she had started 30 years earlier of traveling with Dana and the other grandchildren. Gram told Dana, "I want to take your kids out on a trip like I did when you were children." What an audacious thing to want to do at 91. Not surprising given Gram's longtime love for cruising, and her independent attitude. (Gram continued in her career until well into her eighties, only stopping due to failing eyesight.) Dana was very hesitant to let the kids go on a cruise with Gram alone. Gram would be 92 by the time she traveled with the great grandkids. Dana told her, "I don't think that it's fair to put on the kids the burden of something happening to you. And they are a lot to handle." Gram responded, "Ok fine, why don't we all just go. I'll take you all." After Gram quickly reached that compromise, Dana's concern was alleviated. She assumed this would be a one-time event. "I thought she would take my children, my husband and myself on a cruise because that is what she really wanted to do and we felt like she could not do it herself anymore and it would be done. Gram's passion was cruising and that's what she wanted to do."

In August 2010, virtually 30 years to the day of 12-year old Dana's first cruise with Gram, Dana, her husband Andrew, son Flynn, daughter Callahan and Great Gram embarked on the *Windstar Windsurf* in Barcelona, Spain to Nice, France. Aside from a cruise in Mexico with her parents as a young teen on Sitmar Cruises (now P & O Holidays), for Dana it was the first time cruising in almost 25 years. Flynn and Callahan, and Andrew, would get to experience their first cruise on one of the world's most exclusive vessels. "It sort of spoiled them rotten going on the Windstar Cruise line as their very first cruise!" With a capacity of only 310 passengers, the five-mast, seven-sail, 6-decks *Wind Surf* yacht was the flagship of the luxury Windstar fleet—its largest and most well-appointed craft. The Freeman family and Gram were "somewhat of a square-peg-in-a-round hole" on the grand *Wind Surf*. "We were definitely an anomaly; even for my demographic in the mid-forties, I was not the typical Windstar cruiser. My kids were the only kids on ship. So as a family we were definitely seen as an oddity. Gram was the oldest on the ship and my kids were the youngest." Nevertheless, Dana described the *Wind Surf* cruise as incredible. So, much so that Great Gram and Dana's family decided to take another cruise the next year. "When we got home from the trip—I don't even think Gram's luggage was unpacked—Gram said, let's go again; so where are we going next year." It turns out *Cruising with Grandma* became a tradition—beginning with Gram at 92-years old and taking place over the successive four years—of Gram taking Dana, Andrew, Flynn, and Callahan on a cruise. Not just any cruise; Gram was partial to small luxury craft. So, after first experiencing *Wind Surf*, the Freemans got to experience a Mediterranean cruise on Seabourn, another cruise line that Gram was very fond of, departing from Rome traveling to Mallorca, Spain.

Great Gram, 92, with great grandkids Flynn, 11, and Callahan, 8, on the first cruise with Grandmother on the *Wind Surf* in 2010.

Dana recounts that the second cruise, like the first, was an amazing experience. This time they traveled on the *Seabourn Spirit*, an ultra-luxury ship even smaller than the previous year's *Wind Surf* at only 208-passengers, with included fine dining, open bar, all-suite cabins and a complimentary shore excursion program. Dana recalls, "It was in November of 2011 so it was a little cold, but it was incredible. Prior to the second cruise with Gram, since we were spending so much quality time with her, we decided to purchase a grandma journal." A grandmother journal is a keepsake for documenting stories, experiences and feelings often completed jointly with a grandchild. Dana continues, "They're blank books and they give you prompts to talk to your grandparents about their life story. From that second cruise on we carried it with us, and at dinner, on the deck, or in our cabins we would ask her stuff. What did your first apartment look like? Who did you go to the prom with? Who was your first boyfriend? What was your least favorite subject in high school? Those kind of things." Dana's family and Gram got to spend quality time together that had a real richness to it that would have been lost in a different setting that lacked the intimacy of a cruise, especially on a small ship like *Spirit*. "We were a captive audience; captive is the wrong word because that sounds negative, but I say that in a good way."

With the second cruise late in 2011, the third cruise was in early 2013. Dana, family, and now 95-year old Gram planned a big cruise; this one was back on Windstar, on its namesake vessel, the *Windstar*, and it was a Panama Canal cruise. At only 148 guests, it was almost as if Gram and the Freemans were on their own private yacht. I point out to Dana that I ask every person profiled in *The Joy of Cruising* what is on their bucket list, and Panama Canal is at or near the top choice. Dana's kids were getting the opportunity to experience a bucket list cruise as pre-teens! Their Panama Canal cruise did not disappoint. The *Windstar* departed from Costa Rica, and sailed through the Panama Canal to Panama. The experience was awe-inspiring. Dana notes, "Windstar Cruises did an amazing job because the *Windstar* is so small. Each afternoon there was a lecture about the Panama Canal—building the Panama Canal, what you would see, or the history of it. So it was really nice for me and my children to have that educational piece while going through it. Of course, I had never experienced going through a lock, and I really enjoyed Costa Rica and Panama and the places the cruise stopped."

Andrew paddling around 95-year old Gram in Costa Rica during their 3rd cruise together; that's the *Windstar* in the background.

On her 96th birthday, July 2014 Gram sailed with Dana and family out of Venice on the newly christened *Windstar Star Pride*; shortly before their cruise the *Star Pride* was acquired from Seabourn where it had operated as the *Seabourn Pride*, an identical sister ship to the *Seabourn Spirit*. It was to be Dana and Gram's last trip together. "I was really hesitant; Gram wasn't feeling well. I was concerned about the quality of medical care we could get abroad should something happen. We were sailing out of Venice across to Croatia, Montenegro, and then back up the other side of Italy to end in Rome. I was nervous because Croatia isn't as developed in terms of medical care as maybe the mainland of Europe—Italy, France, or London or whatever. Gram might have been in her 90's but she was still as stubborn as ever and insisted that she was going no matter what."

Celebrating Gram's 96ᵗʰ birthday on the night of departure on the *Windstar Star Pride*.

Dana paused, and stated poignantly, "I knew going into it that if Gram was going to die at sea, that I had to be at peace with it and that she would go out doing what she wanted to be doing—traveling. There are not many 96-year olds that get to travel with their grandchildren and great-children at that age and doing something as far-flung as going on a cruise to a bunch of places."

Dana described sailaway as phenomenal. There are no other ports quite like Venice to depart from. Traditionally, Windstar plays the "1942: Conquest of Paradise" during every sailaway. It made the moment even more poignant as Dana knew this was likely the last time they were going to conquer parts of the world together. That night at dinner, the crew brought Gram a cake and everyone sang Happy Birthday to her in the dining room. Gram was the belle of the ball that night.

The *Star Pride* crossed over to Croatia and Gram was doing fine in the first couple of cities. Then they stopped in Dubrovnik; it was going to be a long stop—over 12 hours. As it was especially hot, they decided to stay on the ship and then disembark in the evening to go to dinner. Dana stated, "We were out to dinner at a beautiful little restaurant on a side street in Dubrovnik. And Gram actually had a stroke at dinner.... yeah." Dana paused. "You know, it was...it was...I didn't know what was going on. I knew that we needed to call an ambulance. If we had been in France where I could speak French, or even Italy or Spain where you could manage to communicate a little bit, but in Croatia the language barrier was incredibly difficult. We did manage through the kindness of the waiter and some strangers dining near us, and we got her to the emergency room."

Gram and Dana eventually got back on the *Star Pride*, but never left the ship again. They continued with the cruise and Andrew and the kids were able to visit the other ports. Shortly after returning to Vermont, Great Gram died. Dana said, "I don't reflect on that trip thinking oh my God, we never should have done it. I know that we did what she wanted to be doing, and that gave me and my family great joy to experience cruising and learn about the passion of cruising, and why cruising is such a great opportunity to see the world and travel, all through Gram's eyes."

Even before the saga of *Cruising with Grandma,* Dana's children already had an appreciation for and familiarity with travel. Dana notes both Flynn and Callahan were on an airplane before they were six-months old. "They both got a social security card and a passport all within their first couple months of life." Dana said, "My kids have seen so many countries in such a short span: Costa Rica, Croatia, Italy, Spain, France, Montenegro. They have seen so many things and places in such a short amount of time. Who knows where they will want to travel when they get older." I suspect the legacy of *Cruising with Grandma* will have a long-term influence on Flynn and Callahan, just as cruising and traveling to many places with Gram as an adolescent influenced Dana's adult career. Flynn and Callahan have not cruised since, but they have already demonstrated an affinity for travel. Flynn started traveling abroad in high school; he went to leadership training camp in York, England during the summer of his junior year. Flynn is now a college student at George Washington University and has applied to study abroad. He is studying political science and wants to do an international relations experience where he is based in Europe and is able to travel to other neighboring countries. Dana said "I think part of that stems from learning to travel and that it is ok; he loves it and wants to explore and see as much as he can. I'm sure that is inspired by his experience with Gram. And Callahan applied for a Galapagos trip this year with her high school. The fact that Flynn and Callahan want to travel so young alone comes from Gram, who definitely expanded their horizons and makes them want to see the world."

Cruising with Grandma has already had some influence on Dana and Andrew's travel as well. Dana and Andrew returned to the *Windstar Wind Surf*—the initial ship of the *Cruising with Grandma* saga—for their first cruise since Gram's passing.

Dana Freeman Travels has tried to stake out a specific niche in writing about travel as opposed to writing about travel broadly. Dana tends to focus on unique destination information or unique things to do in a destination, with an emphasis on food, luxury and—unsurprisingly, given her family travel roots—multigenerational travel. "I think that's a great way to travel. There is no better time to be with your family than when you are relaxed and on vacation. That's a lot better than getting together with your family over dinner! And I love to explore new places." I asked Dana to give me an example of what she means by unique. "Ok, I was on a river cruise on the Danube. Basic excursions are included at destinations on a river cruise—usually a walking tour of the city." In Vienna, Dana instead chose to expand upon her experience by booking and then writing about a tour with a company called Urban Adventures. "Their tagline is 'Locals Know.' You go out in a small group with a couple of tour guides and go where they live—the restaurants and bars and art exhibits they frequent. We rode the underground, and the tram, and the bus; we went to the markets and we went to the coffee houses—stuff that you would never see with a regular tour. I like to get into the weeds and do those kinds of things. I never ask the concierge where should I eat. I like to ask the taxi driver where he eats. I like to experience a place the way local residents do."

Dana likewise tends towards the unique and different in cruising. All of Dana's cruises have been on small luxury ships, several of course with Gram. Her most recent cruise was in 2018 on the river cruise down the Danube on the *Viking Atla,* another small luxury ship. In keeping with her attraction to the unique, Dana has taken to sailing on windjammer cruises off the coast of Maine. A windjammer is a vintage tall sailing ship; that is, it relies on sails that harness the wind to power the ships movement. They may hold as few as single-digit numbers of passengers, and accommodations are generally much more frugal than the kind of small luxury ships described above. For instance, a single bathroom (referred to as the "head") may be available. Dana likens sailing on a windjammer to "camping on the water." There is a subcategory of windjammer sailing that involves more luxurious amenities and itineraries, also covered by *Dana Freeman Travels*.

As with all the passionate cruisers profiled in *The Joy of Cruising*, I wanted to know what's on Dana's bucket list. Consistent with Dana's preference for small, luxury-oriented ships and her preference for more unique travel, Dana aspires to take a barge cruise. Also known as hotel barge cruising, barge cruising represents a tiny sliver of the luxury cruise niche. Hotel barges are working barges—flat bottomed boats used principally for river transport of cargo—that have been retrofitted with luxury accoutrements for the purpose of transporting passengers. (Most hotel barges are converted industrial barges, but some have been purpose-built to serve this luxury niche.) Almost exclusive to Europe, especially France, barge cruisers are smaller than river cruisers and move at a much slower pace. The passenger load of hotel barges typically ranges from several cruisers to a couple dozen, who are pampered by a crew that does the cooking, cleaning, piloting of the vessel, and chauffeuring during included shore excursions. "As you know, my preference is small ship luxury sailing. At eight passengers or so, that is the ultimate in small ship sailing. They're beautiful. That's my dream cruise." Dana said.

Another bucket list item for Dana—pretty much the opposite of barge cruising—is a transatlantic cruise. "I know so many people dislike the days at sea; they get bored. I actually love the days at sea. I'm a beach and ocean person, so I enjoy being out on the ocean. You really get to enjoy the ship, its amenities and the company of the people that you are with without the pressure to get off at each port and go see and do as much as possible. So to me a transatlantic cruise would just be a dream—lay on the deck with your book and just relax. I would love to see what it feels like leaving and not knowing when you are going to see land for days on end."

What does the future hold for *Dana Freeman Travels*? "Travel as much as possible; I love to experience new places and then share them with my readers. I love to share good photography with an explanation of how you can do this too. Maybe you don't have to do it in the same way that I did it, or see the exact same thing, but I want to give my readers a good jumping off point to do their own research."

Dana wants to be her readers' travel muse, as Gram is hers.

Gram's travel journals.

SHERI GRIFFITHS: CRUISETIPSTV

I first became aware of Sheri Griffiths in the spring of 2018 when she was named one of the "10 Travel Influencers Changing How We Vacation" by *Porthole Cruise Magazine* for her popular YouTube series *CruiseTipsTV*. *Porthole Cruise Magazine* stated, "When it comes to planning the best cruise vacation, there's no better follow than Sheri Griffiths." *CruiseTipsTV* was created in pursuit of Sheri's passion for family cruise travel, and to share videos with other cruisers looking to make their cruise experience the best it can be. The *CruiseTipsTV* channel now has close to 500 videos, 60,000 subscribers, garners over 600,000 monthly views and has grown to 11 million total views. While Sheri is the host and on-camera presence, *CruiseTipsTV* is a family production along with her husband and ten-year old son, referred to affectionately by her audience as, respectively, Mr. CruiseTipsTV, and Junior Editor. The family production originated out of another family event—conversation over family dinner when Junior Editor was only five years old. Their conversation went something like: "We're going on a lot of cruises. What if we made a little cruise packing video helping people to learn about

packing for a cruise…it will be terrible and no one will watch it….
I'll hate it…let's just do it, why not?…everybody else is on YouTube.
Why can't we do it? We are passionate about cruising."

Sheri Griffiths, *CruiseTipsTV*. That's *Carnival Imagination* in the background.

CruiseTipsTV started off with modest intentions and modest
production values. Sheri nor her husband had any formal training in
broadcasting, although they did have videography training from their
years as wedding videographers, and had video editing experience
from editing their family vacation videos. Furthermore, Sheri, the
sole on-camera presence, was terrified of public speaking, although
it did help that Sheri danced until 17 or so, so she wasn't totally new
to the "performance" aspect of being in front of the camera. It also
was beneficial that Sheri had studied media and communications
in college where she earned a degree in communication studies at
University of California-Santa Barbara. It was with that media and
technology background that *CruiseTipsTV* premiered with "What to

Pack for a Cruise" in October 2013. "When I tell you it was terrible...
it was so bad. I can't even watch it now." Despite Sheri's declaration
to the contrary, ratings from the 84,000 viewers of the video over
the years are overwhelmingly positive and Sheri and her family were
definitely on to something as people started commenting and awaiting more videos.

The next several videos were of a similar style: primers and
how-to tutorials on subjects like saving money on a cruise, and avoid-
ing illness, and they consisted of Sheri in a "studio" setting providing the audience cruising tips in an engaging manner. Shortly after
the start of *CruiseTipsTV*, Sheri's husband, Mr. CruiseTipsTV, began
conducting ship tour videos and posting them in combination with
the tips videos. Increasingly, *CruiseTipsTV* received a lot of demand
from its viewers first to vlog, that is, to video and write about their
cruising exploits beyond just offering tips; then the *CruiseTipsTV*
viewers implored Sheri to turn the camera around. "In our early
days, all of our episodes were filmed in the studio—my house—and
were pre-recorded. When we reference that our subscribers wanted
us to turn the camera around, they were referring to showing our
surroundings, and also turning to selfie mode and showing ourselves in the cruise environment. Things really started to change for
us when our community said, 'Hey, we want you to take us on vacation.' So, we started filming vlogs. That was the big turning point for
CruiseTipsTV—when we started letting people into our lives."

Sheri stated that live streaming brought them a lot closer to
their audience; that is when *CruiseTipsTV* went from a YouTube
channel to a community. *CruiseTipsTV* conducts a live stream a
couple of times a month. For the last two years, during the month
of October, *CruiseTipsTV* conducts "Vlogtoberfest," a month-long
daily vlogging event.

Born and raised in southern California, Sheri did quite a bit of traveling in her youth—just not cruise traveling. Her family camped often each summer, and traveled to Puerto Vallarta, Mexico for a few weeks each winter where Sheri's father owns a condo. "We would cook our own food and had a beat up Volkswagen we'd pile into to drive into town to stock up on groceries. We were a family that went camping a lot. We kind of grew up in a rustic environment—it was very much the opposite of cruising." However, Sheri was accustomed to the water, as some of those camping trips entailed bringing a boat to Lake Havasu on the border between California and Arizona.

Sheri also got to experience travel abroad once in her youth. Her family traveled to Australia and New Zealand for a month-long journey when Sheri was 16.

On completing high school, before heading off to college, Sheri went on her first cruise, which was a high school graduation present from her mom. At 17, Sheri cruised with her mom and 12-year-old brother on *Carnival Ecstasy* to the Western Caribbean. Sheri's most vivid recollection from her first cruise was the food. "We were overwhelmed by the food—three meals a day, a buffet; I grew up with three brothers and we were kind of fighting for food; didn't get to have three course meals!" Most memorable to Sheri from that first cruise was experiencing another first—scuba diving. Sheri got to scuba dive on Grand Cayman. "My mom let me go on a resort dive—one of those that you don't have to be certified. It felt like a rite of passage…to do something on my own, really by myself with a bunch of strangers on a shore excursion. It was life altering!" While the scuba diving experience may have been life altering, cruising itself was not initially. Sheri didn't really develop a passion for cruising based on that first cruise. "It was there, an interest, but didn't really become a passion until much later when my husband and I first cruised together."

The cruising passion came for Sheri and her husband on Sheri's second cruise 13 years later, a week on a *Diamond Princess* Mexican Riviera cruise departing out of Los Angeles. "I said to my husband, 'We have to do a warm-weather vacation.' We had previously traveled to Paris for Christmas, and during college we lived briefly in Europe. I said to my husband, 'We have to go somewhere warm and I really want you to experience a cruise.' Although her husband had not cruised before, together they had been exposed to travel abroad and gained some appreciation for other cultures. "We lived in Madrid, Spain while my husband completed his final year of University in the Education Abroad Program. During that time, we traveled to the Canary Islands, France, England and Wales."

The *Diamond Princess* Mexican Riviera cruise reignited in Sheri what was so wonderful about cruising that she had experienced at 17, and she and Mr. CruiseTipsTV together developed a new passion. "My husband just absolutely fell in love with cruising. To observe the joy he felt, and for me to relive all that I loved on my first cruise, but to go on a very big and much grander ship compared to *Carnival Ecstasy*, and with my husband instead of my mom and brother.... To experience all that tradition—dressing up for dinner, walking hand-in-hand on the promenade, sitting on the balcony and smelling the ocean air. We both fell totally in love with cruising. And, besides being at sea, adding to the 'spark' was the fact that we did not have to fly. We could drive a few hours to Los Angeles and then escape to Mexico without having to step foot on an airplane. So we were really truly able to unwind."

Sheri has been on a total of 31 cruises. Most of her cruising has been on Princess and Carnival. Sheri has also cruised on Norwegian

Cruise Lines quite a bit, as well as a little with Holland America Line, Royal Caribbean, and MSC Cruises. Sheri's family cruises depart about half from the west coast, to Mexico and Alaska, and half from Florida and other destinations. She is partial to the Princess Grand class ships—*Grand Princess, Golden Princess, Star Princess*—which despite the "Grand class" name are Princess' smallest ships at about 109,000 gross tons and 3000 passengers each, although among the world's largest when the class premiered in 1998. Sheri also really likes the *MSC Seaside*, the technologically advanced ship that entered service in December 2017 built specifically for the North-American market and featuring a number of innovative design touches like the skywalk—a glass-bottom bridge alongside of the ship which looks straight down into the ocean, a couple of art deco pool settings on opposite ends of the ship inspired by Miami's South Beach condominiums, panoramic glass elevators on the back of the ship with a view of the ocean, and a waterpark with black waterslides with a transparent section that juts out over the sides of the ship. (When I took my granddaughter LaKi on a surprise cruise last summer, *Seaside* with its imposing tangle of duel waterslides was docked next to the ship we were going on—*Celebrity Equinox,* a fine ship but one that lacked any waterslides. I had to do my best to divert LaKi's attention away from the massive, distinctive waterslides on *Seaside,* as she's never met a waterslide that she did not want to conquer.)

I asked Sheri what is it she liked so much about *MSC Seaside.* "One of our favorite features of *MSC Seaside* is the Bridge of Sighs, a narrow glass walkway that extends over the back of the ship. You can't help but catch your breath when you look down."

Sheri walking on the Bridge of Sighs, *MSC Seaside*.

Sheri's cruise on *Seaside* also produced one of her family's most memorable experiences on a cruise—an excursion to the Blue Hole in Ocho Rios, Jamaica. The Blue Hole is a breathtaking series of waterfalls with scenic views and photo-friendly vantage points for the less active traveler, and for the adventurous—from swimming, climbing the falls, swinging from ropes into the water, to cliff-diving. Yes, Sheri and family chose jumping off cliffs! "The Blue Hole is a kind of off-the beaten-path waterfalls that go from up a hill; and what you do is you hike up through the waterfalls and you progress back down to the bottom by jumping off waterfalls into giant blue lagoons of water. We took our little son on this and the little guy had more courage than we did jumping off 30-foot cliffs into the ocean with absolutely no fear at all. I think as a family the joy we felt on that day was unforgettable."

Sheri cliff-diving at the Blue Hole, Ocho Rios, Jamaica.

Another memorable Ocho Rios, Jamaica adventure;
Sheri and family tubing on the White River.

Sheri cited several other memorable cruise experiences that were as unforgettable as those in Ocho Rios: The simple pleasure of enjoying the hot tub with 5-year old Junior Editor in 40-degree weather on the side of the *Diamond Princess* in Alaska while approaching a glacier. Or, on a stop in Loreto, Baja California while on a *Star Princess* cruise, Sheri and her family took a private tour on a panga (small fishing type boat) to Loreto Bay, near Isla Coronado. "Out of nowhere, hundreds of dolphins surrounded our boat and surfed the wake for what felt like hours. We plunged our GoPro into the sea and captured video of the dolphins following the boat. The camera also captured their vocalizations, which was a beautiful surprise when we arrived home and pulled our footage in to the editing bay."

Sheri said that another memorable cruise experience involved her "accidentally" swimming with whale sharks in the Sea of Cortez during a stop in Port of La Paz, Mexico during a cruise on the *Star Princess*. How do you accidentally swim with sharks, I ask incredulously? "Well you book a tour and it gets windy. We had booked a tour to Isla Espiritu Santo, where you go and snorkel, frolic in the water, and see sea lions, but the wind picked up and we couldn't get across to this island in La Paz." Isla Espiritu Santo is a small island with picturesque beaches and a habitat for ocean wildlife including dolphins and sea lions, but the tour operator deemed it too windy to go. As an alternative, Sheri and her family were offered the opportunity to go on a whale shark excursion. Sheri said, "So they said, 'Well, we can't make it; how about we go snorkel with whale sharks instead?' We are like, what on earth are you talking about?" Sheri and Mr. CruiseTipsTV had already ruled that out as a possibility when they were considering excursions prior to boarding the *Star Princess*. "We had ruled that out as an excursion of choice—let's dive in the water with giant animals…I don't think so! But it's a very pop-ular activity in La Paz, and given the circumstances, we ended up going for it. Of course we left my son in the boat. That was one of the most memorable, adrenalin-filled days of our cruising lives." I can't say I am surprised Sheri ended up going for swimming with sharks; recall she scuba dived at 17 without being certified, and jumped off cliffs at The Blue Hole in Jamaica without any prior experience!

One of Sheri's most fun times onboard a cruise ship was a very short inaugural sailing on Norwegian Cruise Lines' new flag-ship *Norwegian Bliss,* which premiered in April 2018. "I took Junior Editor along on that two-night media sailing, and it was on that ship that he fell in love with the children's center (he had previously been reluctant to hang out in the kids' venues on cruise ships). The staff was so engaged and played active sports with the kids, as well as other activities including making jewelry for their mothers. Junior LOVED the waterslides on this ship, and Mom got to race the Go Karts as well—definitely a FIRST at sea! *Norwegian Bliss* is an amaz-ing ship, purpose built for Alaska, and our family hopes to sail on her again." Sheri has cruised to Alaska an amazing four times, and hopes to make a full-length voyage on *Bliss* her fifth.

* * * * *

While Sheri is an influencer that many thousands of cruisers, fans, and followers on her multitude of social media platforms look to for cruising advice and to experience cruising vicariously through Sheri and *CruiseTipsTV*, she maintains what seems an ideal work-life balance and is able to compartmentalize the various aspects of her personal and professional life. "The core of my life is that I am a wife and a mom." Despite being a busy professional with a couple of disparate careers, Sheri thrives spending time gardening vegetables, or in the kitchen cooking with her son, with loud music playing. In her non-*CruiseTipsTV* professional life Sheri is a busy managerial employee for a Southern California firm that she has worked for 21 years. Despite being somewhat of a "mini-celebrity"—after all she has many thousands of fans and followers, and is a recognized influencer—Sheri told me that at work her cruising versus professional life is separate and largely unnoticed. There are a handful of fans, but for the most part her co-workers may know about Sheri's cruising life but are not really cruisers themselves. Although, for colleagues who are about to go on a cruise, she is recognized as "that lady, Sheri, she knows things!" Otherwise, she receives no special treatment and has the same limitations as anyone else including peak work times, coupled with a finite amount of vacation. "I have to work within the confines of my corporate job. I think that surprises people; people think we cruise a lot more than we do. We only average two to four cruises a year, and four would have to be some special circumstance."

Sheri and her family wrapped up 2018 with a very special cruise to Asia on the *Diamond Princess* where they visited Asia for 12 nights. They cruised 2800 nautical miles from Tokyo to Singapore— with stops including Hong Kong, Taipei, and Vietnam, along the way. This was their first cruise abroad as a family. I asked Sheri what were the highlights of the cruise? "Waking up to a rare, sunny view of Mt. Fuji in the port of Shimizu, which is usually shrouded by clouds, taking a thrilling rickshaw ride through the chaotic streets of Ho Chi Minh City in Vietnam, and visiting the Fushimi Inari Shrine in Kyoto, Japan." Quite a way to close out the year.

For 2019, Sheri has booked another family cruise abroad—a Mediterranean cruise with MSC Cruises. "We are planning to cruise to the Mediterranean with *MSC Meraviglia* to experience their Yacht Club product, a surprisingly affordable 'ship within a ship' experience that offers exclusivity and some great inclusions, like a private restaurant, access to the thermal spa, and unlimited premium beverages." Sheri is also considering exploring the Southern Caribbean and perhaps visiting Northern Europe in 2019.

Sheri has already cruised to a couple of destinations that are on many bucket lists: Alaska four different times—*Princess' Diamond, Sapphire, Grand, and Golden*—and the Panama Canal. Nonetheless, Panama Canal remains on Sheri's bucket list. To my surprise, it is possible to only do a partial transit of the Panama Canal; that is, through one set of locks, which is what Sheri did with her mom, husband and son. "That was on *Caribbean Princess,* Thanksgiving 2017. That was a 10-night cruise from Fort Lauderdale and was a partial transit through the new Agua Clara locks. We chose the partial transit because the cruise was short enough to accommodate our work schedule—10 days vs. the standard 14-15 day full crossings." On Sheri's bucket list is to do a Panama Canal full passage. Also on Sheri's bucket list is Tahiti and its surrounding islands.

The near future is promising for *CruiseTipsTV* as they have recently introduced—to much early success *CruiseTipsTV Academy,* a one-time fee based course enabling cruisers to access in-depth education about cruising. The first offering of *CruiseTipsTV Academy* is the "Intro to Cruising Master Class" online video program. "*CruiseTipsTV Academy* came about because newer cruisers had the same questions but we couldn't answer their questions fast enough, and we couldn't answer their questions sequentially and provide them with a start-to-finish education. What people really needed was not to sift through our almost 500 videos, but rather the opportunity to start with the cruise research process, through booking, planning, packing, boarding and on through to what to expect about dining, tipping, disembarkation, etc. So we created a course.

It's been incredible—through the first several weeks we already have over 500 students. We have a private Facebook group for the course, live streams, downloadable packing and planning lists, coaches who are experienced cruisers, and more."

Longer-term, Sheri said, "What the future holds is a bit of a mystery, but some of our goals are to continue to vlog our experience in new destinations. We also hope to expand our website, to continue creating learning opportunities for our student community, and possibly to create a membership site. YouTube is an unpredictable platform, so it's important for us to look to other platforms while keeping our YouTube production and live streams going."

Whatever ways evolve for *CruiseTipsTV* to get their videos and other content to their fervent and growing fan base, I am confident Sheri, Mr. CruiseTipsTV, and Junior Editor will adapt accordingly. Coupled with their passion for cruising, the future is bright for *CruiseTipsTV.*

THE TRAVELING WIFE CRUISING AROUND THE WORLD: LUCY WILLIAMS

*T*he *Traveling Wife Cruising Around the World* is more than just a catchy tagline for Lucy Williams. It literally is a way of life by virtue of the fact that Lucy—a former cruise ship employee—is the spouse of a cruise ship officer. In her thirties, and having visited nearly 80 countries, Lucy's story would fit well in Chapter 13, Cruising's Young and Restless about several amazing millenials and cruising. However, the circumstances behind her intriguingly titled story and attendant blog, *The Traveling Wife Cruising Around the World,* are interesting in their own right. And, Lucy Williams' story is well-suited for *The Joy of Cruising's* section, The Influencers, given *The Traveling Wife Cruising Around the World* blog is all about cruising tips and helping cruisers make the best choices, her extensive presence and following on social media, and Lucy's comprehensive website, Lucy Williams Global, www.lucywilliamsglobal.com, with its continuously updating graphic of a world map pinpointing Lucy's current location.

Born in UK and raised on the south coast of England, Lucy stayed in her home town working in the jewelry trade until she was 24, when she responded to an advertisement in a jewelry industry trade magazine to work onboard a cruise ship in a jewelry shop. Lucy applied and within a few months began her life aboard cruise ships. Lucy worked onboard for nearly ten years. She worked in the jewelry shop for three years, and then ascended into management and was on the shop management team for over six years. The shop management team is responsible for all the retail onboard—not just the jewelry shop.

After working onboard cruise ships for a year, Lucy met her future husband, Paolo, one of the ship's officers. They managed to get assigned to the same ship for a while. Paolo then proposed to Lucy. "I met Paolo in the summer of 2007 onboard and we got married in England in 2012." For a few years after getting married Lucy continued as part of the shop management team. "I stopped working onboard as the company would no longer put my husband and me on the same ship, so I chose to leave my position and just travel with my husband." So, Lucy began traveling as the "traveling wife," as the term is used onboard, and ultimately branded her blog with "the traveling wife" phrase. I was curious about the term "traveling wife." At first I was wary of using the term "traveling wife"—it reminded me of "housewife" which some may find offensive—but since Lucy used the term liberally, and it is incorporated in her brand, I assumed it was commonly used in cruise ship parlance. Lucy told me, "Onboard the term 'traveling wife' is used for the ship officers' wives that travel with them." How common is it for there to be "traveling wives," I asked? She told me, "It varies, but there are a lot of wives that do travel with their officer husbands. Usually until their children have to go to school or if their children are grown up or they are child-free like myself. Many officers meet their future wives onboard as there are a lot of female crew onboard."

Lucy Williams in Bora Bora, French Polynesia.

Lucy's husband Paolo is from Italy. "When I'm not onboard, I spend my time between England and Italy. I spend most of the year cruising between different countries. I now feel like a citizen of the world, as I am never in one place for very long, but I call home England and Italy; I'm a 'Britalian' as I like to call it!"

Paolo is the Food & Beverage Director for a well known American cruise line, and Lucy travels with him while he is working onboard. Lucy finds life onboard as a traveling wife to be very different as she is not a crew member, but does not quite feel like a passenger. "It is like you are an in-between," she says. "I did not set out to marry an officer and stop working; it just happened. I did want to continue working onboard, but it wasn't meant to be. So, I treat travelling onboard as my home life; it is not a vacation. If I treated it like a vacation, I would be the size of a house as I travel for three to four months at a time!"

Lucy and Paolo on board.

Lucy and Paolo dine and socialize with the ship captain and other senior officers and their traveling wives when "on duty." I asked her to talk about the majority of time when she is not on duty—what is life like? "I live in crew quarters. My husband's cabin is very nice. It is a suite that has a bedroom, dressing area, bathroom and day room. I can't complain! The other passengers are obsessed with where I live and eat and it usually is the first thing they ask me when they find out I am married to an officer. I eat all around the ship like a regular passenger or in the officer's mess, depending on whether I am dining with my husband or doing my own thing in the daytime."

I asked Lucy, what do you do when Paolo is working and you do not need to accompany him? She told me, "I treat ship life like my home life. I like to have a routine and ship life is not always as glamorous as it looks. I spend a lot of time on my own, although when Paolo has breaks I see him then, so my days often work around his schedule. We often meet for lunch. On the days at sea I go to fitness classes in the morning, have coffee and read my emails. In the afternoon I write articles for my blog if I'm feeling inspired. I'm always talking to the passengers onboard and the questions they ask me inspire many of my blog posts. I like to read, maybe watch some television, and of course, when the weather permits sit outside on deck and relax."

"Most evenings I will have a casual dinner with my husband. Evenings onboard can vary, as some nights there are cocktail parties or hosting dinners, especially on formal nights. I feel like I am always getting dressed up! In a one-week cruise there are two formal nights, and more on longer cruises. On port days I will either go on a tour or just for a walk around the port. Sometimes my husband may join me for lunch off the ship. When he can come ashore with me it is lovely. What other job gives you the opportunity to have lunch and explore different and often exotic locations?"

Paolo and Lucy at Easter Island.

"Being a traveling wife is a nice life, but it does have its pros and cons like anything else. Sure, I could stay at home, but I much prefer to be onboard and see the world. The main thing is to be with my husband; it makes his and my life nicer. He works four months on and two months off. I travel most of his contract with him. When he is off it is great to be home together."

After a year of cruising as a traveling wife, Lucy felt she needed something to keep her mind active; Lucy and her husband were going on a world cruise and she thought there was no better time to start a travel blog. In January 2017, *The Travelling Wife Cruising Around the World* was born. The blog focuses principally on cruise ports, cruising tips, packing tips and guides, and travel in general when not on a cruise ship. Lucy has a unique perspective from which to author such a blog given her work onboard as a crew member nearly ten years and another couple of years as a cruise passenger as a "traveling wife." In addition, she spends time in her native country of England and in her husband's country of Italy, so she is never short on travel stories. "I started writing this blog, as I was seeing all these beautiful places, but only posting photos on my Facebook profile and not really sharing my experiences, I thought why don't I share in a different way and write a travel blog from my perspective. I have a wealth of knowledge between working onboard and traveling as a passenger—I have seen it from both sides of the coin. I thought it might be good reading for those interested in travel and cruising. The blog also allows my family and friends to know what I've been up when at sea – it does save time in those long distance phone calls and emails!"

Curious about the contrast between what Lucy refers to as "both sides of the coin," I wanted Lucy to reflect on her experience working versus traveling as a passenger. Specifically, with regard to working, I ask, "What would you say is the most interesting aspect of working onboard?" Lucy told me, "Working with many different nationalities and making lots of friends. I am still friends with the majority of people I met in my first year of working onboard. Working a six-month contract at a time you become very close with your colleagues as you work and live together—they become your family. The other interesting thing about working onboard is seeing how people behave on vacation! Some are sensible and act like they would normally whilst others go absolutely crazy! The other thing that still amazes me is how the ship works. So many things are made onboard—from the daily newspaper to the bread. Everyone works as a team. Turnaround, that is, embarkation and disembarkation days are crazy as everyone works so hard. The passengers do not realize sometimes that the ship is turned around in four or five hours. Luggage is taken off, cabins are cleaned top to bottom and sheets changed, food, drinks, toilet paper, shop stores, spa stores, artwork, etc., are loaded onboard. All the passengers disembark. Then the new ones embark and we start again a new cruise. Just like that!"

Regarding Lucy's perspective as a passenger, I asked, "Once you became a passenger, what were you most surprised by?" Lucy laughed. "Not much, as I have seen everything! Paul, I could tell you so much, but I have to be careful not to upset the people that might read the book!"

Of course that response just piqued my interest! Not wanting to press Lucy to betray any confidentiality, I implored her to share a general observation that surprised her. "I think the tamest thing I can say is that it surprises me how many people book a cruise that don't really know where they are going! For example, they book a cruise to Hawaii, they don't know what ports they are going to and did not realize how many sea days there would be from Los Angeles.

Obviously, this doesn't apply to most passengers, but I have come across quite a few. It takes all sorts!"

As a "traveling wife" Lucy has been on over 60 cruises totaling approximately 600 days and has visited over 80 countries. Consequently, Lucy has experienced travel to virtually every part of the world including Alaska, Baltic, British Isles, Iceland, Californian Coastal, Mediterranean, Mexico, Panama Canal, South Pacific-French Polynesia and a world cruise comprised of ports of call in United States, New Zealand, Australia, Far East, Middle East, Northern Africa, Europe, Central America, and South America.

I was intrigued about Lucy's world cruise. Several of the individuals I spoke to for *The Joy of Cruising* have a long-term goal of a world cruise. And, those who have gone on a world cruise would like to do so again. When I discuss world cruises with friends who are casual cruisers, I get a mixed reaction. When I mention the length and number of sea days, I get reactions of either incredulity ("oh, that's too much time on the ocean") or awe ("wow, I wish I could get the time off from work to do one of those.") Lucy told me, "In 2017 my husband was assigned to a ship that was going to do a world cruise. The world cruise is one of the best cruises to go on as you see so much in 111 days. We went to 36 ports, 25 countries and six continents and spent 73 days at sea. I had worked a world cruise before, but it was a different route so I got to see a lot of new places for the first time. My favorite parts of the world cruise were visiting Petra in Jordan and seeing the Big Buddha in Hong Kong. The world cruise was not just about visiting the ports though, I got to know a lot of people over the cruise. Some stayed the whole trip, while others came on for segments. Meeting new people is something I love to do and I left this cruise with lots of new friends. There were a lot of sea days, but you needed those to recover after long days in port sightseeing. This cruise was one of the best I have been on and would recommend it to anyone that enjoys long cruises."

A collage of Lucy's world cruise: (l. to r.) at sea; Rabaul, Papua New Guinea; at sea; onboard; Bora Bora, French Polynesia; Bora Bora; Tahiti, French Polynesia; Trapani, Sicily; Guam, Micronesia

Having seen so much of the world, Lucy has a multitude of wonderful memories. 'I have great memories from all itineraries. The world cruise was a fantastic experience, travelling the world and meeting some amazing people from all walks of life. My favorite itinerary is the Mediterranean as you can be in a different country everyday, but the best part is the food! Food and culture is the best part of cruising the Med."

This impressive cruise history was all attained just since 2015 when Lucy started cruising as a passenger with her first cruise to French Polynesia. It doesn't include the hundreds of cruises and destinations Lucy experienced as a crew member—so many that she doesn't remember her first as a 24-year old jewelry shop hostess which was her first time ever on a cruise ship.

Besides the many cruises Lucy has been on with her husband, either as co-workers or as a married couple, I was curious if they cruised much for leisure, perhaps on a different cruise line. Lucy said, "My husband and I have never gone on a cruise together as a vacation. I never cruised before working onboard and my husband cruised only as a child, but as an adult just worked onboard."

Despite Lucy's far-reaching travel experience, she still has a lot on her bucket list. "My future travel plans are to keep travelling! You would think after working onboard for so many years I would be fed up of cruising, but I love it! Cruising is the best way to travel. Unpack once and relax. I am a travel addict and even though I spend my life traveling there are still places on my bucket list! I would love to go to New York, explore more of China to experience the Great Wall and the Terracotta Warriors, see more of Australia and New Zealand, Tokyo in Japan and go on Safari in Africa."

Lucy holding a block of ice at Endicott Arm Glacier Tour in Alaska; Lucy was on this cruise during her interview for *The Joy of Cruising.*

What about Lucy Williams Global, and *The Traveling Wife Cruising Around the World* blog—what does the future hold? "I will continue to share information on cruise ports, give cruise tips and share my travels around the world along with any travel tips I pick up on the way. I love building a travel community, and helping people with their cruise and travel questions, and it makes me feel useful. Ultimately, I would love to turn the blog into a travel television show one day! Who knows?"

SHIPS AND CHAMPAGNE

If the phrase *Ships and Champagne* connotes elegance to you, then I suspect Flavia Gray is smiling. Flavia Gray from Surrey, UK has an award winning cruise blog—named a top 50 cruise blogger and nominated for UK's Wave Award in 2017 and 2018—that evokes luxury in numerous ways beyond its name. The first thing you notice is the logo, a silhouette of a model-figured woman from the waist up in an au courant form fitting dress and matching hat; just below the image are the words: *Ships & Champagne, A Luxury Cruise and Lifestyle Blog by Flavia Gray.* As expected, the blog posts tend toward articles and reviews of higher-end cruises, and the blog also includes posts featuring couture and lifestyle.

Flavia Gray is a single mother of two who after working a succession of sales and marketing jobs saw her singing hobby turn into a full-time career. After working for a few years as a singer in bands performing at weddings, anniversaries, and other private parties as well as in pubs and clubs, it became clear to Flavia that what she enjoyed and was quite good at was not going to provide her with a reliably constant stream of income. Reluctantly, Flavia contacted an employment agency in order to pursue a more traditional work environment. Given her background in sales and marketing, within days of contacting the employment firm Flavia was offered an interview. It was for a position with Royal Caribbean as a Cruise Specialist—an entree to a career that I suspect many of the readers of *The Joy of Cruising* would have been very enthused about in their thirties. Flavia, however, was not all that excited, as the opening involved a position in a call center, which was far from the ideal environment given Flavia's extroverted personality.

Flavia reflects back on the day she arrived for her interview with Royal Caribbean with amusement. "My attitude was already negative and when I saw one of the employees arriving at the office in jeans and tee shirt, I was quite disgusted. Only later did I learn that Friday was 'dress down' day." Long before she was blogging about couture and style, Flavia was cognizant of how people should present themselves—even though her presumption about the employee's attire was incorrect!

It turned out it wasn't so much an interview as a written assessment administered to a roomful of applicants. Applicants would move on to an interview with Royal Caribbean staff only if the assessment score was adequate. Flavia dutifully took the exam, still not particularly enthused about the position. In fact, Flavia had arranged an interview for later that day with a previous employer and was just going through the motions at Royal Caribbean. While waiting for the assessment to be scored, the applicants were shown a video of a Royal Caribbean cruise ship. Flavia had never cruised before. It was at that moment of watching that video that Flavia's life was changed forever. "I mean really, really, changed," Flavia told me. "The ship was huge; it looked like a lot of fun and it had a pool and a kid's club. Then there were endless other things; I just kept thinking, what, there's a rock wall; what, there's a surf simulator; what, there's a mini golf course; a theatre, parades, parties, nightclubs. My mind was blown." Now Royal Caribbean had Flavia's attention. She was captivated by what was on the screen. "Now I wanted that job; I had to have that job, I had to get on that ship. It was like everything else just melted away and I had one vision: getting onboard that cruise ship with Lucy, my daughter."

An interest in travel always lingered in Flavia's background. When she was a child, Flavia's parents would take her to Los Angeles to visit relatives. The sunshine, palm trees, beaches and the American way of life left a lasting impression on her. "It really grabbed me and I have always wanted to go back." As a young adult before her daughter was born, Flavia loved visiting the Gulf Beaches in Florida. Once Lucy was born, visiting Florida as a single mom was just not the same. Single motherhood and an active child on the beach brought with it special challenges requiring Flavia's undivided attention. "As a single parent I didn't have the luxury of another pair of eyes. My days of lying in the sun, listening to music and dozing off were over," Flavia said.

Now Flavia found herself fantasizing. This cruise ship on the screen meant there was a way she could travel again, and even as a single mom. Normally a cruise would be out of reach financially for Flavia, but she had recalled one of the Royal Caribbean staffers mentioning something about free or very cheap cruises during their presentation to the applicants. "I had to get on that ship, and I had to get this job. That was that." Flavia did get the job with Royal Caribbean. She set out to make her fantasy of traveling with her daughter a reality.

The Royal Caribbean call center training was rigorous and comprehensive, providing Flavia with in-depth knowledge into

Royal's products, services, and system. It also included training on Celebrity Cruises and Azamara Club Cruises as they were all under the same parent company.

It was six weeks before she was allowed on real telephone calls, and once that began, she was subject to constant monitoring and mentoring on her performance and was accountable for a stringent set of criteria to meet on each call. Flavia and her call center colleagues faced financial consequences for failing to meet the call standards as determined by the Royal Caribbean Quality Assurance team. There were many times Flavia wanted to rip her headset off and quit. But her mind kept going back to that video about the cruise ship. So, she resolved to get past the six-month probationary period, take her daughter on a discounted Royal Caribbean cruise, and then quit!

Despite the demands and tedium of call center work, Flavia thrived and frequently exceeded sales milestones. As a result, she was offered a free "familiarization" trip (familiarization trips are for employees and travel agents, but not everyone is lucky enough to get one; they are usually based on sales performance.) Flavia could not believe it. The fantasy was about to become a reality in the form of a four-night cruise on *Grandeur of the Seas* departing from Palma de Mallorca, Spain and docking in Málaga, Spain. Flavia was overcome with gleeful anticipation. "I did panic a bit I must admit," Flavia said. "I wondered if it would really be everything I had expected. What if Royal Caribbean had just told me it was great, but in actual fact when I get onboard I am going to hate it and be stuck on the ship with a bunch of people I don't like? Suddenly I started to worry."

"When we arrived at the port there was a huge ship, just like the one in the video. Then as we turned the corner there was what seemed in comparison a small, not so impressive ship behind it. Oh no, that was the ship we were going on, not the lovely big one. Now I was really worried."

Flavia on *Grandeur*, her first cruise.

Flavia boarded and found that "small" ship to be quite nice and it did not feel small at all. In fact, once onboard she found it to be huge. The ship was gorgeous, with a lovely chrome and beech atrium with marbled floor and a ceiling that seemed to extend to the sky. The first food venue Flavia and her colleagues tried was the buffet with a seemingly endless array of choices. After eating they went to the sundeck and Flavia laid out on a sun lounger. She felt like she was back at the beach, only there were really friendly waiters wearing Hawaiian shirts saying hello and asking if anyone wanted anything. She also found the other cruisers to be very personable. The cruise was off to a great start and getting better and better.

Flavia kept hearing others talking about the sail-away: go find one of the many ideal vantage points on the ship, with a cocktail in hand for sail-away. Flavia chose to join the group of Royal Caribbean employees that she was sailing with on the top deck. Cocktail in hand, steel drum band playing and guests joining members of the Royal Caribbean entertainment team to dance on the deck stage, the anticipation was thrilling. That larger ship, the *Liberty of the Seas*, the one Flavia mistakenly assumed was meant for her to board, went off first. Despite already being captivated by the more modest ship she boarded, Flavia watched wistfully as the "ship like the one in the video" sailed past. Someday....

In time they started moving. Flavia was overcome with a sense of excitement and adventure. As the ship moved away from the port and the waterfront homes appeared smaller and smaller, Flavia just felt free. It was in that moment that Flavia fell in love with cruising.

Flavia would soon be offered another, even more impressive opportunity to experience her newfound love. After her first cruise in May 2011, she earned a place on the inaugural sailing of *Celebrity Silhouette* in July 2011. It was awarded to the person who had made the most bookings for *Celebrity Silhouette* within a qualifying period. Celebrity Cruises is a more premium cruise line owned by Royal Caribbean International. Flavia's experience cruising on *Celebrity Silhouette* was incredible before the ship ever left port, beginning with them being flown to Rome and given a balcony stateroom—85% of the *Silhouette* staterooms have balconies. Celebrity Cruises ships are more luxurious than Royal Caribbean, and Flavia felt more suited to this type of cruise line. The most noticeable difference she found on the new, more premium cruise ship were the furnishings. Flavia found them to be much more comfortable. "You just melt into your chair." The other differences that were very apparent to Flavia were the service and the quality of the food. She found both of these to be impeccable on Celebrity.

Flavia worked with Royal Caribbean for several years, although she never grew fond of the call center environment. Flavia took three more cruises during her time with Royal Caribbean. The more she cruised, the more her passion for cruising grew. She also spent a lot of time onboard the cruise ships in port. Flavia became a member of the Promotions Team, which involved escorting visiting groups around the ships tours and answering their questions. She thrived in this role because it meant more time onboard. "There is something about being on a ship that I love, regardless of whether it is for a few hours or a few days. Any opportunity I get, I am onboard."

Flavia's passion for cruising came through in her interactions with customers. They trusted and enjoyed talking to her. At the same time, this was a bit of a problem within the confines of the call center job description and work environment. Flavia was eager to find a way to perform her job on her own terms.

In 2013, Flavia left Royal Caribbean to start her own travel business from home. It afforded her the opportunity to get on board other cruise lines. Flavia was able to discover MSC Cruises, Ponant Cruises, Princess Cruises, P&O Cruises, Cunard, Fred Olsen Cruises, Disney Cruise Lines, Crystal Cruises, Oceania Cruises, Regent Seven Seas Cruises, Cruise and Maritime and Azamara Club Cruises. It was challenging, however, to raise the funds necessary to market her new business. So, Flavia created a blog to convey her knowledge of and experience with cruising as a means to market her travel business. Initially the blog was positioned as a way for people to consider her services as a cruise travel agent, and the blog carried her name. After a couple of years gaining experience as a travel agent, Flavia found creating her blog and conveying her insight to prospective cruise customers to be more satisfying than making cruise bookings. She decided to focus more of her effort on the blog, and since she leaned towards luxury cruising, she rebranded the blog as *Ships and Champagne* in 2015. It is much easier for a travel agent to get onboard a cruise ship than it is for a blogger, so Flavia was able to continue to use her travel agent status to gain more content for the blog.

Flavia at the Bionic Bar on *Anthem of the Seas*. Yes, those robotic arms mix and serve your cocktails!

Flavia onboard Ponant Cruises luxury boutique vessel, *Le Boreal*. Photo by Andrew Sassoli-Walker.

Flavia had cultivated a number of relationships with cruise journalists and bloggers, and she sought their counsel regarding the transition from travel agent to cruise writer. One person in particular

Flavia respected, admired and trusted was John Honeywell, better known as Captain Greybeard, a legendary journalist and cruise writer in UK. Flavia considered Captain Greybeard a true gentleman; she reached out to him a couple of times when she wasn't sure of the correct way to write something, and he was always very friendly and helpful. Their rapport grew, conversations were more frequent, and they became online friends. John was someone Flavia could ask for honest and expert advice in the cruise journalism industry. When Flavia's childhood hero, George Michael, died on Boxing Day (December 26) 2016, she wrote a heartfelt tribute to whom she considered an amazing person, as writing was the only way she could positively channel her emotions. Given the sensitivity and timing, Flavia asked John if he would take a look at it for her before she posted it on *Ships and Champagne*. John read it and told Flavia it was "really beautiful and very well-written." Later that day John shared the tribute on his Facebook page with the message "To make up for not breaking the news, here's a link to a touching tribute to George Michael written by a friend."

John Honeywell passed away suddenly in 2017. Indicative as to what an icon John was to the cruise industry, Royal Caribbean installed a telescope on UK-based *Independence of the Seas* in his memory, with a plaque inscribed with his motto. Though immensely sad about Captain Greybeard's passing, Flavia is very proud that her writing hero's final interview was for *Ships and Champagne*. Flavia recalls being on a cruise when she got the news of John's passing. Through her tears Flavia looked out at the blurry sea and recalled John's motto: "Any day at sea is better than a day in the office." It was at that point Flavia decided to become a full-time cruise writer.

Cruisers Like You and Me...
Sort Of

BILL AND ROSIE, AND MARK AND LEANNE, AND KAREN AND JERRY

*T*he *Joy of Cruising* features a number of cruise industry person-alities who embody passion for cruising, and organizations who facilitate ways for others to pursue their own passion for cruising, such as theme cruise purveyors. These individuals and organizations are either covered in the media, are part of cruise media (cruise writers and bloggers), or show up in search results. However, there are millions of "regular" cruisers whose stories of passion for cruising are just as enthralling and fascinating. Of course, there is no typical "regular" cruiser that could be portrayed in *The Joy of Cruising* in a way that represents this entire group. There are innumerable interesting stories and like a snowflake, each one is unique. Everyday I browse the cruise-related internet discussion forums, blogs, and social media and come across individuals I would love to have a conversation with, and I believe many others cruisers and prospective cruisers would like to be "a fly on the wall" in the room when that conversation takes place.

Just in the days around when I wrote this chapter of *The Joy of Cruising*, I read the following from "regular" individuals in a single discussion forum thread on the topic of the frequency with which people cruise:

"Wife is working and I am self employed. We cruise 6 to 7 weeks a year."

"...we cruise 40-60 days a year"

"two years ago 62 days on cruise ships, last year 75 days.

"we take at least 16 cruises per year"

Prolific cruising, that is, number of cruises or days sailing or how close one is to the next tier in the various cruise lines loyalty incentive programs, by itself doesn't necessarily make one's story compelling. A single cruise may be a source of incredible stories. In a previous chapter I discussed Elizabeth Hill who had never cruised before when she embarked on the inaugural cruise for *Independence of the Seas* after being chosen as ship Godmother. Nevertheless, I would love the opportunity to speak with the prolific cruisers in that discussion thread about cruising frequency. I want to learn what motivates them to spend so much time, and money, to do what they do. I want to experience cruising vicariously through them. For the most part I can't; they are just faceless voices in cyberspace, dispersed throughout the country and beyond as I am to them; I am just a voice on the internet. I suspect if I could ask them about their cruise exploits they would wonder: Who is the guy? Believe me, I tried— and sometimes the responses were essentially "Who is this guy?"

I did get a chance to have a conversation with some of them. Perhaps I can get an inkling of "what would someone have to think and believe" to make these individuals do what they do by experiencing cruising vicariously through Bill Raffel, a retired salesman and entrepreneur from Milwaukee, Wisconsin whose cruising exploits I envy. Or Mark Weston, an Australian salesman. Mark and I both love cruising. I cruised a couple of times last year. Mark cruised last year also; twenty-one times! Or Karen Ahr, who lives near the water, goes to the beach virtually every weekend, and when not at home in Southwest Florida is likely on the water in a cruise ship in the Caribbean.

Bill and Rosie

Bill and Rosie Raffel, from Milwaukee, Wisconsin have been married 41 years. They have lived in the Milwaukee area all their lives. Bill and Rosie are passionate about travel. They also attend about thirty Milwaukee Brewers games including a road trip each year. Bill's hobbies are photography and making videos of the cruises they take, and they both enjoy spending time with their large extended family in the area.

Rosie and Bill on the Navigational Bridge of *Serenade of the Seas*.

Bill is a retired sales executive and entrepreneur, and Rosie works as a nurse. Rosie plans to join Bill in retirement in a couple of years and then they will cruise a lot. How do I know that? Did they tell me that? They did not have to. I am not really venturing out on a limb by surmising what Bill and Rosie will do in a couple of years. Just look at how they have chosen to live out their cruising passion up-to-now.

Bill and Rosie have been on 60 cruises and have several more booked through 2020. They have cruised on Norwegian, Carnival, Princess, Celebrity, and Royal Caribbean cruise lines. Bill and Rosie have cruised the Caribbean extensively; numerous Pacific Coastal cruises; and, amazingly, Alaska four times, Panama Canal four times, and a transatlantic cruise. Passionate about cruising indeed. And Rosie is not even retired yet. Earlier I conjectured about Bill and Rosie's plans when Rosie retires. Later, Bill said to me, "Once Rosie retires our cruise plans go into warp speed, with a possible 121-night World Cruise in our future."

When discussing highlights of their cruising life, most travelers focus on the exotic, picturesque destinations, beautiful vistas, breathtaking views and experiences, the slightly rocking relaxation and solitude of the ocean, as well as the aesthetics, amenities, and wow factors of particular cruise ships. Of course aspects of cruising, like destinations and experiences matter to Bill as well. After all they have been to Africa on a three-week Safari, Australia to scuba dive on the Great Barrier Reef, and Hawaii, and the aforementioned Alaska and Panama Canal among other amazing experiences. But when I inquired about his cruising highlights, Bill focused on something different. "The highlights of our cruising are not the places we have been, but the people we have met. Rosie and I love interacting with people and hearing about their lives and stories. Our best friends are not from our local neighborhood, but instead are from around the cruise world," Bill told me. An example of one of the group of cruisers that Rosie and Bill have befriended is the Pink Boa Cruisers. The wearing of a pink boa (and pink fedoras and tiaras) has become a symbol of the friendships made through cruising. The Pink Boa Cruises are over 10 years old and span the United States. Their motto is FUN ~ FEATHERS ~ FRIENDS.

Pink Boa Cruisers from *Harmony of the Seas* 2017. Bill front, Rosie to his right.

It comes through in Bill's videos about his cruises where it is very apparent that Bill is not just a people person, but has made interactions with others on a cruise—whether friends Bill and Rosie travel with, as they often do, or people they meet on the cruise— an integral part of his cruise experience. It is not only apparent in the sixty or so videos of Bill's cruises at his YouTube channel. Bills gregariousness also is apparent in the comments to his videos that viewers have left on his YouTube channel where you see numerous mentions of Bill causing some cruiser, or prospective cruiser to laugh out loud; or others conveying gratitude to Bill for bringing back fond memories of a cruise they also took on the ship Bill featured in a video, or for previewing a cruise that they too are booked on; or even mildly chastising Bill for leaving out of a video his trademark phrase "Gooooooood Morrrrrnnning!" It is not unusual while on a cruise for someone to ask Bill if he is the guy that has cruise videos on YouTube. They inevitably, bring up the Gooooooood Morrrrrrnnning catchphrase present in Bill's videos.

Bill and friends in front of The Ultimate Abyss, a ten story slide on
***Harmony of the Seas*. Not just a photo op! Yes, they did the slide!**

Bill has assumed a role of an ambassador for cruising, actively working to pass on his passion for cruising to others. On Cruise Critic, the leading cruise community website, Bill often takes a lead role on cruise roll calls—where cruisers meet up and make plans with others who will be on the same cruise—and tries to put together group excursions and activities, and provide as much information in general to new and less-seasoned travelers. Bill also is a member of many Facebook cruise groups, and moderates one, which is how we met.

Besides frequently cruising, cultivating his YouTube channels and participating heavily with cruise social media, Bill has come up with a more practical means of pursuing his passion. Upon retirement, Bill became a work-from-home travel agent so that he would get first-hand information directly from the cruise lines, be able to take advantage of group pricing, and receive commissions on his bookings. Bill has become a busy agent, serving the needs of one very demanding client—Bill and Rosie Raffel.

Bill and Rosie closed out 2018 with the first family cruise with their granddaughters. Bill said, "Seeing the world of cruising through their eyes was very interesting and amazing. The passion to cruise and travel has been passed to another generation in our family."

At the DreamWorks Character Breakfast on *Harmony of the Seas*: Bill (left), Rosie (right,) with grandkids, 5 year-old Lillian and 20 month-old Violet.

"Cruising is not just a vacation; it is a mindset and a way of life to those of us with a cruise passion!"

Mark and Leanne

Mark and Leanne Weston have resided in Paradise Point on The Gold Coast in Queensland Australia the past 33 years. Mark, 59, has spent his entire career in sales for various industries. For the last 18 years, Mark has been in sales in an industry somewhat related to cruising: he has sold pontoons, also known as docks. Mark sells pontoons within the recreation and commercial marina market. As he works on commission, and is good at what he does, Mark has a great deal of flexibility, enabling his cruise life and professional life to easily co-exist. Mark is in no hurry to retire; he works from a water-front home and does what he wants, when he wants, so he doesn't see how retirement can be better than his current life. Mark can cruise for a month or two, go back to work for a month, and that pays for another month or two of cruising. "So I may as well keep doing what I do," Mark says. When on land, Leanne spends much of her time with Mark, often accompanying him on sales calls when not caring for her elderly mom or spending time with her grandkids.

Mark and Leanne in front of the *Radiance of the Seas.*

The Weston's have been married 38 years and still love every day together. They have the same likes and dislikes—fortunately cruising is one of their mutual likes—and love to do everything together. That's pretty important if you have spent over 1300 days together at sea, with many more planned. Mark and Leanne have three children and five grandchildren.

Mark and Leanne Weston typify the kind of cruisers who first sparked my interest in writing about travelers' cruising pursuits, admittedly driven largely out of intrigue. What would a person have to think and believe to cruise 21 times in a single year? Besides interest in Mark and Leanne's backstory and motivation, someone who has cruised a total of 123 times has to be a fount of amazing stories, anecdotes and experiences.

Many of the Weston's cruises have been on glimmering, massive, technically advanced cruise ships. Yet Mark recalls fondly their very first cruise in 1982 on an old, small vessel which lacked any of the features and amenities today's cruisers are used to. Mark and Leanne sailed on the *TSS Fairstar*, of Sitmar Cruises. The *Fairstar* was 18 years old at the time and had been repurposed twice before its reincarnation as a cruise ship, starting its life as a British troopship, and then pressed into service transporting British emigrants to Australia under an Australian government contract. The *Fairstar* cruise ship lacked stateroom phones, televisions, and could fit in the promenade of the Royal Caribbean *Allure of the Seas*, one of the ships the Weston's sailed on in the past year. Nevertheless, Mark and Leanne had a blast on that first cruise; clay pigeon shooting and fishing off the back of the ship, and downing 20-cent beers. That, in retrospect, rather pedestrian cruise inspired a passion in Mark and Leanne that would result in dozens of cruise adventures that enabled them to explore the world, meet numerous fascinating cruise mates, establish lasting friendships, including some who would become future cruise partners, and experience a lifetime of memories. Yet there is much more they plan to do.

Following that first cruise, Mark and Leanne cruised infrequently in the ensuing several years as they raised their children, cruising every few years, sometimes with the kids and sometimes just as a couple. They did a couple of cruises on Star Cruises, the dominant Asia-Pacific cruise line at the time, sailing out of Singapore around Asia. In 1991, Mark and Leanne returned to the *Fairstar* and took their kids, who were just 8, 10 and 12 years old, on a 14-day cruise out of Singapore visiting China, Vietnam and Hong Kong.

Besides their occasional cruising in the nineties, the Westons initially did mostly land-based travel, frequently as a family. They traveled 15 trips to Bali, an island paradise in Indonesia known for its lush tropical flora, beautiful white sand beaches in the south, and black sand beaches in the north, and surrounded by coral reefs. Bali was a desirable destination for Australians given its reasonable pricing and only 5-hour flight. One year the Weston's visited Bali four times. Even though these trips were wonderful, affordable holidays for the Weston family, as is the case with most who have had a taste of the cruising life, they were hooked by cruising. They longed to do that on a steady basis and began to focus their holidays on cruising.

Altogether, Mark and Leanne have completed 123 cruises. Many cruisers with such a prolific cruising history tend to be partial to one or two cruise lines to maximize their loyalty rewards, which virtually all major cruise lines utilize for brand building and to keep you away from competing cruise lines and even land-based leisure and travel. Mark and Leanne are at or near the top tier of the loyalty programs for a couple of cruise lines, yet they have cruised on a diverse mix of lines: Royal Caribbean, Carnival, Princess, Holland

America, Celebrity, Norwegian, Costa, Star Cruises, Sitmar, P&O, and even the *SS Leonid Sobinov*, owned by the Soviet Union-based Black Sea Shipping Company. Mark and Leanne's "home" ship is the *Carnival Spirit* as its permanent home port is Sydney, Australia, although still a fairly long drive or several hours dealing with airports. *Spirit* is changing its homeport in 2020 to Brisbane, which is only a one-hour drive from where Mark and Leanne live. "Oh dear, that may become our future home," Mark said.

In recent years Mark and Leanne have tended to focus on just Carnival and Royal Caribbean, and have tried several classes of ship from small to mega. As amazing as Royal's mega ship *Allure of the Seas* was when they tried it in 2018, they like the smaller Royal ships better. They consider Royal's *Ovation of the Seas* probably the most exciting ship they have been on, with the sky flying and surfing simulators, bumper cars, roller skating, and the North Star, a robotic arm observation deck that extends far above the ship offering breathtaking views of the ocean. "We are hoping with the new port being built in Brisbane Royal will also be putting a ship here."

I asked many cruisers about the highlights of their cruising life, and what cruises remain on their bucket list. In comparing the responses I receive with discussions of highly desirable itineraries in the cruising media, I find that many frequent cruisers have done at least one and sometimes a few of the itineraries considered to be bucket list cruises. Mark and Leanne have done virtually all of the itineraries often mentioned as bucket list cruises. They have cruised the South Pacific, New Zealand, the Mediterranean, Hawaii and Tahiti, Asia, a 7-week cruise around South America, a cruise around Cape Horn and up to San Francisco, as well as Transatlantic, and Transpacific cruises. Consequently, Mark and Leanne say that they don't have much of a bucket list as they are already doing whatever they want to do now "because that is what we love." They have not yet done Alaska but plan to do so in the next few years. They also want to do a Baltic cruise. Mark mentioned perhaps an Africa cruise, as their son-in-law is from Kenya.

Most of Mark and Leanne's cruising has been done in the past 10 years, with the last five years averaging 12-15 per year. It was actually friends that really got Mark and Leanne hooked on cruising some years ago. Hard to believe Colleen and David, a retired couple from Tampa, Florida have done a lot more cruising than the Westons; they spend nine months out of the year cruising. I asked Mark how David and Colleen influenced them to cruise as much as they do. "Just seeing how David and Colleen basically live on board, I thought: what a life; we can do this. So, we are in training, to be just like them."

2018 was the Weston's biggest with 21 cruises. With that many cruises, choosing highlights becomes a daunting task. A three cruise stretch over two months last summer was among those highlights: *Carnival Spirit* for a back-to-back cruise that took them from Sydney to the South Pacific Islands of Noumea, Mare, Mystery Island and Lifou last July; then a cruise again on *Spirit* in August with friends from Canada that Mark and Leanne met cruising some years ago. "They spent a month with us prior to a 10-day South Pacific cruise, so we first visited Sydney and the Blue Mountains." Mark said.

In September, Mark and Leanne flew to Seattle to board Royal Caribbean *Explorer of the Seas* for a total of 28 nights, first doing a 7-Night Pacific Coastal including a two-day stop in San Francisco, followed by a 21-Night Transpacific Hawaii Cruise that ended in Sydney. After just four days home, the Westons flew to Venice for 49 more nights cruising!

Mark and Leanne closed out their whirlwind year of cruising by reuniting with their "cruise muses," Colleen and David, sailing with them on a series of back-to-back-to-back-to-back cruises on Royal Caribbean *Rhapsody of the Seas* itineraries departing out of Venice November 3 with ports of call including the Greek Isles, Croatia, Adriatic, Barcelona, the Canary Islands, Bahamas and ending in Tampa December 22. Mark and Leanne finally got home on Christmas day, for a respite until their next cruise which commences January 24, 2019 and will have them on Royal Caribbean *Explorer of the Seas* for seven back-to-backs for a total of 64 days. And then home for 16 days before flying to Barcelona to board the brand new Royal Caribbean *Spectrum of the Seas* for a back to back visiting Rome, Naples, Athens, Suez Canal, Jordan, Dubai, Muscat, Coachin, Penang and ending in Singapore 30 days later. Damn, I am exhausted just writing that!

After the celebration, Leanne and Mark on the top deck of
***Carnival Spirit* with the Captain Vittorio Marchi.**

With such cruising frequency, it is not surprising that Mark and Leanne have garnered some attention from others. They have been covered in local media and were featured in *Woman's Day* December 2017. To celebrate their 100th cruise in September 2017 they chose a cruise on *Carnival Spirit*. Carnival feted them like celebrities. To Carnival they are, having been deemed by Carnival as the most prolific cruisers with Carnival in Australia, with 398 nights as of the end of 2018. Onboard the *Spirit* Mark and Leanne were honored by Carnival Cruise Line Australia senior management at a ceremony on the top deck including the ship Captain, Maître'D, Hotel Director, Cruise Director, and other ship management, and the ceremony was attended by the media.

Cruising has permeated the lives of the Westons. Besides the bonds resulting in lasting friendships and seeing the world and spending weeks at a time with friends on the ocean, two of the Weston children were married on *Carnival Spirit*. Even the Captain came to the weddings. Mark and Leanne were the first Carnival Australia Diamond members—Carnival's highest tier in its loyalty program, that is first to achieve 200 nights with the company.

**Not only was Mark's son Jaye married on Carnival Spirit—
he takes it with him everywhere he goes!**

When they cruise out of Sydney, from the minute the Westons step foot in the cruise terminal, the staff know them and accommodate them in the waiting area before others are let in. They are first to board and their cabin is always ready as soon as they step on board. Mark and Leanne dine with the Captain on every Carnival cruise.

As seasoned cruisers, nowadays Mark and Leanne generally do back-to-back cruises. "I don't want to pack and fly anywhere for just 7 days; I usually prefer a month plus, but I am happy doing four consecutive seven day cruises rather than a single 28-day cruise with the same people. Its fun when everyone else is getting off and you get to stay and do it all again," Mark told me. Being in sales, Mark is naturally gregarious and loves to meet and talk to people. Virtually every cruise they go on, no matter where in the world it is, they run into other cruisers they know. Mark and Leanne place a high value on the social aspects of cruise traveling. "Cruising for us is all about the people, the crew and staff and the passengers you meet. At home we have a handful of really good friends, but at sea we have the whole ship. Just love it, dining out, shows, drinks in the hospitality lounges with other frequent cruisers, sharing stories with like minded people."

People often ask Mark about expense. Mark tells people that cruising doesn't have to be expensive. Sure it can be, but he and Leanne typically book much less expensive inside cabins, since they rarely spend much time in their stateroom. Mark says, "What we save on, say, four cruises by booking inside cabins rather than a balcony pays for the 5th cruise." They usually budget AUD$100 (approximately $74 US) per person per day. Mark reasons that while they are away for a month or two at a time, they are not paying for food, fuel, power, entertainment and dining out, drinks, etc. at home, so if you take that off the AUD$100 per day, it probably nets to AUD$70 per day.

"Does anyone else have our addiction—10 cruises done for the first half of this year, 11 more before Christmas…?" Mark asked the Facebook cruise group discussion board last year. His query elicited over 900 responses, the most I had ever seen regarding a single post. Of course, Mark's post captured my attention, and I was just as curious as to what the commenters would say. So, I read several hundred responses—more than half—before my eyes started to glaze over. By far most reflected a mix of awe, envy, "go for it" encouragement, and a fair amount of religiosity (there were dozens of iterations of "you are blessed"). Of course, this being the Internet there was a smattering of haters and snark. "Get a life!" "Buy a boat!" Yes, there are those who see Mark's passion as some kind of problem. I say, what a good problem to have! What do you say to that Mark? "Cruising life away one port at a time," Mark replied.

Karen and Jerry

I have reached out far and wide to passionate cruisers to try to convince them to share their stories with readers. Cruisers from Australia, New Zealand, United Kingdom, both coasts of the United States—as well as many in between the Pacific and the Atlantic—agreed to talk to me about their passion. When I heard of Karen and Jerry Ahr, I knew I wanted to talk to them about cruising, but I did not have to "reach out" very far. I did not know them, but they were right down the road from where I live in Fort Myers, Florida.

Karen and Jerry Ahr are like so many friends and neighbors I encounter in Southwest Florida who are among those I refer to above as from "between the coasts," drawn to this area by the sunshine, and by the proximity to the water, to retire, work from home, or some ideal medium between the two. The Ahr's relocated to Fort

Myers in 2010. Karen and Jerry experience closeness to the water virtually throughout the year: they live minutes from Fort Myers Beach and go to the beach every weekend—when they are in Fort Myers. Otherwise they are on the ocean, cruising an average of ten times a year. Add to that an annual stay on the beach in Punta Cana, Dominican Republic, abutting both the Caribbean Sea and the Atlantic Ocean.

Karen and Jerry from a cruise on their favorite cruise ship.

Karen and Jerry have sailed on 113 cruises mostly with Royal Caribbean; they just sailed on their 100th Royal cruise. They have also cruised with Celebrity, most recently *Celebrity Silhouette* in 2016, and Princess, where they sailed on *Regal Princess* in 2017. The Ahr's typically stay in regular balcony cabins, but the nicest state-room they recall was a suite on *Harmony of the Seas*, one of Royal Caribbean's Oasis-Class ships, the largest vessels sailing. Karen and Jerry are partial to the Oasis-Class just because there is so much to see and do. Karen's single favorite ship is the Oasis-Class *Allure of the Seas.* "Just something about that ship that really "speaks" to me. I love all the Oasis-Class ships, but *Allure* is my favorite." They also like all the glass and brass of Royal's ornate Radiance-Class ships, which are less than half the size of Oasis-Class ships.

As beach enthusiasts, Karen and Jerry cruise virtually exclusively to the Caribbean. St. Thomas, Sint Maarten, Antigua, St Lucia, Grenada, and Barbados are their favorite ports of call, but for the most part they love all of the ports along the Southern Caribbean route. Always a highlight for them is watching the ship come into the ports at these islands. "The water coves; it's just so gorgeous looking into the bays and seeing the water and the cities at each port."

From Karen and Jerry's cruise ship coming into port at St Thomas.

When I asked about their most memorable experiences cruising, surprisingly the response didn't involve some pricey excursion or exotic destination or iconic view like Magens Bay in St. Thomas, but rather simple, touching interactions with others while cruising. "Many years ago while in St Lucia, we went to a beach area called the Wharf. We met a local family that invited us to see what they were cooking on the edge of the palm-lined woods. They were the nicest family and invited us to lunch. We talked to them for a long time and were amazed as to how much they knew about the United States. Way more than we know about their country," Karen told me. She also mentioned a lasting memory about a member of the crew on *Serenade of the Seas*. "Our cabin steward would have his guitar and sing to us as we came back to our cabin each evening. He was super sweet. We still talk about him." Despite all the cruises, all the money spent, it is these kinds of person-to-person experiences that continue to bring a smile to Karen's face. "We have had staff come up to us after a couple years of not seeing them, and they still know us by name. That is pretty special."

Karen and Jerry's first cruise was on *Monarch of the Seas* in 1994. After 14 years of matrimony, they decided to take the belated honeymoon they finally could afford and to give cruising a try. Karen and Jerry flew to San Juan and sailed *Monarch* to the Southern Caribbean and immediately fell in love with all aspects of the cruising experience. They were amazed from the moment they stepped on the ship, and with their penchant for appreciating beaches well-established, they found the visits to ports in St Thomas, St Maarten, Antigua, Martinique, and Barbados mesmerizing. To this day, even after all their 113 cruises that first cruise remains their most memorable. Karen's says, "At that time *Monarch* was the largest cruise ship in the world. We were so "wowed" about everything—the staff, ship, food, islands, etc. It is what got us hooked on cruising and what keeps us loving to cruise to this day."

Belated honeymoon on *Monarch of the Seas* in 1994.

After finding their *Monarch* experience wonderful in so many ways, Karen and Jerry started cruising once a year, gradually increasing to twice a year, then by 2008 they started taking multiple cruises each year until now, where career flexibility and finances enable the Ahrs to cruise many times every year. They have another 18 cruises booked through 2020. Their bucket list cruise is to fly to Tahiti and do a 10-12 day South Pacific cruise. Karen and Jerry closed out 2018 with their 113th cruise, hitting their 100th cruise milestone with Royal Caribbean with a Christmas cruise on *Mariner of the Seas.*

Karen and Jerry's lifestyle jibes well with cruising whenever they want. Jerry is a retired hospitality executive. Karen is a Certified Public Accountant who after many years in private industry started her own practice in 2008 and currently works from home. Cruising fits so well with Karen's lifestyle that for fun she became a travel agent several years ago. Like Bill Raffel earlier in this chapter, she works only with certain "demanding" clients. Karen said, "My real job is a CPA, but because we travel so much, I decided I might as well make some commissions doing it, since I booked all my travel anyway as well for my friends and other family." (Spoken like a CPA!)

Karen expressed a sentiment to me that I heard variations of over and over from cruisers I spoke to for this book: "Cruising is our passion and everything we do revolves around when the next cruise is."

A CRUISING MINISTRY

I have known Cindy Williams, the epitome of a passionate cruiser, for virtually my entire life. However, I haven't seen and communicated regularly with Cindy in decades. During the years that we were not in regular contact, Cindy and her husband Ken created an amazing cruising story spanning nearly the entire world. I found out about it by happenstance, but I am glad that I did. Cindy's cruise story is both fascinating and inspiring.

I used to visit the former Cynthia Adams and her siblings regularly at her family's apartment in New York City where she was born and raised. At the age of fifteen, Cindy and her family moved south to rural Virginia, and our interactions became infrequent. I completely lost communication with her when she embarked on a career with the United States Army. It is from there that Cindy's world traveler exploits began. Cindy states, "I did a tour of duty in Misawa, Japan, visited the Philippines and finished my military career in the Panama Canal Zone. Upon my return to the United States, I became a wife and mother. I worked in several different career fields such as Clerk of Court, Secretary, and Assistant Protocol Officer for the Defense

Language Institute. I worked for The Department of Revenue and as a Sign Language Interpreter. It's a wonder I had any time to slip in a cruise or two here and there along the way."

Cindy and Ken on board the new *Carnival Horizon's* transatlantic crossing from Barcelona to New York in May 2018.

When speaking about her extensive travels both abroad for professional and leisure travel, as well as vacationing across the United States, Cindy stated, "The thing about traveling via planes, trains, buses and automobiles, then staying in hotels and going to restaurants over the years is that you have to do virtually all the work yourself and you are usually exhausted from being cramped in a tight seat for hours on end. Then you have to locate somewhere to eat or go grocery shopping and cook the food yourself. You really can't totally relax and unpack in a hotel—at least I can't. You end up living out of your suitcase. That to me is a bummer. With cruising, once you board your ship, you don't have a worry in the world. You don't even have to worry about how to entertain yourself. You just position yourself in the areas where activities are going on and you will be entertained. The food is on a continuous flow. You can always find something to eat, or you can always order room service."

Cindy's interest in cruising was piqued long before she joined the Army and had the opportunity to experience cruising on her own. She recounts, "When I was twelve my mother had the opportunity to go on the first and only cruise of her life. She came back radiant from her once in a lifetime experience and her glowing reports and recollections ignited a desire in me that has become a passion in my life." (In the interest of full disclosure, Cindy and I are cousins. For those who have read my previous book, you will remember Paul "Bunyan," my larger-than-life-dad who hovered over most aspects of the story. Cindy's mother Elizabeth, who was so affected after her only cruise, was Bunyan's sister.)

Both Cindy and Ken's first cruise was in August of 1993 on the *SeaEscape* from Florida to Freeport, Bahamas. Their inexperience showed as they selected the cruise on an impulse. Cindy states, "We knew nothing about cruising or the considerable differences in the various cruise lines, so when it came time to choose a cruise we saw a flyer for *SeaEscape* on the counter in a restaurant we happened to be eating at and proceeded to book the cheapest cabin available." Cindy and Ken's first cruise turned out to be a disappointment from the standpoint of accommodations and service, but it didn't dampen their enthusiasm for cruising. She said, "I'm so glad I finally found Carnival Cruise Lines. I was exclusive to them for many years until for our 27th wedding anniversary we wanted to cruise to Hawaii. Carnival had limited cruises going to Hawaii at that time, and the ones they had were not sailing during our desired time frame. That's when I discovered Princess Cruise Lines." Princess travels to more exotic destinations and offers longer itineraries. After Cindy and Ken both retired, they started doing longer cruises, including a world cruise. Cindy states, "Princess had the longer 30, 60, 90 and 111 day cruises. Once you've tasted those cruises it's kind of difficult to go back to the 7-15 day cruises."

In total Cindy and Ken have sailed on 42 cruises and currently have three cruises booked for 2019. They estimate that they have sailed the circumference of the world approximately three times. When I informed Cindy of my plan to write a travel-oriented book and expressed an interest in learning more about her travel background that I had heard so much about, Cindy proceeded to send me an itemized list of a couple hundred destinations around the world that she and Ken had visited. Virtually every corner of the planet was represented: every major island in the Caribbean; China; Australia; New Zealand; Iceland; Sweden; Russia; France; UK; Scotland; New Guinea; Chili; Peru; Ecuador; Dubai; Egypt; Israel; Alaska; Hawaii; Cuba; and, on and on.

The *Celestyal Olympia* in Kusadasi, Turkey en route to Israel in 2017.

Cindy and Ken at Santorini, Greece on the *Celestyal Olympia* cruise.

At Lake Towada, Japan during a stop on *Island Princess* in 2018.

I asked Cindy about her most memorable cruise experience. Of course that first cruise on *SeaEscape* makes her list for all the wrong reasons! Other than *SeaEscape,* Cindy notes it was their first world cruise on the *Pacific Princess* out of Los Angeles from January 22 to May 16, 2017, with ports of call highlighted by Mumbai, Dubai, Venice and China—111 days and over 40 ports of call in all. Another was a cruise to Spain, Croatia and Rome aboard the *Carnival Horizon* in April through May 2018. Cindy recounts, "The Gaudi architectural works of art, the Leaning Tower of Pisa and the Sistine Chapel were wonders to behold."

Formal night on the *Pacific Princess* world cruise; Ken and Cindy had just visited Mumbai, India.

Cindy states, "I like to cruise places I've never been before on a ship I've never cruised on before and take part in activities I've never experienced before: walking across a multi-tiered wooden suspension bridge suspended in the trees, or parasailing, zip lining, river tubing, cave tubing, camel riding or, riding in a Tuk-Tuk (three-wheeled form of transport common in Asia)." With Cindy having seen so much of the world, I wondered what adventure could be on her cruising bucket list. She told me, "My next major cruise venture is to sail around Africa. I'd like to take a genuine African Safari and get a taste of and exposure to both Africa's modern as well as historic flavor." This bucket list experience is booked on the *Sun Princess* to Africa, India, and Singapore departing out of Australia in January of 2020.

Cindy cited one memorable aspect of her 25 years of cruising that didn't pertain to a single cruise, but rather the very concept of cruising and the benefits it could bestow on others. Cindy knew there were many who desired to try cruising but were not in a financial position to do so. A devout believer who is active in church, Cindy saw cruising as a way to minister to others. Cindy stated, "I grew to love cruising so much that I wanted to share this cruising experience with others. Many of my friends caught the cruising bug and cruised with me regularly; others though, were just not able. I wished that everyone could experience the joy I experienced. I saw friends and relatives and other individuals working in their weary work-a-day world, needing a break and never seeming to be able to get one. I feel I was motivated by the Lord to ask different ones to come cruise with me, and when they replied that they had no resources to undertake such a venture, I simply told them, 'Don't worry, God's Got This.' At first this would happen once every few years. Then, as time progressed, I started noticing that we were giving away cruises more frequently until it was happening almost annually." Cindy's cruising "ministry" has enabled approximately 21 individuals to cruise.

Cindy said, "I watched one young lady who was nervous, uptight and withdrawn, take off her shoes and dance playfully in the fountain in Costa Maya. I've seen people weep over the beauty of the lush foliage, flora and fauna in Honduras or sit awestruck during an onboard musical performance. I would be all day trying to recount the myriad of expressions of joy and wonder I've seen in the eyes and on the faces of these deserving individuals. The overall feeling I've taken away is that cruising—even if just for a few days—seems to allow people to be someone else, somewhere else, and take in all the architectural eye candy or all of nature's splendor in a safe and carefree environment. That to me is priceless!"

After 40 years, having reunited from a distance via *The Joy of Cruising*, Cindy and I are planning to reunite in person on a cruise!

CUBA CRUISING

Despite being only 90 miles away from the southernmost point of the United States, Cuba is often on the bucket list of US cruisers right next to cruises to such far-flung destinations as Alaska, Antarctica, Hawaii, Galapagos, South Pacific, and more. Among a number of appealing factors to travelers, cruising to Cuba brings with it an unquestionably desirable aspect that few other ports of call have: rarity. Simply because Cuba has not been accessible to cruise travelers for very long. Consequently, a Cuba cruise is on the to-do list of a number of cruisers, particularly seasoned cruisers who have experienced other Bahamas and Caribbean itineraries multiple times. Coupled with the fact that there are some restrictions, both logistical and government imposed, a Cuba sailing has an exclusiveness, a cachet to it. That in part explains why older cruise ships, albeit refurbished and outfitted with features popular with cruisers such as Food Network star Guy Fieri's "Guy's Burger Joint" on Carnival ships, elaborate water slides, and onboard Cuba-themed venues and enrichment activities, get repurposed and repositioned for Cuba sailings, and can command a significant premium over comparable length itineraries to other destinations for that same ship. A collateral benefit to cruise lines of older ships sailing to Cuba is that their smaller size relative to the newer mega-ships cruise lines are increasingly introducing are able to dock; Havana's existing pier cannot accommodate mega-ships.

Cuba's classic cars by *Couplestravel (Joan and Jim Sloan)*.

In addition to its colorful and vibrant street life, music, pastel-colored structures and Art Deco architecture, what sets Cuba apart from any other ports of call is its abundance of classic cars, a consequence of the late Fidel Castro's ban on car imports after the 1959 Cuban revolution.

Cuba's classic cars by *paulandcarolelovetotravel.com*.

Havana with Paul and Carole

In November 2017 Paul Morgan and Carole Morgan-Slater were able to tick Cuba off their bucket list with a combination of a land-based and cruise holiday. Paul and Carole flew from London to Havana for a 4-day stay prior to embarking on MSC Cruises *MSC Opera* for a two-week Caribbean cruise.

Paul and Carole live in the city of Gloucester, UK, and they love to travel, as chronicled in their eponymously titled blog: *pauland-carolelovetotravel.com*. Besides travel, Paul is a passionate Tottenham Hotspur football fan and Carole loves gardening and drinking wine. Since meeting over 20 years ago they have bonded around their mutual interest in travel. Paul credits Carole with passing on to him her wanderlust ways, formed mainly when she worked for a couple of years for Celebrity Cruises. "My time at Celebrity gave me a taste of what the world had to offer and increased my hunger for travel, and since that time I have traveled whenever finances and work have allowed," Carole notes. Paul added, "To this day, my travel highlight is Thailand; I had never been keen to visit the Far East but as in most cases Carole talked me into it and it's one of the best things she has ever done!"

Paul and Carole on Royal's *Mariner of the Seas*; Princess cruise ship in the background.

Paul and Carole have visited 41 countries. They have cruised 14 times and sailed from UK to France, Spain, Portugal and the Canary Islands, and Norway, culminating with their Caribbean cruise from Havana. Besides MSC, they have cruised with Royal Caribbean, Cunard, P&O, Celebrity, and Marella cruise lines.

After arriving in Havana, prior to joining the *MSC Opera*, Paul and Carole stayed at the Memories Miramar Hotel. For the standard of hotel they wanted they learned Havana was certainly not cheap. Memories Miramar was fairly nice but they quickly realized that 4-star lodging in Cuba is very different than 4-star accommodations in Europe.

As soon as Paul and Carole arrived in Cuba they noticed the classic cars everywhere. I was curious about Paul's reflections on this as he has worked in the car industry for 28 years and currently owns P&C Cars, a pre-owned automobile dealership. "The majority of the classic cars are actually not really classic; they are Cuban copies running more modern diesel engines, but if you look hard enough you can still find some original American classics still running the old V8 petrol engines which sound amazing!" Paul told me. Paul advises that if you are planning a trip around Cuba in a classic car, make sure you shop around as prices vary a lot. Despite the lack of available parts for these frozen-in-time cars—causing residents to re-use parts from cars that are no longer functional, re-purposed from old Russian vehicles or even to improvise parts out of non-automotive items—the locals are intensely proud of the classic cars. Paul noted that the locals have some concern about cars now being imported from Russia, China, Korea, and Japan due to loosened restrictions on new car imports and worry about the classic cars declining. "We did smile when a stretch Russian Lada drove past; not something we have ever seen before! We loved our evening tour in the classic cars; however, the fumes can become overpowering, so going long distances wouldn't be something we would choose to do," Paul said.

Paul and Carole pointed out that other alternatives for transportation in Cuba are buses and taxis. While they did not ride the local buses, they observed they always seemed packed. "We did spot a bus pull up and get filled with locals carrying mopeds and a man even hauling an 8 by 4 sheet of plywood!" In addition to the classic cars used for tours, classic cars—in significantly worse condition—are also used as taxis in Cuba. These vehicles are typically used to transport locals. Tourists in Havana often use the "Coco" taxi. They are yellow vehicles with bucket style seats on a 3-wheel frame with a round fiberglass body; apparently, the name comes from the word coconut given the vehicle's shape. "You see these everywhere and as with everything in Havana, prices do vary so don't be afraid to bargain hard," Paul said.

"My Mojito in la Bodeguita, my daiquiri in El Floridita" supposedly said Ernest Hemingway of two of the most famous bars in Havana. Despite the mythology of this saying—and the dubiousness of its authenticity—there is a hand-scrolled sign with that statement and Hemingway's autograph in La Bodeguita del Medio, along with inscriptions on the walls from the likes of Harry Belafonte, Nat King Cole, and Fidel Castro. Paul and Carole tried a couple of times to get into La Bodeguita, as well as El Floridita, but they were always too packed. They did manage to sample a few mojitos and daiquiris in other bars that drew them in with alluring live music. "In Old Havana we found a bar called Cafe Bosque Bologna on Obispo Street. The daiquiris were excellent. We sat down and noticed that just behind our table was an area where there were turtles, which was a bit strange, but we soon learned the reason they were there is that the Cubans believe that they bring them good karma," Carole said.

"In San Francisco Square right opposite the cruise terminal is a bar called Restaurante Cafe del Oriente, a lovely bar with a seating area outside, ideal for watching the world go by and inside a very talented piano player where we spent a wet afternoon having a fun sing-song. The Mojitos here were excellent too!"

Paul and Carole had a lot of fun with their Havana bar crawl but offer a word to the wise: "If someone comes up to you in the street and recommends that you try out the nearby restaurant, or have a drink in a bar, and you follow them there, you'll end up paying more for your meal and your drinks. The restaurant/bar will be expected to pay the hustler a commission, which will be added to your bill."

Havana street life.

Music is pervasive throughout Havana. Paul and Carole heard music coming out of houses, bars and restaurants. It is not unusual to see locals hanging out and dancing to it as well, and they loved that aspect of Cuba. When there is live music either in bars or out on the street, it is normal for one of the band members to come around asking for tips. Similarly, be prepared to pay if you take pictures of the locals on the streets. Of course, that is common at a number of cruise ports of call, but Havana street life presents an abundance of photogenic characters. "The man with a rat on his head, the lady who had her cat in a stroller in baby's clothes; street life was certainly entertaining" Paul said. "We paid 1 Cuban Peso for a photo of a vibrantly dressed lady smoking a cigar."

Speaking of cigars, Paul warns not to buy Cuban cigars from the street sellers. Paul and Carole were told they may have anything in them like grass, newspaper, and who knows what else, and they should only purchase them from a proper tobacco shop. Along with Cuban cigars, there are plenty of ways to add to the Cuban economy; Paul and Carole brought home a couple of bottles of the excellent Havana Rum, and there were plenty of souvenirs to be had such as some great Cuban classic car pictures.

Besides the delightful food and drink, classic cars, vibrant street life marked by music, colorful characters, and vivid murals and street art, a highlight for Paul and Carole was the Malecón. The Malecón is a five-mile-long promenade along the shores of Havana harbor. Carole told me "The Malecón is also known as the largest sofa in the world; locals and tourists visit the Malecón for an evening stroll, to meet friends for music, drinking and dancing or to just simply sit down and gaze at the city and the sea. This is how we imagined Havana: vibrant, lively and full of life."

Paul and Carole had a fantastic time in Havana and consider it one of the most interesting destinations they have ever visited. They ended their holiday at the gorgeous beach resort town of Varadero, one of the largest resorts in the Caribbean, Varadero is primarily visited by European and Canadian tourists because of U.S. government restrictions that make it difficult for U.S. citizens to visit Cuba as tourists. Then came their 14-day cruise on *MSC Opera*!

Paul and Carole look forward to being able to cruise more in a couple of years when Carole is able to retire from her nursing career. Then, Carole says, "We will be able to lead the nomadic life that we have dreamed of!" In the meantime, Paul and Carole will continue to travel as much as possible given career demands. They recently completed a two-week cruise on the *Marella Discovery* to Norway and the Arctic Circle. This year they will be headed back to their favorite destination, Thailand, on a land-based holiday, and have a cruise booked to Greece and around the Adriatic, another part of the world they are very fond of.

Longer-term, Carole would love to do a world cruise, but Paul is not so sure of all the sea days and spending several months on the same ship. They are currently looking at navigating much of the world on a single holiday but using a combination of cruising and rail, which will enable them to experience different ships. Other bucket list cruise aspirations include New Zealand, the Pacific and Hawaii, a Panama Canal cruise and a cruise around Asia.

"Our joys of cruising include sitting on the aft or promenade decks and watching sunsets over the ocean followed by exceptional food with superb service. Including the variety of entertainment and waking up somewhere new in the world to explore really does make cruising a unique experience and something we will be doing as long as we can breathe!"

Barbara and Bill's Quick Jaunt to Havana

It took Paul and Carole 10 hours to fly from UK to Havana. Just in the time it took them in the airport checking in and then retrieving their luggage in Havana, Barbara Stewart and William "Bill" Stewart, who live in Fort Myers, Florida drove two hours down Florida's "Alligator Alley" and boarded a cruise to Cuba. (Yes, that stretch of FL I-75 runs alongside swamps teeming with gators.) One of the benefits for cruisers living in south Florida—besides the sunshine—is the easy access to several cruise ports and South Florida's proximity to a bucket list location. In fact, when I asked Barbara if there was any special motivation in cruising to Cuba, she told me it was suggested by some local friends as an easy, long weekend trip.

Empress arriving in Havana at dawn (left); docking next to *Carnival Paradise* (right).

"The ship left Miami on a Thursday evening and pulled into Havana just as dawn was breaking on Friday. The ship stayed in port until Saturday evening at 8 PM and very slowly returned to Miami, docking Monday morning." Barbara and Bill cruised from Miami to Cuba on a Royal Caribbean "Immersive Cuba Cruise" on *Empress of the Seas* in September 2018. *Empress* is one of those ships repurposed and perfectly suited—older and smaller—for cruises to Cuba, and had a multi-million-dollar refurbishment in 2016. *Empress of the Seas* inaugurated Royal Caribbean's presence in Cuba in April 2017, and at over 1600 passengers became the largest ship the Havana port can accommodate.

Barbara, a university administrator, and Bill a real estate professional, aren't frequent cruisers, but of the four cruises they have taken they ticked off two destinations that many cruisers have on their bucket list: Alaska and Cuba. Their Alaska cruise in 2005 would have checked several bucket list boxes for me: it was a two-week Alaska Sea/Rail adventure that departed Anchorage by rail to Fairbanks, then a motor coach to Skagway and then a cruise on *Holland America Line Volendam* to Vancouver, British Columbia. Along the way the Alaska cruise included a helicopter ride landing on a glacier, a seaplane trip to a salmon hatchery, and an excursion to Denali, also known as Mount McKinley, the highest mountain peak in North America. Barbara and Bill's first cruise was in 1988 on Sitmar Cruises *Fairsea*, a 10-day Eastern Caribbean cruise where they introduced their two young sons to cruising. They followed that up two years later with a Key West/Mexico cruise on Chandris Cruises *Britanis*.

On arriving in Havana, the Stewarts and the couple they traveled with chose a full day Havana tour with CubaTrip Compass, which offered them the option of picking what they would get to see or letting the tour company take them to the places they considered important. The couples chose a mix of each—listing some places they really wanted to see, and letting CubaTrip Compass direct the group to other landmarks. Their excursion was comprised of a walking tour of the old part of the town, Old Havana, and a driving tour of the newer part of the city, New Havana.

Barbara and Bill's tour was in a 1957 Chevrolet Bel Air. "The car was large enough for Bill and me, the couple that accompanied us, the tour guide, and the driver, a young man who owned the car. He had retrofit air conditioning into the car so it was very comfortable, and much more fun than the tour bus that the ship's tour would have provided. 1950's car buffs will swoon over the variety of lovingly restored vehicles."

The tour guide and the 1957 Chevrolet Bel Air.

Among the highlights of their tour was El Floridita. "We went to El Floridita, the night club associated with Hemingway, and we were delighted by the performances of three different groups. I think the live music in Havana was the happiest part of the adventure."

Another place Barbara and Bill got to visit that Ernest Hemingway frequented—as did Clark Gable, Spencer Tracy, and John Wayne—was historic Sloppy Joe's Bar (originator of the sloppy joe sandwich). Sloppy Joe's Bar was an iconic gathering place frequented mainly by Americans in pre-revolution Havana. Consequently, after the revolution Sloppy Joe's Bar closed and remained closed from 1959 until just several years ago when it was restored in its old location, replete with much of its original façade after 50 years.

Bill and Barbara at El Floridita, Ernest Hemingway's Havana haunt.

Sloppy Joe's Bar, deemed "one of the most famous bars in the world." A hangout for American celebrities for decades (and originator of its namesake sandwich), it recently reopened after the revolution shuttered it for nearly 50 years.

Their tour guide took them to visit a "private" restaurant, La Casa Restaurante. La Casa Restaurante is one of Havana's oldest paladares. An outgrowth of the political-economic structure of Cuba, and their existence controlled by the government, a paladare is a privately run dining establishment in the home of a Cuban. They are considered a way of bringing tourists closer to the people and the Cuban culture. "At La Casa Restaurante we were serenaded by a trio of gentlemen and it was so enjoyable I bought their CD."

The tour also took them to Jaimanitas, also know as Fusterlandia, so named after Cuban artist José Rodriguez Fuster who resides in the poor neighborhood. Fuster painted murals and crafted tile mosaics on the outside of homes, businesses and public structures in Jaimanitas, and he maintains his studio and a gallery in his home. "José Fuster's amazing art museum/home showcasing his passion for mosaic art was quite unique."

Barbara and Bill visited numerous other places highlighting the vibrancy, history and music of Cuban culture. Despite the beauty of Cuba and the colorful street life, Barbara told me her lasting memory of Cuba was the general condition of the country. "What made the biggest impression on me was the relative poverty and the poor condition of the old buildings and the lack of modern conveniences. Their tour guide said that she, and many other Cubans, considered Castro's alliance with the USSR instead of the US his biggest mistake."

In addition to seeing the street life of today's Havana and many of the cultural icons of both modern day Cuba as well as modern links to Cuba's storied past, Barbara and Bill got to see many reminders of Cuba history from the revolutionary period and before it. "Having lived through the Cuban Missile Crisis as a child it was amazing to see the remnants of that era. Sad to see what has been lost in the way of history as so much has not been preserved."

Barbara and Bill saw many reminders of the revolution.

Retirement is in the not too distant future for the Stewarts and cruising is in their plans. "We are interested in a European River cruise and a Scandinavian Cruise that would include St. Petersburg, Russia. The Greek Isles also look fabulous. Several friends have done trips to New Zealand and Australia that included cruising. But I think I will need to win the lottery!"

Joan and Jim: Cuba and Jazz

Cuba was a natural destination for Joan and Jim Sloan, a Philadelphia couple who now live in Wilmington, Delaware. They are long-time avid travelers who fly, sail, and drive to several destinations every year. Illustrative of their passion for travel, here is their next few months "itinerary:" As I write this in December 2018, they are en route to Aruba for a week; then will bring in the New Year in Ghana; they travel to Costa Rica in February, St. Martins in March and will embark on their annual trip to Puerto Vallarta in April! If you think that by April they will be finished traveling for 2019, you don't know Joan and Jim. At the very least, I would wager that they will spend the 4th of July week in New Orleans at the annual Essence Music Festival, which they attend regularly. In fact, it was at Essence that I got to know the Sloans and learn about their travel passion.

I first met my "travel mentors" in Wilmington, Delaware where Cheryl and I owned a retail establishment. The Sloans were regular customers at our shops, and we maintained a casual acquaintance. By happenstance, we ran into the Sloans in New Orleans during our own annual jaunt to the Essence Music Festival. Over charbroiled oysters and a beverage or two, the Sloans regaled us with their travel exploits all over the world. Since then I have jokingly said about the Sloans when describing them to others, "I want to travel like Joan and Jim when I grow up." (We are almost the same age!)

The neighbors ran into each other in New Orleans: Jim, Joan, Cheryl, Paul.

The Sloans' diverse travel pursuits all over the world have included a number of cruises, and in February 2017 they ventured to Cuba on *The Soul Cruise*, a unique seven-day R&B themed-cruise branded as "The first ever soul music cruise from the United States to Cuba!" The cruise was on *Fathom Adonia* (now *Azamara Pursuit*). Fathom Cruises was established in 2015 to conduct "social impact travel" cruises from Miami to the Dominican Republic, and Cuba, where in May 2016 *Adonia* was the first United States cruise ship to dock in post-Castro Cuba. Joan said, "*Fathom Adonia,* a 750-passenger ship provided intimacy, specialized in culture tours, and provided Cuban-inspired foods throughout our weeklong cruise."

The *Fathom Adonia* inaugurated cruises to Cuba after President Obama announced a more open approach to Cuba in December 2014.

The Soul Cruise was a new venture by Capital Jazz Productions, who produces the annual DC-area *Capital Jazz Fest,* one of the nation's oldest and most well-attended jazz festivals, and *The Super Cruise,* their flagship ocean-going version of the *Jazz Fest. The Soul Cruise* was headlined by a number of R&B stars and comedians including Kem, Lalah Hathaway, Mint Condition and more, and was hosted by Grammy-award nominated singer Eric Roberson.

(Roberson had also hosted *The Super Cruise* Joan and Jim previously attended.) "We were excited about going to Cuba—which was on our bucket list—and were expecting a great time as we had gone on the *Capital Jazz SuperCruise* the year before and were blown away by the amazing artists and non-stop music and partying into the wee hours of the night."

Joan and Jim were fortunate enough just to be sailing to a bucket-list destination, but as with most cruises, "getting there is half the fun." (One of the greatest travel industry advertising campaigns ever was Cunard Cruise Line's 1950's "Getting There is Half the Fun!") In the case of the *The Soul Cruise,* that slogan was more apt than ever. Joan said, "*The Soul Cruise* did not disappoint with a line up that included jazz singer and keyboardist Frank McCombs, soul crooners Avery Sunshine, Kenny Lattimore, Naturally 7, comedian Michael Colyar and more. To spend late nights in 'Frank McCombs' living room,' an intimate space where artists popped in and joined in the jam sessions was one of our favorite experiences. And of course there's no one better to host than entertainer extraordinaire Eric Roberson."

Not surprisingly, after this second music cruise Joan and Jim vowed that cruising for them had to include music, so they went on the *Blue Note Jazz Cruise* in 2018, and are booked on the *Capital Jazz SuperCruise* to the Caribbean January 2020 on Royal Caribbean *Independence of the Seas.* (In the section "Theme Cruising: Two Passions in One," *The Joy of Cruising* examines theme and music cruises more closely and discusses the phenomenon experienced by cruisers like Joan and Jim—once you go on a theme cruise, it is very likely you will continue to do so.) And the Sloans have become friends with Eric Roberson. In fact, he generously gave his time and talent to host a benefit concert for the American Cancer Society along with their daughter Tswana Sewell, who at the time was Director of Distinguished Events for the American Cancer Society. Along with Joan and Jim, Tswana met Eric on that first *Capital Jazz SuperCruise*.

Joan and Jim with their friend and *The Soul Cruise* to Cuba host, Eric Roberson.

For the Cuba cruise, Joan and Jim sailed out of Miami and the itinerary was comprised of three ports of call: Havana, which included an overnight stay, Cienfuegos and Santiago de Cuba. "It was nice to have a "hotel at sea" as we had heard that accommodations in Cuba were uneven. At each port we had a number of cultural exchange activities to chose from. We chose a walking tour of Old Havana, a day long Dancing Through Havana tour and the revolution tour in Santiago."

On the walking tour of Havana the Sloans learned a lot about the culture and Cuban way of life, and of course saw lots of classic cars and were amazed at how many of them appeared to be in mint condition.

Street life in Havana.

Joan with street performer at Morro Castle fortress at the port of Old Havana.

Habana Compas Dance Company. The colorful chairs the dancers are
sitting on were also used as powerful percussion instruments.

Joan and Jim enjoyed the dancing tour the most. "It was fun
with three different dance activities, but it also was very exhaust-
ing. We began early in the morning with two hours of group salsa
lessons. Our instructors were high energy and engaging, and Jim

and I came away feeling like we were ready to go out salsa dancing. Our next stop was to a ballet company and school where we met with the dancers who were all graduates of the university, and we enjoyed a performance that contrasted African and European ballet. Our group decided to make a donation of ballet slippers for the company as they were not made in Cuba and costly. Lastly we went to see a performance of the Habana Compas Dance Company. The dancers were classically trained and were accompanied by powerful percussionists who mixed traditional and contemporary dance style. Each dancer played an instrument hand crafted by the director. It was amazing to see them use their chairs as percussion instruments."

Jim in front of the bullet-riddled Moncado Barracks, site of a failed Castro incursion.

In Santiago de Cuba, after Havana the second-largest city of Cuba, and where the Cuban Revolution began in 1953, they visited a number of revolutionary sites and observed numerous buildings that were still bullet-riddled. "We visited Castro's grave and saw the changing of the guards which was very impressive. We were also very warmly greeted in Santiago, as a large percentage of the population is of African descent and they were pleased and surprised to see so many African-Americans traveling together in Cuba."

Having ticked off a bucket-list item, Joan and Jim have added a new one regarding Cuba. "We would love to return to Cuba with more time to really get to know the people, explore the countryside and beautiful beaches, and to get more of a taste of the nightlife and the music for which they are famous."

Now both retired, Joan from 24 years at Independence Blue Cross in Philadelphia in Marketing, Sales and Strategy, and Jim as an administrator from the Philadelphia School System, the Sloans have amped up their travel even more. Whenever I reach out to them they are as likely to be in another part of the world as to be at home in Delaware. They have seen so much with six cruises, and land-based travel to 28 countries, across three continents, and travel to 29 states of the United States. I asked them what a bucket list looks like for travelers like them who have seemingly done it all. Joan told me, "Next up on our bucket list includes trips to South Africa, Brazil, South America and Singapore. But we've also talked about having a theme for our travel like 'chasing sunsets and views' or 'we'll travel for food'; visiting the seven wonders of the world or all 50 states.' Wherever we 'land' it will be because we seized an opportunity to experience a different culture and/or the wonders of the natural world."

In addition to ticking off that bucket list, going on their new-found pastime of music-themed cruises, and of course their annual trek to Essence Music Festival, there is a new and exciting travel-related future ahead for the Sloans. Joan told me, "We are both trained in travel writing and Jim in travel photography, and now that we have more time, we plan to pursue this as our third act, called *Couplestravel.*"

SEVENTEEN SEAS

*P*assengers who had balcony cabins on the port side found themselves with a fine view of the Ocean Terminal building. Lyall
Wellington reckoned he and Ngaio could just about reach out from
their balcony and help themselves from the plates of those dining in
the restaurant named inappropriately California Pizza Kitchen. "That
reminds me of a man on our last cruise," offered Jovial Joe, always ready
to respond to such a promising lead-in line. "We'd just boarded and
were unpacking our bags before the ship left port and got under way,
when I heard the fellow from the cabin next door berating the steward
in the passageway. 'Where's the purser's office?' he was demanding. 'I
paid for a cabin with an ocean view, and all I can see is the bloody
wharf.'" Jovial Joe paused, looking around at his audience for effect – he
knew how to tell a story. "The steward, he was a little guy from Manila,
Fernando his name was. Well, Fernando was quick, and right away
he said 'Never mind the Purser, I can see to that for you, Sir. I'll have
it fixed for you by the time you come back from dinner.' "Sure enough,
after dinner everyone on our side of the ship had a sea view. I reckon
Fernando earned himself a good tip on that voyage."

—Excerpt from Seventeen Seas, chapter Walking Forward

Bronwyn Elsmore is the author of a large number of published works—short stories, articles, and books. She has won several short story competitions, been winner of the Playwrights Association of New Zealand's playwriting competition three times, and earned other writing awards. Bronwyn is a well-travelled writer; her travels have taken her to every continent except Antarctica, 78 countries in all. Much of that travel has been via cruises; 14 months of Bronwyn's life has been spent on cruise ships. The excerpt above is from Bronwyn's work, *Seventeen Seas*, part novel, part creative non-fiction. *Seventeen Seas* follows a half-world cruise taken in 2008 that sailed from the South Pacific through 10 countries, 15 ports, across 17 seas, for 46 days.

Bronwyn Elsmore is a New Zealander by birth and by choice. Bronwyn has lived in various parts of New Zealand and has spent periods of time outside of that country in Hawaii, Singapore, and Fiji. She is now settled in Auckland, New Zealand, also known as New Zealand's Queen City and City of Sails because of the activity on its glorious harbor. Although as Dr. Bronwyn Elsmore she spent many years as an academic—including serving as a university professor—she has always considered herself first and foremost a professional writer. Over her writing career, Bronwyn has been an advertising copywriter, freelancer, contract writer, editor, education writer, writing mentor and tutor, as well as widely published author across a wide range of genres, fiction and non-fiction, short stories, articles, and a dozen books. She is also a playwright, with 12 plays staged in New Zealand theatres.

Bronwyn's first cruise experience was in 1992, a Pacific Ocean voyage on Princess Cruises *Island Princess*, famous for appearing in the romantic comedy television series *The Love Boat*. (*Island Princess* and *Pacific Princess* were sister ships and were both used in the series as *The Love Boat*.) It was not an auspicious introduction to cruising. The 20,000 ton, 698-passenger ship, diminutive by today's standards, ran into the outskirts of cyclone Betsy, and bucked and pitched for days. There were few people in the dining room at mealtimes. Bronwyn recalls that when the *Island Princess* reached the first port, Vila, Vanuatu, the storm had done substantial damage. "We were sad for the people of the island, but also glad at their assurance that our visit contributed to their battered economy." On that first cruise, and reinforced on subsequent cruises in different parts of the world, Bronwyn learned from the locals just how much a visit by a cruise ship can help them economically.

On a later Pacific cruise, on another ship on a wild night, a high wave smashed in the window of a cabin two doors away from Bronwyn's. Several cabins and the corridor were flooded, rousing the cleaning crews from their beds. Bronwyn has experienced further rough days in other seas, many transits of pirate-frequented waters, and being on a ship that lost power in the Bermuda triangle. Despite these experiences that she thinks of as all part of the adventure, Bronwyn has always felt quite safe aboard ship.

Bronwyn's cruises have taken her to approximately 160 different ports in Europe, Africa, Asia, the Baltic Sea, Oceania, North and South America, mostly on Princess, P&O, and Star cruise lines. She notes that repeat visits on subsequent cruises always provide welcome reminders of her previous visits there, and it is always good to see the changes and development since last at a particular port of call, but it is new places she most likes to experience. In fact, destinations are foremost in Bronwyn's mind when selecting cruises, more so than the ship itself. "I don't understand passengers who see the ship as a hotel and don't go ashore at ports. I select cruises according to the destinations, and this way I have been able to visit so many places on the globe I would not have gotten to via land-based travel. True, a port of call usually is just for a day, but that can be enough to get the flavor of a place and assess if I'd like to return for a longer stay.

Single days on fairly remote islands in the Java Sea have stayed in my memory long afterwards, and I doubt I would have got to such places as Falkland Islands, Costa Rica, Namibia, and many other places by any other means."

In response to my inquiry about her most memorable experience, Bronwyn told me that rounding both the Cape of Good Hope on P&O's *Aurora* in 2016, and Cape Horn on *Sea Princess* in 2017, were extra special. She notes that on occasions such as these voyages you really appreciate modern cruise ships and feel for sailors who manned tiny sailing ships at the mercy of winds and currents. Where they scudded along on top of the waves, today's powerful engines drive through safely and surely, with stabilizers largely keeping the decks steady.

"In the case of Cape Horn, we were in luck. After much anticipation and praying for good weather as we sailed further and further south, we achieved the feat that most ships try to avoid. Around breakfast time we stood on deck, clad in polar fleece and padded jackets looking at Isla Hornos. The sky was grey, temperature just above freezing, wind at 4 on the Beaufort scale. Almost balmy for that part of the world, even in summer, given just 650 kilometres (404 miles) of stormy sea separates it from the ice of Antarctica. The engines were managing the legendary currents, the surface of the top of Drake's Passage was as smooth as can be realistically hoped for, and there wasn't an iceberg in sight. We were at the meeting point of the great oceans. On one side lay the Pacific, on the other the Atlantic. Across a short expanse of water stood a peak with scattered low vegetation. With the aid of binoculars and telephoto lens I could see the long building topped by the lighthouse that still serves to signal to mariners the end of the earth."

**Bronwyn (right) and her sister at "the end of the world",
last stop before rounding Cape Horn.**

Right up there with Bronwyn's most memorable experiences were interactions with monkeys at exotic ports of call on two different cruises. On a very memorable visit to a small island with no permanent residents, Palau Sikuai, Indonesia, Bronwyn was bitten by a monkey. "Well, it was a cute little thing and I did try to pick it up for a cuddle." That resulted in her one and only visit to a ship's doctor, to get a tetanus booster. "I passed on the offer of a series of rabies shots." While on a different cruise, when visiting the Batu caves near Kuala Lumpur, Malaysia, a large macaque, "not nearly as cute," leapt onto Bronwyn's shoulder, grabbed her glasses and raced away. "When it found they had the wrong prescription for its eyes, and it couldn't eat them, it threw them away—fortunately undamaged and recoverable! Once again, a pack of medicated wet wipes in the day bag proved useful."

Bronwyn's eyeglass prescription didn't suit this long-tailed macaque.

The premise of *Seventeen Seas* came about a few years ago after Bronwyn sailed on a half-world cruise, though other cruises also contributed to the creation of characters, as they helped build a picture of the variety of passengers. Bronwyn had always been interested in observing group dynamics; she has a doctorate in world religions and is a recognized authority on religions and spiritual interaction. Over previous cruises and other trips Bronwyn had been fascinated with how people react and interact when in unfamiliar places, and when finding themselves in close proximity to others over a period of time. "I find that passengers on cruise ships, most of them in the second half or later part of their lifespan, have often lived fascinating lives. They have had a variety of careers, possess many skills, and can talk intelligently on a very wide range of subjects." Bronwyn used this idea to create the characters in *Seventeen Seas*. They are not specific people she met on any one cruise, but are composites created to represent the variety of fellow cruisers one is likely to meet on board.

Seventeen Seas contains both non-fiction and fiction aspects, or creative non-fiction. Bronwyn prefers to call it a travel book with a difference. The account of the cruise—itinerary, ports, and some events on board and ashore—are non-fiction in that they recount actual events. The characters are fictional but based on many who have cruised on ships Bronwyn has been on, and people cruisers are likely to encounter on any such voyage. Bronwyn chose the fun aspects of the trip; the lighter moments of passengers' experiences aboard and ashore as they cross the world. "I had a lot of fun writing *Seventeen Seas,* and I must have got something right because people have told me those characters could well have been their fellow passengers, and some incidents could have occurred on ships they have been on." As one review reads: "It was so funny because as I took a walk down memory lane I could put various people that I met on the different cruises to the characters in this book. This book has humor and it would be a good book to recommend to someone who is about to embark on their first cruise." *Seventeen Seas* was published in 2012.

I asked Bronwyn what the future holds with respect to her cruising. She responded, "With 78 countries on my been-there list, sometimes I wonder if I should just sit back and take it easy, but I suspect I'll be tempted again in the future when I think about somewhere I still haven't ticked. I have yet to visit Korea, so that may well come up before long. When I do get too old to travel, I'll have so many great memories of places all around the globe. And if I need a further reminder, I have enough certificates to attest to the fact that I've done such things as crossed the equator, the international dateline, rounded the Horn, transited the Suez and Panama canals, won ship trivia challenges, etc., to paper a wall."

Cruising's Young
and Restless

CRUISING'S YOUNG AND RESTLESS

When I set out to chronicle the stories of passionate cruisers doing interesting things I assumed it would be mostly about individuals who had been "around awhile," principally because cruising requires ample resources both financial and time. Generally, the older you are the more likely you are to have those resources available. Of course there are exceptions to every rule, and the young passionate cruisers profiled in *The Joy of Cruising* are testaments to that. Emma Le Teace, *Cruising Isn't Just for Old People*, profiled in Chapter 14; Jason Leppert, *Popular Cruising*, profiled in Chapter 17; and the three dynamic young individuals discussed in this chapter, respectively: Danny Bradley, *The Cruising Baker*, Matt Mramer, *Cruising with Matt*, and Marcus Adams, *Sparkx*, average 29 years old. Between these five millennials (people born between the early 1980's and the early 2000's) they have cruised well over 200 times to virtually every corner of the globe that can be accessed via cruise vessel. Everyone of them has experienced one, and in some cases several cruises typically thought of as bucket list experiences. Almost all pursue their passion for cruising on a part-time basis. Besides their relatively young age, the only commonality they all share is that they started their cruising life at a very young age, as early as a toddler, and on average ten years old. (Hey that bodes well for my granddaughter; we just returned from the *Anthem of the Seas*, her fourth cruise we've taken together and she is nine years old.)

There is clearly a trend towards cruise passengers becoming younger. This trend manifests itself in a number of ways, with the most dramatic being the design of the cruise ships themselves. I have alluded several times in *The Joy of Cruising* to the ongoing movement for the cruise lines to introduce bigger and bigger ships, but in addition to cruise ships increasingly being "up-sized," cruise lines are also installing a number of youth-friendly attractions which appeal to millennials as well as families with children. In 2018, Norwegian Cruise Line launched *Norwegian Bliss*. Paraphrasing from the NCL press release, here are some of the fun, creative, youth friendly innovations highlighted: "...*a two level electric-car race track*. The competitive track, the longest at sea at nearly 1,000 feet, will rev up the hearts of all who race around her many twists and turns... After burning rubber at the race track, guests can test their agility at the *open-air laser tag course*... The ship's *Aqua Park* also includes two multi-story waterslides. Not for the faint of heart, the high-speed *Ocean Loops* free fall slide includes two exhilarating loops, one that extends out over the side of the ship and a second see-through loop that stretches down to the deck below, sure to offer a wet and wild ride. The tandem *Aqua Racer* slide allows guests to race side-by-side on inner tubes for more than 360 feet, with a translucent section that provides stunning ocean views as guests twist and turn to the finish line." There are many other examples I can point to which underscore this "theme parkification" of cruise ships. Basically, if it is a popular land-based attraction, it is likely already on new or recently refurbished cruise ships, or coming soon. Bumper cars, carousels, trampolines, bowling alleys, skydiving simulators, zip lines, IMAX movie theaters? Already on cruise ships. Several years ago I took my grandkids on a cruise that stopped in Grand Turk. The Grand Turk Margaritaville featured a FlowRider® surf simulator, which my grandkids loved, and I thought was an ingenious attraction which resulted in some priceless videos of them falling off, or successfully navigating the boogie board. At that time, I assumed Grand Turk Margaritaville had a FlowRider® because it was the world's largest Margaritaville; it was unimaginable to me on a cruise ship. Well now there are FlowRiders® on half the Royal Caribbean ships, and my grandkids had a ball on the FlowRider® surf simulator on *Anthem*.

LaKi on the bumper cars on *Anthem of the Seas*.

In 2020 Carnival Cruises will introduce the first roller coaster at sea, BOLT, on the *Mardi Gras*. While Carnival is the most popular cruise brand with its affordable pricing and promotion exuding "fun" as exemplified by Chief Fun Officer, Shaquille O'Neal, Carnival doesn't crack any lists of the world's largest cruise ships. *Mardi Gras* will be Carnival's first foray into super-sized ships—the first in Carnival's new XL-Class. At 185,000 gross tons, which is 50,000 more than Carnival's largest current ships, *Horizon* and *Vista*, doubtlessly *Mardi Gras* will be jam-packed with millennial-friendly attractions.

I can't help but wonder if in the next decade or so a cruise ship will be introduced that brands itself as a floating theme park! By the way, along the lines of a theme park, Royal Caribbean is building one, sort of, not on a cruise ship but as part of a cruise. Royal Caribbean is in the process of redesigning Coco Cay, its private island in the Bahamas that is a stop for its Caribbean cruises, under a $200 million project called "Perfect Day at Coco Cay." The renovation of Coco Cay will comprise 125 acres of thrilling attractions: a water park featuring 13 water slides, including Daredevil's Peak, what will be the tallest slide in North America; a 1,600-foot zip line; a helium balloon ride; the largest wave pool in the Caribbean and more. Perfect Day at Coco Cay is the first of a series of private island renovations and Royal Caribbean plans additional Perfect Day destinations in Asia, Australia and Caribbean.

Yet another new innovation appealing to millennials is cruise lines jumping on the burgeoning craft beer trend. The *Carnival Vista* launched in 2016 was the first North American cruise ship to have its own brewery. Carnival followed that up with the launch last year of *Carnival Horizon* with another brewery, Guy's Pig & Anchor Bar-B-Que Smokehouse and Brewhouse, a partnership with Food Network star Guy Fieri.

Its arguable as to whether cruise lines are adding these millennial-friendly attractions on their ships and private islands *because* of increased millennial passenger demand, or to *generate* increased millennial passenger demand. What is unarguable is that—driven by the increased demand for cruising by younger cruisers—the growth of theme cruising that is targeted specifically to younger cruisers is explosive. Theme cruise providers are largely independent entrepreneurs looking to capitalize on existing demand, and millennials are flocking to cruises geared to their lifestyles, such as *Ship-Hop* featuring Hip-Hop and R&B music, *The Grown and Sexy Cruise, Latin Dance Cruise, The Groove Cruise,* with its non-stop electronic dance music experience, *Welcome to Jamrock Reggae Cruise*, and more.

The Cruising Baker-Danny Bradley

He had me at *The Cruising Baker*. With that name, that clever "mash-up" of passions, I just knew *The Cruising Baker* needed to be in *The Joy of Cruising*. That probably sounds shallow on my part, doesn't it? There is nothing shallow about Danny Bradley, also known as *The Cruising Baker*. Dr. Bradley, as he's formally known, studied psychology focusing on consumer and cyber psychology, individual differences and autism. He has completed his BSc in Psychology, MSc in Lifespan Neuropsychology and just completed his PhD in Psychology at Bournemouth University!

Danny lives in Poole, Dorset, UK on the South Coast of England and has lived in Dorset all of his life. In fact, Danny's first cruise, in celebration of his eighteenth birthday, was his first time outside of the UK. Danny's introduction to cruising was on Royal Caribbean's *Independence of the Seas. Independence* had been warmly welcomed into the hearts of Britain's cruisers.

Danny in front of *Britannia* docked in Antigua.

Independence of the Seas was christened a little over a year earlier during a ceremony in Southampton by its godmother, Elizabeth Hill of Chesterfield, UK (profiled in Chapter 4 of *The Joy of Cruising*). Among the world's largest, most advanced ships, the *Independence* sailed Danny and his family to the Italian Mediterranean, with port of calls including Rome and Pisa. Despite the fantastic locations at which the ship docked, Danny was even more awed by the *Independence* itself, with its ice rink, boxing ring, royal promenade with shops and restaurants, climbing wall, FlowRider® surf simulator, and West End London-style entertainment. The grandeur of *Independence* left a lasting impression.

Ever since his first cruise only ten years ago, Danny has been passionate about cruising. Since then he has cruised another twenty times. All the while, Danny was pursuing his studies, working at creating and managing websites, and, as the name of his blog suggests, Danny bakes–which he also blogs about.

Danny's first cruise ship: The magnificent *Independence of the Seas*

Besides that first cruise on Royal Caribbean, Danny has sailed on six ships on P&O Cruises, three on Princess, one on Celebrity, and an August 2018 "bucket list" transatlantic cruise with Cunard on *Queen Mary 2*. I write this with a mix of intrigue, envy, and joy on behalf of my new friend; Danny gets to check off one of his bucket list items before he is 30! Danny's cruises have sailed to Norway, Scandinavia, Northern Europe, the Mediterranean, Iberia, Canary Islands, and throughout the Caribbean; quite remarkable for someone who ten years prior had never travelled out of the UK. Clearly, Danny's thirst for exploration was ignited and his passion for cruising inflamed by that first experience on *Independence of the Seas*. Danny has made up for lost time; not yet 30 years old Danny has cruised more than the average traveler cruises in a lifetime.

Danny cites his cruises to Norway among his personal highlights. He has been fortunate enough to cruise around Norway numerous times. Danny loves Norway and it is his favorite destination—he suspects what might account for part of the reason he loves it there so much is because he is nearly a quarter Scandinavian, according to AncestryDNA! Danny has sailed as far north as Longyearbyen on the largest island in the Svalbard archipelago north of mainland Norway, a stunning location near the North Pole surrounded by picturesque mountains and glaciers, and populated by reindeer that comfortably co-exist alongside residents. Danny has cruised Arctic Norway at the height of both summer and winter. He describes it as a glorious place with 24 hours of light in the summer and dark in the winter. The lasting memories Danny has from cruising Norway and experiencing excursions include seeing the Northern Lights lighting up the sky and streaking across the cruise ship; taking in the awe inspiring views and magnificence of cruising the Norwegian Fjords; husky sledding in the arctic sun through magnificent white fields of snow; snowmobiling in the arctic; and, the Ice Hotel, an entire hotel, including the chairs and beds, made out of snow and ice blocks from the nearby Torne River (even the glasses in the bar are made of ice).

Husky sledding in Tromsø, Norway.

Sailing through Geirangerfjord, Norway onboard Princess Cruises *Grand Princess.*

Many have taken more cruises then Danny but have not had the time or otherwise been in a position to cruise longer than a week or two. Danny has already experienced a 20-night Caribbean and Azores cruise on P&O *Britannia*. The splendor of the Caribbean made the *Britannia* cruise a holiday to remember, and Danny's favorite port of calls were the stunning islands of Grenada and Antigua. Danny blogged about his experience on the extended cruise and the reception the blog received was incredible. "This was the first cruise I ever blogged 'live' from onboard; readers did seem to appreciate me posting from directly onboard and I try to do this whenever possible, internet permitting." Consequently, Danny was asked to publish his reflections about the cruise on the World of Cruising UK website.

Then there are the highlights of the bucket list cruise which Danny had just completed when we finished our interviews. On August 24, Danny flew to New York, spent a couple of nights in Time Square and got to experience a little of New York City before embarking on *Queen Mary 2* for a transatlantic cruise back to Southampton. "New York City was amazing. I only had a short amount of time to spend so had to prioritize what I wanted to do. But my absolutely highlight was going to The Top of the Rock...breath-taking! The views are simply stunning and it was an experience I will never forget." Top of the Rock is an observation deck atop Rockefeller Center, considered the best panoramic view of New York City; coincidently it was built to resemble the deck of a cruise ship.

"Crossing the Atlantic on *Queen Mary 2* was very special. Everything about Cunard exudes luxury and sophistication. The service and food was outstanding. We had great weather most of the week onboard and the seas were calm and serene the whole voyage back. *Queen Mary 2* is a true ocean liner and very unique. At the moment she is very close to securing the top spot of my all-time favorite ships."

The Cunard *Queen Mary 2* Grand Lobby.

Danny closed out his cruising in 2018 in November with a post dry-dock mini-cruise on Cunard *Queen Elizabeth*. Given the pace of Danny's cruising in the last ten years, it is safe to say that there will be a lot more in the next ten. Near-term, Danny has booked

Princess Cruises *Sapphire Princess* for May 2019 and has a couple of cruises planned in 2019 on *Britannia*. He is booked to return to the Mediterranean for the first time since 2015 in August with *Britannia*, and a mini-cruise in October. In 2020, P&O *Iona* will be launched and Danny is already booked. "I will be sailing on *Iona* within the first month of her maiden season to the Norwegian Fjords." Longer-term, Danny would like to try a few cruise lines he has not yet experienced. Those high on his list to try are Holland America Lines, Norwegian Cruise Lines and Marella Cruises. Iceland, Greenland and the Baltics are high on Danny's destination list and if he can get past the requirement for the very long flights to and fro, Danny is considering cruises which take in destinations such as Africa, Asia, and Australia.

Danny's remaining (!) bucket list is long and ambitious. Based on his past ten years of cruising, something tells me he will exhaust the entire list, which includes cruising with the luxury lines of Viking Cruises, Oceania Cruises and Silversea; cruising Alaska, ideally in conjunction with a transatlantic cruise back to the UK from New York; touring Canada; and, staying in San Francisco and cruising under the Golden Gate bridge. As a corollary to his Norway cruises, Danny aspires to cruise to Antarctica and see the Southern Lights. Danny has cruised as far north as possible; he would like to do the same southward. Finally, his bucket list contains the "holy grail" of passionate cruisers, a world cruise.

A word about *The Cruising Baker* blog: mixed in with the cruise trip reports, interviews, features on existing and upcoming ships, and yes, recipes for lemon drizzle surprise, is something that caught my eye and is worthy of mentioning. From a young age, Danny and his family have worked with and been surrounded by children and young adults who have various special educational needs and disabilities, and this extended on to Danny's psychology studies and work with autism. Danny notes on the blog, "A topic close to my heart is accessibility and inclusion for everyone." Danny has several posts on his blog pertaining to accessibility at sea, including an interview with a physically challenged cruiser regarding her perspective on accessible cruising.

I don't know how Danny finds time, but besides cruising and blogging, Danny, of course, loves to bake, hence *The Cruising Baker*. I know that I had a little fun with the name earlier, but Danny is very serious about his baking. "I've been baking since before I can remember. Hours spent in the kitchen with my Mum and Nan (grandmother) creating many tasty delights has ingrained a love for baking so deep that it will always be a part of who I am. When she passed away, Nan gave me her beloved cookbook that we used to bake together, and it is something I still have and treasure. It's a real family thing. In secondary school I took a general certificate of secondary educations exam in food technology and completed a whole project on bread! I love baking bread—the smell, the process, the creativeness. Fantastic. I definitely bake for pleasure and relaxation and, although being far from an expert, I hope that sharing my love for baking and the recipes I have will help share this passion with others. For me, combining my love of baking with my passion for cruising was a 'no brainer'; they are two of my biggest passions."

When not cruising, blogging, studying, researching, caring for others, or baking (whew!) Danny also has a keen interest in reading and writing, and has a deep love for animals, especially dogs. He keeps tropical fish and loves to Aquascape—think garden landscaping but in an aquarium. I think the following quote from Danny summarizes him well: "Experiences and love are more important than any material things."

Danny's New York Cheesecake

Ingredients for the base:

160g digestive biscuits

1 tbsp caster sugar

85g unsalted butter

Ingredients for the filling:

900g full-fat soft cheese

250g caster sugar

3 tbsp plain flour

2 tsp vanilla extract

finely grated zest of 1 lemon

3 large eggs + 1 yolk

200ml soured cream

- Making sure you have an oven shelf positioned in the middle of the oven, preheat to 180C/160C fan/gas mark 4.

- Prepare a 23cm springform cake tin by:

- Taking the base of the tin and placing a square piece of baking paper (larger than the tin) over the top.

- Clip the tin together trapping the baking paper in place, with excess left hanging out of the bottom.

- Lightly grease the sides of the tin with butter.

To make the base:

- Crush the digestive biscuits into fine crumbs. I find the easiest way is to put the digestives into a sturdy bag and crush them using a rolling pin. But you can also use a processor or crush them in a bowl. Once crushed, mix the caster sugar so that it is evenly distributed within the biscuits.

- In a saucepan, melt the butter. Add the crumb mixture and stir until the butter has been adsorbed and the mixture is evenly moist throughout.

- Place the mixture into the tin and spread evenly. Press the mixture down firmly using the bottom of a dessert spoon or rolling pin, or something similar. If needed, use your fingers to make sure the edges are firm as well - take care as the mixture may be hot to touch.

- Bake in the oven for 10 minutes. Leave to cool while you make the filling.

To make the filling:

- Increase the oven temperature to 220C/200C fan/gas 7.

- In a bowl, beat the soft cheese until it becomes smooth and creamy. If using a stand mixer, use the paddle attachment on a medium-low speed setting for about 2 minutes.

- Add the sugar and beat until fully incorporated. For a stand mixer, turn the setting to a low speed for this stage onwards.

- Add the flour and a pinch of salt. Beat until smooth making sure to scrape down the sides and base of the bowl to ensure all ingredients are incorporated.

If using a stand mixer, swap the paddle attachment for a whisk attachment - continue on a low speed. If making by hand, continue using your spoon. Add the vanilla extract and lemon zest. Then slowly add the eggs, one at a time. Again, scrape down the sides of the bowl regularly.

Add the soured cream and beat until incorporated. The mixture should be light and smooth. Do not over-beat as incorporating too much air may cause your cheesecake to lose its smooth top and crack/bubble.

Pour the mixture on top of the biscuit base you prepared earlier. Place in the oven and bake for 10 minutes.

After 10 minutes, turn the oven temperature down to 110C/90C fan/gas ¼. Bake for a further 45-50 minutes. When cooked there should be a slight wobble to the cheesecake and still be cream in colour on top, going slightly golden around the edges.

Turn off the oven and prop open the oven door. Leave the cheesecake in the oven to cool - this prevents the top from cracking. Ideally it should stay there to cool for at least 2 hours, then remove from the oven.

When completely cool, loosely cover with foil and chill in the fridge for a minimum of 8 hours, but ideally overnight.

Run a pallet knife around the edge of the tin, releasing any edges that have stuck. Unclip the tin, remove the cheesecake and slide onto a plate. Once on the plate, slide the baking paper out from underneath - this is easier said than one. But the oversize baking paper should make this considerably easier.

Decorate and enjoy!

Cruising with Matt

I have a special affinity with Matt Mramer. Sure, I envy his cruising life, where at age 25 he has already had 13 cruises and has sailed as far away as the Mediterranean and the Greek Isles. At 25 I had zero cruises and the furthest I had been away from home was to California for a job interview after business school graduation! The connection I have with Matt is not just due to our mutual interest in cruising. After I heard of his cruising story as a millennial, I research him and learned that Matt is a recent graduate of Florida Gulf Coast University where I currently work as an administrator. I am proud that an FGCU student is making a difference in the world of cruising so soon after graduating.

Matt in front of Vittorio Emanuele II Monument in Rome where he
cruised to on *Celebrity Reflection* in 2015. Nice shirt, Go Eagles!

Matt spent much of the past year as the Director of Video and
Multimedia Content for Cruise.com, meaning that Matt was responsible for every part of the content creation process at Cruise.com
from concept to completion. In addition to creating a variety of marketing and training videos, Matt was often working hand-in-hand
with cruise lines to create engaging ship tours and overviews. Prior
to his time in the cruise industry, Matt spent a year as the broadcast coordinator for the National Basketball Association's Orlando
Magic. Both of those sound like roles that would have been wonderful opportunities for many of us in our twenties. "I loved my time
with the Magic and I learned a great deal about the inner workings
of the NBA and of a high-quality broadcast. I wasn't a fan of the
Orlando area, and I decided to relocate to Miami in hopes of being
closer to the cruise industry and in a city that I felt had more to
offer me."

Matt is originally from Cleveland, Ohio. He left the Midwest to move to Fort Myers, Florida to attend FGCU. Matt currently resides in Miami, Florida. When not cruising or using his video skills to create unique projects, Matt can be found exploring his other passion, sports. He loves to golf and you can always count on him rooting for the Cleveland Browns every Sunday. Matt is an avid cruiser and usually cruises at least annually. He has cruised with Disney, Norwegian, Carnival, Royal Caribbean, and Celebrity cruise lines. Matt's first cruise was in 2003 on *Disney Wonder* when he was just ten years old. Matt cruised again at 14-years old when he sailed on Royal Caribbean's *Freedom of the Seas.* I asked Matt if as a teen he was already smitten with the cruising bug or did it develop gradually. He told me, "I'll never forget falling in love with cruising. It certainly wasn't a slow and steady proposition. After my family's trip onboard the *Freedom*, I knew that cruising was something that I wanted to spend my life doing."

10-year old Matt with his mom on *Disney Wonder*.

Matt's most memorable voyage was a 12-day graduation cruise on the *Celebrity Reflection* in 2015 with ports of call in Rome, Naples, and the Greek Isles. "In Mykonos (in the Greek Isles) we rented all terrain vehicles for $40 for the day and just explored the island on our own, cruising from beach to beach and enjoying the local cuisine. In a previous cruise we rented scooters in Roatan; I really love the ability to explore on my own and find hidden gems that are never included in the guided walking tours and such. I love to really connect with different areas and cultures of the world and this is usually my focus when I stop in any new port."

2018 was an exciting cruise industry year for Matt. He got the opportunity to tour *Norwegian Bliss*, the new flagship for Norwegian Cruise Line's Breakaway Plus class, during her US inaugural tour in Miami in May. In July he cruised on the *Norwegian Sky*. Matt wrapped up the year by sailing in September on *Carnival Horizon*, Carnival's newest ship which launched in the spring of 2018. *Horizon* is packed with some of those millennial-friendly attractions mentioned at the beginning of this chapter such as the SkyRide, a pedal-powered bike-like contraption suspended high above the ship that rides along an 800-foot-long track, an IMAX Theatre, the Water Works aqua park, and Guy Fieri's Pig & Anchor Bar-B-Que Smokehouse | Brewhouse. "It was my first sailing with Carnival, and I enjoyed it more than I thought I would. There were a few things that stood out, most notably the great number of food offerings. *Horizon* has a fabulous selection of included dining outlets, in addition to some of the most affordable specialty restaurants at sea. The rooms were spacious and comfortable, and my room in particular even featured a bathtub in addition to the stand-up shower. Lastly, you can definitely tell that Carnival is geared towards kids and families with the extensive sky park and Dr. Seuss Waterworks installations sprawling throughout the top decks of the ship."

Matt also enjoys land-based travel. While he loves his Miami beaches, he finds differing landscapes exciting as well, particularly when it includes the opportunity to play or see golf. He was able to experience Denver and other parts of Colorado for the first time in September, exploring the mountains and taking in the beauty of nature. "I'm dying to get to Thailand and explore that beautiful country. I'd also like to explore much of Europe and Asia that I haven't been fortunate enough to see yet. South America also makes the list without a doubt."

I asked Matt what he considers as his ultimate travel aspiration. "Taking a golf trip to Scotland and Ireland to learn about the history of the game and test my skills on those old links courses is something that I absolutely have to do before my name is called. I also would love to explore the middle east beginning with Oman and Dubai, both places where I'd also like to tee it up at some point. I don't really have one spot that I can zero in on; there is so much of this world that I'd love the opportunity to see and explore."

Matt feels strongly about the importance of stressing that cruising is for everyone and not just older folks and retirees. With all of the incredible advancements in the cruising industry over the last ten years, Matt feels "there is something out there for every type of traveler. I'd also like to stress the social environment of a cruise; I've made many lifelong friends from all across the country and the world onboard my cruises. No technology is such a nice respite from the BS that has started to consume our world, and I really love disconnecting for a week and reconnecting with other people, having conversations and living life fully present."

I asked Matt what best illustrates his passion for cruising. He reflected for a while and then told me the story of the path he took to end up with his job at Cruise.com. "I moved from Orlando to Miami with no job, no connections, nothing except a roommate and a place to live. I have always dreamed of being a part of the cruise industry, and I felt that I had a better chance of doing that by coming to the cruise headquarters of the world here in Miami. I moved my life to Miami with no promises because I believed that I could create something special if I just got a chance, and I'm so thankful to have that chance with Cruise.com."

Of course Matt got the position, despite having no work experience in the cruise world. But he brought with him to Miami that passion for cruising first inflamed as a 14-year old on *Freedom of the Seas,* and that passion came through in his interview. He also brought along a video he had made. Serendipitously, after near tragedy, Matt had taught himself video editing. In the summer of 2017, Matt and his dad cruised together on the *Norwegian Escape*, and Matt made a video of that trip. Only a few months after the cruise, Matt was involved in a terrible accident when someone hit him while he was riding on his scooter. Matt was lucky to survive as he suffered a broken neck, several broken ribs, separated shoulder, and a severe head wound among other injuries. While convalescing, Matt had a spurt of creativity, in part due to his circumstances. "Being in a neck brace for three months, there wasn't a whole lot that I could do and so I decided to teach myself how to edit videos, since I had already done so much work editing audio for the Orlando Magic." Matt created a polished video of his trip with his father and attached it to his application to Cruise.com and credits it with helping to solidify his status as the right person for the position of video editor. "I think it caught the eye of the company as something modern, fun and eye-catching."

**Matt, thankful to be alive, and thankful to be enjoying a
sunset onboard *Norwegian Sky* last summer.**

Matt's long-term dream is to host a cruising TV show dedicated to exposing people to the amazing world of cruising and all the incredible options that are available with a cruise. "I feel like I'm so close to achieving that dream and I look forward to taking steps over the next few years to network and make the connections necessary to turn this dream into a reality." Matt recently left Cruise.com after concluding that he can best pursue his passion for cruising and his long-term dream through his own trips and projects rather than spending his time focused on Cruise.com initiatives and objectives.

Matt plans a big step towards making his long-term dream a reality with a cruise he has planned for February 2019 on *Norwegian Jade* where he will be filming a pilot episode for his show concept. "I look forward to bringing people into the world of cruising with my passion and personality, something that I've been wanting to do for quite awhile. This will hopefully be the first step in making my dream of hosting my own cruise program come to fruition. We will be sailing on the *Norwegian Jade* for a 5-day cruise to Costa Maya and Norwegian's private island in Belize, Harvest Caye. I am traveling with a friend of mine who works in Hollywood with a variety of different video projects and we will be shooting what I hope will be somewhat of a bridge between a vacation vlog and a ship tour video. I plan to show some of the unique things about the ship and the itinerary while also diving into the activities and relationships that await passengers in general in the world of cruising. In addition to amazing ships and destinations, I want to showcase to viewers the soul of the cruise experience and why I believe it to be such a unique vacation option for all types of people. Overall, the objective is to create an episode that is fun and engaging, and something that will catch the eye of production companies and cable networks to potentially invest in the project long-term."

Remember the name Matt Mramer!

Sparkx-Marcus Adams

Marcus Adams lives in Winchester, Hampshire, UK, about an hour from London, where he commutes each day to work as a Policy Advisor to the Mayor of London. Marcus is creator of the cruise blog *Sparkx* (Marcus' nickname during his youth.) Marcus was introduced to travel early on as his dad, a bank executive, did a lot of travelling in conjunction with his work as his responsibilities included developing and organizing all the management incentive trips. Consequently, Marcus got to visit a number of interesting and exotic places. Part of this exposure to travel at an early age included accompanying his parents on cruises. Marcus sailed on his first cruise ship, *Majesty of the Seas*, at just nine years old. He considers it a life-forming event and has been hooked on cruising ever since. Even at nine,

Marcus could appreciate the appeal of cruising. He recalls attending the kids club on board and instantly making new friends with whom he spent time throughout the cruise having fun and making mischief. "I remember one day being at the kids' club and one of the staff saying, 'come on it's time to go and meet your mum and dad to get off the ship.' Wait, I have to get off the ship, leave my friends and do other things? It's funny looking back on it now, but I hear similar stories quite often." (I can relate to Marcus' recollection many years later. Lately other than at ports of call, I rarely get to see my grandkids when they accompany me on a cruise because of the friendships they make and activities they get involved with at the kids' clubs.)

9-year old Marcus with his mum in front of *Majesty of the Seas* **during his first cruise.**

Fast forward three years later to 1996, to Marcus' second cruise, aboard *Carnival Sensation*: "My appreciation of cruising had grown, as I had. I remember the excitement of our first port on this journey, San Juan. I'd heard of San Juan in films, such as James Bond GoldenEye which came out a year before, so I was particularly excited to see what this island was all about. Stepping off the ship in the warm evening, we were welcomed by a Latin extravaganza across the Old Town. Street parties, music and culture all brought this vibrant city to life. I instantly fell in love with the island. It would be a number of years before I came back, but that memory has stayed with me ever since."

As a young adult Marcus continued to return to what he refers to as "my happy place," cruising, and increasingly wanted to share his experience with others. I asked Marcus, "At what point did you develop your passion for cruising? Was it right away in those first couple of cruises as a young boy or did it develop over time? How did you know you were hooked?" Marcus responded, "I think to be honest that first cruise hooked me—I was hooked straightaway. I was the one who suggested the second cruise. Even at that age I wanted to know as much as I could about the industry, the ships, the destinations. I'd collect as many brochures as I could and pore over them to look at everything. After my mum passed away in 2001, my dad and I continued to go on cruises. It was something that brought us together, but also was a strong reminder of my mum. On these adventures, dad and I would live life to the fullest. Cruising with my dad as an adult was a very different experience. We'd enjoy the food and entertainment, as well as finding our favourite bars and watch the world go by."

Today Marcus is up to 30 cruises and counting. He has cruised mostly on Royal Caribbean and has sailed Carnival, although lately Marcus has a particular fondness for Celebrity and Viking cruise lines. Nevertheless, Royal Caribbean will always hold a special place in Marcus' heart. First, he got engaged on a Royal Caribbean cruise ship. In 2014, Marcus was the first person to propose in the North Star on board the new *Quantum of the Seas*. The North Star observation tower is a glass-walled capsule that extends on a giant robotic arm out over the ocean and takes groups of up to 14 cruisers to more than 300 feet above sea level. *Quantum's* first stop was Puerto Rico. "We arrived in the late afternoon and stepped off the ship to find the Old Town alive with street parties and a food festival. Instantly I was taken back to 1996 and found myself reliving these memories with my partner." It was a special night and Marcus proposed on the North Star high over the Atlantic Ocean the following day. Another factor that made the *Quantum* cruise special is that Marcus was fortunate enough during that same cruise to appear as an extra in a 30-second Royal Caribbean television commercial that aired throughout the United States and China—Marcus portrayed a guest enjoying himself at the pool and having dinner. So, Marcus is an answer to a trivia question: Which *The Joy of Cruising* subject has been seen by the largest number of YouTube and television viewers in the world?

Marcus in front of *Celebrity Reflection* in Jamaica.

Marcus in Geiranger, Norway; that's the *Viking Sea* in the background.

Marcus has sailed across the world including the Caribbean, Mediterranean, and Northern Europe. His most recent and upcoming cruises are of particular interest to me. Marcus' last cruise of 2018 was a nine-night New York, Canada, and New England cruise on *Anthem of the Seas*. I was anxious to get a review from him, given my own plans to sail *Anthem* three months later. At the beginning of 2019, Marcus is booked for *Celebrity Edge,* perhaps the world's most anticipated new cruise ship which launched officially in December 2018. Just a couple of months later, Marcus will cruise on the maiden voyage of MSC Cruises stunning flagship *MSC Bellissima*, with its bowling alley, Cirque du Soleil at Sea, and virtual cabin assistants. *MSC Bellissima* will be christened in Southampton, UK, becoming by far the largest cruise ship ever launched there.

Longer-term, Marcus is considering a cruise around Asia including Japan and Vietnam. He is also in the planning stages of an Australia and New Zealand cruise. On Marcus' bucket list are cruises to Alaska, Panama Canal, and river cruising the Mekong in Southeast Asia.

These days Marcus goes on cruises with his partner, with friends and occasionally he cruises solo. His partner had never conceived of going on a cruise when they first met a number of years ago, but being the passionate cruiser that he is, Marcus quickly convinced him they should go on one. Very quickly he was hooked and now takes just as much enjoyment from cruising as Marcus does. Together they've travelled all over the world on ships, experienced amazing cultures and scenery, and met wonderful people along the way.

Marcus created his blog *Sparkx* shortly after his father passed away tragically in 2014. "I needed a positive outlet in my life to support my mental health. So, one day I sat down at my desk and started to write about all my experiences in cruising. I wanted to give back to the travel and cruise community and wanted to share all my experiences and pass on any knowledge that might help others get as much out of cruising as I did."

Marcus describes his blog as follows: "*Sparkx* aims to be a quick, simple and easy go-to place for information and news pertaining to travel and cruising, together with a healthy dose of randomness and fun thrown in for good measure! Given the busy world we all live in, I want people to be able to get and understand information very quickly without getting bogged down." When he is not on a cruise or doing land-based travel, which he also enjoys greatly, or spending his evenings and weekends working on his blog, Marcus enjoys photography and spending time with his dog. He says there is nothing better than getting outdoors and experiencing nature and the world around you.

"Ever since that first cruise at nine years old I have been a lover of cruising. Like many, I find the sea very calming. There's nothing quite like sitting on deck or on a balcony and watching the world go by. For me, it is a safe haven from all the stress of everyday life. This is something I shared with my parents; it was always our happy place as a family. Where else can you wake up somewhere new and exciting every day? What is better than being able to explore somewhere new each day? Well, how about exploring and sharing it with others. For me, the beauty of cruising is not only being able to see and experience new things but being able to share these experiences, both with people you know and those you get to know on the journey."

CRUISING ISN'T JUST
FOR OLD PEOPLE

*C*ruising Isn't Just for Old People. Lest you think I am stating that as a point of view to elicit a reaction and generate discussion or debate, that is not my intention. Besides, despite a widely held myth about cruising being focused on older travelers, the veracity of that commonly accepted belief is becoming more and more arguable. Cruising isn't just for old people! According to the Cruise Lines International Association (CLIA), the world's largest cruise industry trade association, millennials and generation Xers (generally 20-50 year olds) are cruising more than ever before, and they rate cruising over land-based vacations.

For one thing, cruising is becoming more affordable, which puts it more in the reach of a younger, less affluent demographic. The average price of a cruise is less than it was ten years ago. Cruise ships are being reimagined to appeal to younger cruisers. Just about every new cruise ship, as well as major refurbishments of existing ships, include family-friendly attractions such as water slides, bumper cars, zip lines, surfing and sky flying simulators, go karts, trampolines, and on and on. Furthermore, the growth in theme cruises is helping introduce millennials and generation Xers to cruising. Consider the *Groove Cruise* (electronic dance music); the *Reggae Cruise*; the *Hip Hop Cruise* and a number of others.

Cruising Isn't Just for Old People is the name of an award-winning blog run by Emma Le Teace. Emma created the blog in 2016 with a vision to dispel the myth that cruising was the domain of an older demographic. The CLIA findings suggest Emma is doing her part!

Cruising Isn't Just for Old People started as a cruise blog but has evolved to become a collaborative community of young cruisers. The site brings together bloggers and cruisers from all over the globe, and all walks of life, who all share a passion for cruising and a belief that cruising is for everybody irrespective of age. Contributors to the site share a wide variety of content, including cruise reviews, top tips about cruise lines and destination guides – all with new cruisers in mind. The foregoing words were written by 23-year old Emma Le Teace on the occasion of winning the 2018 Wave Award for Favorite Cruise Blogger. The Wave Awards celebrate the best of the UK's cruise industry, including several categories for cruise lines and cruise ships, as well as industry operations such as technology, marketing campaign, etc. Emma is from West Sussex, UK, about 60 miles south of London where she traveled to attend "The Oscars of UK cruising" to accept her Wave Award over numerous more experienced and renown cruise writers.

Emma grew up on the south coast and still loves to visit the seaside. When not working at her day job as a data developer for an insurance group, or on a cruise, Emma spends most of her time writing about cruising for the *Cruising Isn't Just for Old People* blog or making videos about cruising for her YouTube channel. Other than that she likes to play piano and recently purchased a guitar, "Which is much harder than it looks!"

Emma holding her Wave Award trophy.

Emma sailed on her first cruise with her family when she was 11-years old. "It was my Gran's idea that we should take the cruise; she is still cruising at 91! This cruise was actually two parts and was advertised as a 'fire and ice' cruise, meaning that we visited both Hawaii and Alaska. The Hawaii part was onboard Norwegian Cruise Lines *Pride of Aloha* (now the *Norwegian Sky*) and the Alaska part was onboard the *Norwegian Spirit*. It was amazing, I had so much fun exploring the ship with my cousins Libby and Fern, and brother Max." Quite a memorable first experience cruising; in a single voyage Emma ticked off two destinations which are on many experienced cruisers' bucket lists.

So, early on Emma's passion was inflamed. Emma next cruised again a couple of times with her family as a teenager. When she decided to go on her first holiday as an adult, Emma said cruising was an obvious choice. Emma sailed a western Caribbean cruise on the *Norwegian Getaway*. "It was great to cruise with NCL again, and it was the first cruise that I had taken with my boyfriend Jono. Jono is 6'3 so I was a little worried about fitting him in an inside cabin, but he had no problems at all. Jono was bitten by the cruising bug and has cruised with me multiple times since." Since that first cruise as an adult, Emma has always had a desire to visit new places. "Cruising really opened up my eyes to different cultures and ways of life. There's not a lot that I love more than learning a little about the history of a country, preferably on a walking tour!"

11-year old Emma, right with her cousin Libby during her first cruise.

Emma has been on a total of 18 cruises. Most of Emma's cruises have been on Norwegian; she has also cruised with MSC, Cunard, Royal Caribbean, Princess, P&O, Viking, and Marella Cruises on diverse itineraries that have taken her on Mediterranean cruises, Canary Islands, Greek Isles, Bahamas, Bermuda, Hawaii, Alaska, Asia, and last year to the Norwegian Fjords on her first ever P&O cruise aboard the *Britannia*. "We took an excursion to Briksdal glacier which was breathtaking to see."

Emma's favorite cruise was Singapore to Tokyo onboard the Princess Cruises *Golden Princess*. She also recently took a British

Isles cruise onboard the *Royal Princess* which she found amazing. "I was really blown away by the places that we visited. Being from the UK myself, I had never really considered a British Isles cruise, but I am so glad that I did. I visited Loch Ness but sadly didn't find Nessie!"

Emma's favorite sail-aways are Miami and New York, both of which Emma finds breathtaking. Among her favorite ports of call is Barcelona. "I've been a couple of times now and find it so easy to get around. There are so many things to see and do." Emma also includes Valetta in Malta, and Gran Canaria in the Canary Islands as favorite destinations.

Emma has cruised so much and to so many exotic locations, that I wondered what was her most moving memory from her cruising experiences. She told me, "In 2018, I visited the Norwegian Fjords with my mum. It was great to spend time together. The weather was cold but we were desperate not to miss a second of the view so we wrapped ourselves up in our duvets and sat on the balcony with a cup of tea. It was perfect!"

Along the lines of powerful moments from Emma's cruising background, I want to single out one cruise in particular which just happened in September of 2018. Emma sailed on a Baltic cruise on *Marella Discovery*. In honor of her grandfather who died from cancer in 2017, during the cruise Emma had her head shaved for the Macmillan Cancer Support *Brave the Shave* challenge. Emma wanted to "give something back" on behalf of those affected by cancer. Emma raised £5000 ($6500) for Macmillan Cancer Support, and she donated her hair to the Little Princess Trust which makes wigs for children who have lost their hair due to illness. Emma said, "I have been thinking about doing this for a while, always waiting for the 'right time'. It was at my granddad's funeral that I finally made the decision. He lived a full life but, even still, life is so short and none of us know how long we will get," said Emma. "The work that Macmillan does is incredible and if I ever had cancer, or anybody I knew had cancer, I would want Macmillan to be there."

At 24, Emma has already cruised much of the world, but she does have a few bucket list destinations as well as embarkation ports in mind: she would love to cruise through the Panama Canal, as well as cruise out of New Orleans. Emma's ultimate bucket list cruise is to the Pacific Islands. "Shame they're so far away and I couldn't get the time off work," Emma says. Somehow I suspect Emma will get there sooner rather later considering the progression of her cruising life to this point. In addition to cruising, Emma has traveled on land-based trips to several places in Europe and the United States. "I also love taking cheap weekends away. I visited Le Harve (northern France) on a cruise recently and it was so expensive to get into Paris that I decided to come home and plan a weekend on the Eurostar instead. It was cheaper for me to go from London to Paris than from the port of Le Harve!"

Emma created *Cruising Isn't Just for Old People* when sailing on her first Cunard cruise, the *Queen Victoria* to the Greek Isles in 2016. "I had no idea that 'cruise blogging' was a thing. Who'd have thought it? I was joking around with my brother about how I would make a website. He jokingly asked me what I would call it and I said *Cruising Isn't Just for Old People*. The rest is history. I aim to write content that will help cruisers pick their perfect cruise. I am a firm believer in the idea that there is a cruise line and ship for everybody; the challenge is finding each person his or her match." I met Emma through her *Cruising Isn't Just for Old People* Facebook group. At the time I was joining every Facebook cruise group that I could in preparation for writing *The Joy of Cruising*. I felt a little sheepish about joining Emma's group as I kind of figured it was aimed at a slightly different demographic—just a little bit younger than I—but I quickly learned that my fears were unfounded!

After disembarking from that Cunard cruise, Emma spent the first six months "stumbling around the internet" trying to learn how to set up a website. Emma works in the information technology field—she writes computer code for a living—but found that it is a different language from that behind a website. After launching her website, she created the aforementioned *Cruising Isn't Just for Old People* Facebook group to create a space for cruisers, and those who aspired to go on a cruise, to chat. Emma said, "If I have a question about cruising or I'd like to share a story or photo, I now know that there is a community of people who want to listen and help." Several of the experienced cruisers profiled in *The Joy of Cruising*—from the UK as well as from the US—participate and contribute to the Facebook group. The *Cruising Isn't Just for Old People* website was launched in September 2016.

Emma ready for formal night on one of the *MSC Meraviglia* Swarovski Crystal staircases.

I asked Emma when she became aware that *Cruising Isn't Just for Old People* was a success. "I blog in my spare time so I never really envisaged it becoming a success. I have been absolutely blown away by the way that people have reacted to me and my community. In 2018 when I won "Favourite Cruise Blogger" at the Wave Awards (an award show run by World of Cruising, a UK cruise magazine) I never expected to win. The cruise blogger category was up first, and when my name was called I didn't know what to do. It was incredible but absolutely terrifying at the same time. I suppose this validated to me that there is an audience of young cruisers who want their voices to be heard. We now have *Cruising Isn't Just for Old People* engraved in a trophy!"

I was curious as to how life has changed for Emma since winning such a prestigious award. She told me she cruises a lot more. In 2018 she sailed on five cruises; prior to that Emma only cruised once every couple of years. "The main difference since winning the Wave Award is that people take my passion for cruise ships seriously. Previously it was a little bit of a joke, but now if anybody tells me that cruises are just for old people I can show them my trophy!" Emma also gets noticed more. "There are two main cruise magazines in the UK, *Cruise International* and *World of Cruising*. I won the Wave Awards (World of Cruising) last year and am again nominated for this year. This year I'm also nominated in the Cruise International Awards, which is really exciting. It's all very exciting and doesn't seem real at all. I'll never quite get my head around it! For something I do in my evenings after work it seems to have struck a chord with fellow cruisers."

Awards or not, the future is bright for Emma and *Cruising Isn't Just for Old People*. She is an engaging subject for interviews in the media and on other blogs, and she is recognized as an influencer in the UK cruising community. For instance, recently Emma was invited to visit Chantiers de l'Atlantique, a shipyard based in Saint-Nazaire, France to explore the *MSC Bellissima,* a cruise ship currently under construction and scheduled to launch March, 2019. Besides the tour in hard-hat, Emma later attended a party literally underneath the elevated cruise ship. "The visit was incredible and something I will never forget," Emma said. (By the way, recall those attractions to draw younger cruises that I discussed at the beginning of this chapter? *MSC Bellissima* will feature Cirque du Soleil at Sea, and will have the first full-size bowling alley on a cruise ship.)

Emma, 2nd from right, under a propeller of the *MSC Bellissima.*

Emma has accomplished so much both in terms of cruising, as well as sharing her reflections of cruising via writing, video and social media at such a young age. When Emma agreed to be in this book, I posted on social media that "I am pleased to announce that Emma Le Teace of *Cruising Isn't Just for Old People,* one of the up and coming 'movers and shakers' of the UK cruising community will be in the *The Joy of Cruising*." A lot of readers endorsed the "up-and-coming mover and shaker" comment. I know several of them and they are quite accomplished in their own right.

Emma, what do think the future holds for *Cruising Isn't Just for Old People*? "Lots of cruising I hope! My site is a collaborative community, meaning that we have content from many writers, some of whom have their own blogs and some of whom are just regular cruisers. We've had 40 contributors to date, and I would love to grow this over the next year or two. I also hope to grow our Facebook community and of course my YouTube channel, my latest venture!"

Cruise Bloggers:
The Readers' Choice

CRUISE BLOGGERS: THE READERS' CHOICE

Cruise enthusiasts who decide to create, cultivate, and curate a blog and sometimes a related podcast epitomize what *The Joy of Cruising* is about: individuals moved by their passion for cruising who choose to manifest that passion in an engaging way when not sailing. Virtually every one of the many bloggers, vloggers, and podcasters I spoke to for this book were motivated to pursue their avocation after an introduction to the world of cruising inflamed an intense interest in cruising more, learning about cruising, and conveying that knowledge to others. Throughout *The Joy of Cruising* are individuals who along with their interesting cruising stories also blog, podcast, and/or have a YouTube channel.

The individuals discussed in the next few chapters are referred to as Reader's Choice cruise bloggers: finalists and winners in the 10Best Readers' Choice New Media Award for Best Cruise Blogger, sponsored by USA TODAY along with its companion site 10Best. com which provides users with travel and lifestyle content.

Danielle Fear, of United Kingdom, creator of *CruiseMiss* was one of only two bloggers outside of the United States selected as a winner of the 10Best Readers' Choice New Media Award for Best Cruise Blogger. Danielle has been writing about cruises and working in the cruise industry since 2010 and created the *CruiseMiss* blog in 2013.

Jason Leppert was a 10Best Readers' Choice New Media Award for Best Cruise Blogger finalist for the *Popular Cruising* blog. Prolific is the word that comes to mind with Jason—both in terms of the sheer breadth of his writing and videography that ranges from cruising to an extensive knowledge, experience and coverage of Disney theme properties—to the frequency and diversity of his cruising.

10Best Readers' Choice New Media Award for Best Cruise Blogger winners Matt Hochberg and Scott Sanders share a couple of things in common: each authors a blog that's dedicated to coverage of primarily a single cruise line, and they both have successful podcasts as companions to their blogs. Matt won for *The Royal Caribbean Blog* which he started in 2010 and is described as "your ultimate source for Royal Caribbean coverage," and he hosts *The Royal Caribbean Blog Podcast*. *The Royal Caribbean Blog* is an unofficial fan blog written for other fans of Royal Caribbean, and is not affiliated with Royal Caribbean International. Scott won for *The Disney Cruise Line Blog*. Since 2012, *The Disney Cruise Line Blog* and accompanying podcast has been an unofficial source of Disney Cruise Line news and information and a place where fans can share Disney cruise experiences.

CRUISEMISS: DANIELLE FEAR

"I don't live in a lavish house, I definitely don't speak the Queens English and I still have many things to learn in this life, but I'm pretty confident in my cruise knowledge—I could put a few people under the table. You see, that's what I do, that's what makes me tick and brings me life, so for me, that's all that matters." Drops mic.

Danielle Fear, known to many with a passion for cruising in UK and beyond as *CruiseMiss*, is the author of the above quote. She didn't really "drop the mic," but I could picture her doing so as I read her quote. To make such a self-assured statement, you have to be recognized as someone who knows of what you speak. Let's see, earlier I mentioned *CruiseMiss* as being one of the winners in the USA Today10Best Readers' Choice New Media Award for Best Cruise Blogger, one of only two UK bloggers to join that venerable list, and many other cruise blogger accolades have been accorded *CruiseMiss*: Best Cruise Blogger; Top 25 Socially Shared Cruise Blogs; Top 10 Cruise Bloggers You Need To Follow; Top 50 Cruise Blogs To Follow in 2018, and more including finalist and highly commended recognition in other major awards such as the UK cruise industry's The

Wave Awards. Perhaps even more of a testament to *CruiseMiss'* credibility and esteem in the cruise writing world is the frequency with which her perspective and insight is sought for expert commentary, quotes, and articles in media such as World of Cruising, Cruise Critic UK, Porthole Magazine and more. Danielle has done radio interviews, email interviews, and provided content for numerous online travel sites.

Danielle Fear at Treasury temple in Petra, Jordan, 2000-year-old architectural marvel.

Danielle Fear was born and raised and still lives in Newcastle upon Tyne in North East England, about four hours north of London. Danielle prefers to be on the move all the time—more than likely on the water, such as the 108 consecutive days she spent in 2018 on a world cruise—but notes there is nothing quite like home. "If I travel anywhere via rail, on the return journey I always make sure I stand at the door as the train passes over the Tyne. The sight of the Tyne Bridge tells me that I'm home—it's a beautiful feeling."

After leaving school and entering the work world, Danielle found she was bored with the monotony of the same thing, day in and day out. Danielle was restless and disappointed in herself for not striving to reach her full potential. Her last regular job before getting involved with writing about cruising was selling sneakers; not Danielle's idea of what she saw herself doing long-term, and it had nothing to do with her burgeoning passion. Danielle had already cruised several times; not a substantial amount, but it was enough to show her that in her heart she was destined to travel.

Danielle finally worked up the courage to venture out, leaving to work for a cruise website. Working on the cruise website afforded Danielle the opportunity to learn as much as she could, and she was even able to avail herself of some online training for selling cruises that normally only travel agents would have access to. Alas, Danielle's foray into the professional travel world did not work out long-term. For 18 months, she was unemployed, but that did not stop her from cruising. Danielle had saved much of her income from her short-lived cruise website job as well as from her prior positions. She deliberately positioned herself financially to continue to cruise because she had already decided that in the long term it was what she needed to do in order to gain content and experience and ultimately build her blog. "I had to make a decision: either invest in my aspiration to be a cruise writer, or do something else." During those 18 months, Danielle spent a lot of money on cruising. That was her passion and she wanted to develop it. She experienced new places and new ships and traveled the world, going on six cruises, one of which was a five-week cruise to the Caribbean from Southampton on P&O Cruises *Oceana*. It was Danielle's first time in the Caribbean and she absolutely fell in love with it, especially the islands of Antigua and Jamaica. The first stop on the itinerary was Antigua, and as the ship sailed into port, she could hear the band playing the steel drums on the pier. "I remember thinking to myself wow, I am in the Caribbean, this is real!" During that time of unemployment and self-discovery, Danielle also sailed the Mediterranean several times and the Canary Islands. She also embarked on her first-ever press trip during that time; it was with Cruise & Maritime Voyages aboard the *Marco Polo*.

During those 18 months Danielle gathered what would become a substantial base of content to draw upon for her future blog. She eventually dropped her own anchor and developed *CruiseMiss.com* in 2013. The focus of *CruiseMiss* was cruise ships and destinations that can be reached via cruise ship. Danielle says, "If it doesn't involve a ship, I'm not interested in it." To grow her readership, Danielle networked, learned as much about each cruise line as she could, and made social media her main outlet for finding people that might be interested in reading what she was writing about—a passion for cruising. *CruiseMiss* became one of the most recognized cruise blogs in the UK. Danielle's work with many different cruise lines, the pleasure she derived and insight gained on her cruises with them, interacting with other travel-related companies, and the many fantastic destinations she visited paid off. "This is what I worked hard for and I'm glad I took the risks to get here."

After launching *CruiseMiss*, one of Danielle's most memorable cruise highlights was the first time she was invited to a cruise ship naming ceremony. Danielle was chosen to attend because of the sailings she had previously been on with P&O Cruises and because of the credibility of *CruiseMiss.com*. The naming ceremony was for P&O Cruises *Britannia*. All cruise ship naming ceremonies are special, but this one was particularly so as Her Majesty Queen Elizabeth 2 had been named as Godmother to *Britannia*, her second time being selected by P&O as a Godmother as the Queen was selected in 1995 to christen *Oriana*—the very first ship Danielle sailed. The naming ceremony was held at the Ocean Terminal in Southampton on March 10, 2015. Danielle said she felt like a kid at Christmas!

"I couldn't believe it. Me, at this big, flashy event. I loved every second of it. I love, and I mean love cruise ships, and one of my favourite times of the year is Christmas. When you are passionate about something, so passionate that it literally is what you eat, sleep and breathe, to have the honor of being included in such a momentous occasion that involves your passion is a massive privilege. I couldn't believe I was there. I could see the Queen and it still didn't feel real. I have been to a few more naming ceremonies since then and for me, they are always a great privilege." Several days later Danielle returned to Southampton to sail on *Britannia's* maiden voyage, a 14-night Mediterranean itinerary with stops in Gibraltar, Barcelona, Monte Carlo, Rome, Ajaccio and Cadiz.

Her Majesty the Queen at the Britannia naming ceremony

Danielle has now been on 57 cruises. She has sailed with cruise lines including Fred Olsen Cruise Lines, P&O Cruises, Cunard, Royal Caribbean, Norwegian Cruise Line, Princess Cruises, MSC, and Crystal Cruises. Cruising has enabled Danielle to travel to America, Belize, Cuba, Peru, Ecuador, Tahiti, Jamaica, Grenada, St Lucia, Antigua, Aruba, Honduras, Australia, New Zealand, Indonesia, Myanmar, Singapore, Malaysia, India, Jordan, Egypt, Greece, Italy, Israel, Spain, France, Morocco, Norway, Sweden, Finland, Russia, Estonia, Latvia, Germany and Holland, among others. Those travels have exposed Danielle to such iconic sites and experiences as the Pyramids at Giza (Egypt); The Treasury in Petra (Jordan); The Sydney Opera House (Australia); the Statue of Liberty (America); the UNESCO Old Town in Tallinn (Estonia); the Aurora Borealis in Alta (Norway); and a walk through the Anne Frank House in Amsterdam (Netherlands).

It all started somewhat reluctantly with Danielle's first cruise with P&O Cruises *Oriana*. She reflects back on it recalling a sense of trepidation leading up to the cruise, and ultimately a fondness at what would turn out to be a life-changing event. "I had never wanted to go on a cruise. It was my idea of a really bad time, but circumstances pushed me to board for a 12-night cruise to the Canary Islands. It was that cruise that changed everything for me. It ignited a passion for ocean travel and travel in general that I'd never felt before. I was addicted to it, I wanted to go and see and do more. On that cruise, *CruiseMiss* was born; I just didn't know it at the time." Sadly, Danielle recently learned *Oriana* is to be sold to a Chinese company and will be leaving the P&O fleet in 2019. "She was my first cruise ship; it's going to be incredibly hard to see her leave British shores. I'll probably never see her again. For those that don't cruise, that may sound odd, but you do hold a special place in your heart for your first".

That first cruise ignited a passion for ocean travel and travel in general in Danielle. She was addicted, and immediately resolved to see and do more. Danielle set out to develop her knowledge and pursue additional cruising experiences in order to better position herself to convey information about cruising to others. "How could I possibly advise people on cruising if I had barely any experience of it myself?"

Danielle loves cruise ships of all kinds, but prefers the smaller, more traditional vessels. Her favorites are the Fred Olsen *Balmoral*, Fred Olsen *Black Watch*, P&O *Oceana* and Saga *Sapphire*. Danielle's longest cruise was on the *Black Watch*: a 108-nights world cruise from Southampton traveling to the Azores, the Caribbean, Central America and the Panama Canal, Easter Island, the South Pacific, Southeast Asia, India and the Middle East from January 5 to April 24, 2018. In total the world cruise visited 23 countries on six continents.

Black Watch is a small traditional cruise ship. She doesn't have all the gimmicks that the larger vessels have. *Black Watch* takes a purist approach to ocean travel, the way it used to be. Its size offers the chance to really connect with fellow cruisers, and if you were travelling solo as some were, that's a huge selling point. Danielle reported that the crew was superb, nothing was ever too much trouble, and that added to the overall experience. *Black Watch* has a single main dining room, a buffet option, a specialty steak and seafood restaurant, and a poolside grill for breakfast and lunch. Entertainment is offered in the Neptune and Lido Lounges, and you can always relax in the Bookmark Café and enjoy coffee with some quiet time. Her outer decks are traditional and tiered, one of the characteristics that Danielle loves about the older ships. There is ample space for everyone to enjoy the sun. The *Black Watch* Promenade Deck is a wraparound, so you can do full laps of the ship, and there are two swimming pools and several hot tubs. *Black Watch* also has a gym, salon, spa and small cinema. Danielle's stateroom was a porthole cabin on Deck 4 of the 8-deck ship. There was a lot more space offered than on some other ships, ideal for shopping in all 36 ports of the world cruise! "I felt comfortable on her, she was my home-away-from-home and I was sad to leave. It was incredible—one of the most enriching experiences of my life. We circumnavigated the globe, passed through the Panama and Suez canals and got to see some of the world's most incredible historical sites. It was nothing short of amazing! We even picked up an owl in the Bay of Biscay as we were heading back to Southampton. How many other cruisers can say that?" Danielle continued, "The whole cruise was a highlight, but some things that stick in my mind are holding a koala in Brisbane, seeing Komodo dragons on Komodo Island, and then snorkelling from the incredible Pink Beach, eating authentic Indian Thali in Mumbai, seeing Petra, seeing the Sphinx and Pyramids in Cairo. The entire experience was truly unforgettable."

There are those that take even longer cruises than Danielle's 108-night journey, but for many of us such a long cruise is unfathomable. I asked Danielle what motivated her to take a cruise for such an extended period of time (as if *CruiseMiss* needed motivation). After having learned Danielle's story her response did not surprise me. "I love to travel, and I love to cruise. That's all the motivation I need for any trip. Every embarkation promises a new adventure, even if you've previously visited some of the destinations on the itinerary."

On the *Black Watch* world cruise at the Suez Canal.

For the short periods of time when she is not on a cruise, Danielle enjoys watching documentaries, especially historical ones. Coupled with the culturally iconic destinations Danielle has experienced through cruising, it is clear that she loves to learn! Danielle also collects authentic African wall masks and now has around 20 of them.

Danielle enjoys land-based travel as well, despite the fact she is not particularly fond of flying. Her "go-to" place when she just wants some "me time" other than on a cruise ship is Amsterdam, which she often visits a couple of times a year. Even then she is able to experience time on the water. "I sail to and from Amsterdam on a ferry operated by DFDS Seaways. It's an overnight sailing from Newcastle, arriving in Ijmuiden in North Holland the following morning and then taking a bus to Amsterdam."

Socializing with friends is also a big thing for Danielle, particularly her good friend Ria whom she met through, of course, cruising. More precisely, through the *CruiseMiss* blog. "We wanted to do the same cruise but not pay the single supplement; although we had never met, we decided we would share a stateroom—worst case scenario, we wouldn't like one another and just have to sleep in the same cabin for two weeks! I met Ria for the first time in the atrium on P&O Cruises *Ventura,* at the beginning of our cruise, and the rest, as they say, is history. She's one of my closest friends!"

Despite having seen so much of the world through cruising, there are still so many places Danielle plans to visit. She would really like to do more exploring of her own shores, and Scotland has always appealed to her. Further from home, Danielle has an ambitious, esoteric bucket list of experiences to check off: spending New Year's Eve in Sydney; swimming in the clear blue seas of Bora Bora; an African Safari; spending time with an African Tribe—ideally the Himba people; swimming with wild dolphin; cuddling a baby elephant; tornado chasing in America! On the water, Danielle looks forward to spending a night aboard the *Queen Mary i*n Long Beach, and her dream destination is an expedition cruise to Antarctica.

"The ocean is truly my happy place, I enjoy coming home, but I am always searching for the next adventure. I think in my previous life I may have been a nomad or traveler. I literally cannot sit still."

POPULAR CRUISING:
JASON LEPPERT

At only 30 years old Jason Leppert was a 10Best Readers' Choice New Media Award for Best Cruise Blogger finalist for *Popular Cruising*. Today at 34, the indefatigable cruiser and writer is now up to 138 cruises, and in addition to serving as editor in chief, "the captain", at *Popular Cruising,* Jason is the Cruise Editor at TravelAge West, founder of *Popular Cruising* and its successful YouTube channel, and contributor to other outlets such as Cruise Travel, Porthole, and Oyster.com. He also annually attends "Comic-Con International: San Diego," the 50-year old entertainment and comic convention which draws over 130,000 over three days to Jason's home town. Jason is the epitome of a passionate cruiser who manifests his passion with driven, concerted action personally and professionally. Given the amount of time he dedicates to cruising, both sailing and writing about it, one would be tempted to conclude that about sizes up Jason's life. However, all things Disney round out much of Jason's personal and professional life.

As a native and resident of San Diego, California—having never lived anywhere else despite having traveled the world—Jason enjoys spending leisure time at Disneyland Resort with his wife Heidi, and professionally covers Disney parks and resorts domestically and abroad for TravelAge West, Oyster.com and MiceChat.com. In addition to Disneyland, Jason has visited Walt Disney World in Florida, Disneyland Paris, Shanghai Disneyland, and Aulani Disney Resort and Spa in Hawaii. Jason has also experienced several Adventures by Disney trips; Adventures by Disney provides a series of planned vacations across various parts of the world where guests are taken on expeditions featuring activities designed for families. In a mash-up of Jason's duel passions, he has cruised on all the Disney Cruise Line ships. "The cruises in my estimation are the best of the best when it comes to Disney; it's where the brand's travel and narrative prowess both magically come together. Heidi and I don't have any children of our own, but as perpetual kids at heart, we adore the line even as adults."

Heidi and Jason at Disney Cruise Line's Port Canaveral terminal.

Jason's 138 cruises have been on every mainstream ocean cruise line in every category from standard to upscale luxury. He has also sailed on numerous river, expedition and niche lines from AmaWaterways to Windstar Cruises. Jason's cruising has covered almost the entire world with the only notable exceptions being future voyages he has planned to the Arctic, Antarctica and Australia/New Zealand. His last voyage of 2018 was a Christmas markets river cruise down the Danube on 95-cabin *Viking Tor*. Also in 2018, Jason cruised *U by Uniworld*, a brand launched April 2018 targeted at millennials and comprised of two sleek, black 120-passenger yachts that cruise rivers in Europe; *Seabourn Ovation*, an ultra-luxury 600-passenger boutique ship; *American Empress*, a Victorian-styled paddlewheel boat operated by American Queen Steamboat Company sailing the rivers of the Pacific Northwest; and, the *Celebrity Edge*, the just launched mega-ship with its first-of-its kind floating entertainment platform called "The Magic Carpet" that reaches heights of 13 stories above sea level.

The revolutionary *Edge* was mentioned to me by a number of the contributors that I spoke to for *The Joy of Cruising*. Jason was among the first cruise journalists to check out the much anticipated *Edge* which was launched just prior to completion of *The Joy of Cruising*. Jason told me, "Celebrity Cruises' latest in the angular form of *Celebrity Edge* does indeed impress. It's truly a game-changer for cruise ship design thanks to its most-talked-about features all the way down to the little details. The Magic Carpet, cantilevered off several decks makes for a fantastic bar and dining venue hybrid, as well as an excellent platform for transferring passengers to tenders to transport them to shore. The *Edge's* Eden restaurant without question makes a bold statement as a restaurant and performance venue. But honestly, the sheer beauty of the ship's smaller designs accumulates to be the most striking. The loft suites are stunning as are the unique asymmetrical meanderings of the outdoor, multilevel jogging track and the atrium's contemporary take on midcentury modern aesthetics to name just a few. In other words, the bar has been raised across the board for other cruise lines."

Celebrity Edge. **The orange frame is the movable Magic Carpet structure.**

Being a cruise writer and influencer has also afforded Jason the opportunity to tour major shipyards and witness keel-laying and christening ceremonies: Meyer Werft in Germany (builder of the Royal Caribbean's revolutionary Quantum class *Quantum of the Seas, Ovation of the Seas, and Anthem of the Seas*); Fincantieri in Italy (builder of Carnival's flagships *Vista, Horizon,* and the under construction *Panorama* due in 2020); and Chantiers de l'Atlantique in France (builder of the world's largest cruise ship, Royal Caribbean's *Symphony of the Seas,* and two just completed "game changing" ships, *Celebrity Edge,* and the *MSC Belissima* with a full-sized bowling alley).

Jason at Chantiers de l'Atlantique in France with his building contractor dad, Mark Leppert, in front of the soon to be largest cruise ship in the world, *Symphony of the Seas*.

How can a 34-year-old accumulate 138 cruises? Well, beside the fact that cruising is both Jason's passion and his profession, he started early! Jason sailed on his first cruise at only two years of age. He is an only child, and his parents wanted to share their passion for travel with Jason early on, taking him on his first cruise aboard the original *Royal Princess*—the one launched in 1984, named by Princess Diana, and occasionally a stand-in for the *Pacific Princess* as the setting for the television series *The Love Boat*. There were two later cruise ships christened the *Royal Princess*. I asked Jason about the first cruise he could remember. "My next cruise was actually another one aboard the original *Royal Princess* only a couple years after the first. And I actually do remember bits and pieces from that ship, especially its observation lounge. It was a quiet place that I enjoyed roaming as a little one. Perhaps that's why to this day I cherish ships that still feature such venues. It's also been quite neat to sail on the current-generation *Royal Princess* that is in operation today, coming full circle." Growing up, Jason also sailed a lot with his family on Crystal Cruises and on Celebrity Cruises.

The "Captain" not yet two years old, on *Royal Princess*.

Recognizing the difficulty of singling out memorable cruises out of dozens, I asked Jason what comes to mind. He said, "That is a challenge, but I must say that expedition cruising has really proven to be a memorable experience for me. The opportunity to visit some of the most remote destinations in Alaska and Micronesia with Silversea Expeditions (*Silver Discoverer*) and UnCruise Adventures (*Safari Endeavour and S.S. Legacy*) has just been a blast. Of course, any time I go on a Disney cruise is always special too, given my affinity for the brand overall. But ultimately, I always enjoy every one of my cruises for varied reasons as they all offer something different and interesting." Expedition cruising, which usually involves small ships in order to be able to access harder-to-reach ports in more specialized and exotic destinations is a burgeoning trend in cruising. Expedition cruises range from Spartan-like led by expedition teams and often location or subject-matter experts where the focus is on exploration to very luxurious craft that blend exploration with an upscale cruise experience. Jason said, "I really think—following the initial rise of ocean cruising and the river cruise boom—that expedition cruising is next to come into its own. Compared to the renowned but aging hardware currently servicing the niche, there are lots of new-builds scheduled to come online with exciting purpose-built features like onboard helicopters and submarines. It's about to become more broadly available to more people, and the price point is likely to go down with increasing competition as well."

Jason developed his passion for cruising early on, but never expected to make a career out of cruising. Jason studied graphic design, photography and video in college, graduating from the University of San Diego in 2007. However, Jason was always a good writer. "After my parents encouraged me to submit a piece relating to cruising to the *San Diego Union-Tribune* newspaper and it was published, I sought out opportunities and eventually found my niche. Now, I'm thrilled to say I truly have a dream job."

Jason started *Popular Cruising* in 2012. He wanted to establish his own voice in the cruising blogosphere, particularly via video reviews, and *Popular Cruising's* flourishing YouTube channel. The site has grown substantially. "I used to write more for the site but currently focus most on my other outlets for print and online photo and editorial pieces. My videos, though, I will always pursue for *Popular Cruising*." In addition to the aforementioned outlets, Jason has contributed to the Travel Channel, Fox News and *USA Today*.

Jason's upcoming cruises represent an eclectic mix of vessels and experiences and is indicative of someone who has already experienced so much of what cruising offers through dozens of cruises. Jason plans to next sail on *Nieuw Statendam*, the new Holland America Line ship premiering January 2019; then, *Regal Princess*; *Avalon Envision*, a new all-suite river cruise ship; *Crystal Serenity* and more into 2019.

"I've had the pleasure of cruising since before I was two years old. To this day, the thing I love most about all my voyages is simply the joy of being at sea, sailing on the beautiful blue expanse. With my love of Disney, the Disney Cruise Line is definitely a favorite of ours, but I truly do enjoy every brand for its unique set of offerings. Now, it's a joy to cruise the world with my lovely wife. When we're not sailing we love going to the Disneyland Resort as often as we can."

ROYAL CARIBBEAN BLOG:
MATT HOCHBERG

Matt Hochberg, a USA Today/10Best Readers' Choice New Media Award winner for Best Cruise Blogger is the creator of the *Royal Caribbean Blog*, and the reassuring voice of the *Royal Caribbean Blog* podcast. I say reassuring because if you happen to be listening to the podcast a lot, including going back into the archives to listen to episodes you might have missed or replaying episodes you've previously listened to, it likely means you are booked on Royal Caribbean and your sailing date is approaching! You are part anxious, and part excited, and Matt (along with occasional guests) calms your anxiety with useful information and stokes your excitement with fun insights. In anticipation of my December 2018 *Anthem of the Seas* cruise, I listened to every episode of the *Royal Caribbean Blog* podcast of the last couple of years (and if *Anthem* was in the episode title, let's just say I listened to it more than once.)

Royal Caribbean Blog is an unofficial fan blog written for other fans of Royal Caribbean International, although it is not affiliated with Royal Caribbean. The *Royal Caribbean Blog* started in 2010, and its accompanying podcast is now up to close to 300 episodes. *Royal Caribbean Blog* offers daily coverage of news and information related to the Royal Caribbean cruise line along with other relevant topics of cruising, such as entertainment, news, photo updates and more.

Matt grew up in Connecticut and currently resides in the Orlando Florida area. His professional background is web development, and he studied information technology at Pace University and graduated in 2004. Matt has enjoyed travel for quite some time, and was a co-creator and for ten years a co-host of the popular WDW Today podcast about all things Walt Disney World. WDW Today did a live broadcast from the *Disney Wonder* cruise ship in 2007—an industry first and presage of things to come for Matt. "We did that from 2005 to 2015, and that got me into the online travel world," Matt said. "My interest in Disney was very high but as my interest in cruising in general and particularly Royal Caribbean started to move up as the years went by, eventually it outpaced Disney and I began to lean more and more toward cruising."

Matt's first cruise was in the early 2000's on the *Disney Wonder*. His parent's took Matt and his siblings on a three-night cruise to the Caribbean. Prior to that they had not even considered cruising as an option, but finally his parents were persuaded by the kids. "We wanted to try it; after all it was Disney, and it was a cruise, and finally my parents caved in to our desires. I think it was my sister's sweet 16 or something like that." The cruise may have been short, but it definitely had a lasting influence on Matt. After that cruise Matt knew he liked cruising and wanted more of it. He finally got to go on another cruise in 2006, the *Explorer of the Seas*. "The ball started really rolling from there as cruising became something I could take advantage of. It's something I developed an enjoyment for quite quickly. When it came to my honeymoon, we knew we wanted to do a cruise vacation, especially after the land-based vacation we considered proved to be too expensive." Matt and his wife Marissa sailed the *Mariner of the Seas* in 2008 for their honeymoon.

Matt and Marissa on *Mariner of the Seas*.

I asked Matt how his passion for cruising was formed and he told me it really started right away once he started cruising. "My passion was formed just from trying cruising out. The idea of visiting different ports, different cities, and returning to this place where you go to sleep and wake up and do it again…. Plus, all you can eat! Man, that combination won me over quite quickly. To me it was just the perfect medium. Up to when my family did that first cruise on *Wonder* we did a lot of car trips. Hop in the car, drive from state to state, seeing all these places. Car vacations, car trips, were a staple of my childhood. Part of me still relishes that. But going on a cruise took away the worst part of those otherwise fond memories of the car trips: sitting in the car, looking out the window and not being able to do anything. You know, really doing something; you try to pass time somehow but.... On the other hand, being on a cruise ship is just totally different. It has all the best parts of the car trips—relaxation, destination—without the worst part, the traveling aspect of it. On the ship there is a lot to see and do and of course eat, and I think that combination really appealed to me."

Matt has taken 30 cruises, primarily Royal Caribbean, although he has cruised several times on Disney Cruise Lines and once on Norwegian Cruise Line. 2018 was quite a year of cruising for Matt as he sailed on two cruises which are on many cruisers' bucket lists, Alaska, and Cuba, and sailed on the world's largest ship, *Symphony of the Seas*. In addition to his stellar 2018 experience, some earlier cruises really stood out for Matt. He loves all the new ships Royal puts out. "*Harmony of the Seas* was amazing. The other one that really stood out is the Radiance class ship, *Brilliance of the Seas*. What I like about going on these smaller getaway ships out of Florida with short itineraries is that it is more of an intimate experience. It not only allows me to get in more cruises, but it allows me to experience a more relaxing 'let's hang-out-by-the-pool' vibe."

Matt particularly likes observing and experiencing Royal Caribbean's evolution. This really comes through in his podcasts. For instance, Matt's enthusiasm was palpable in hearing him talk about the theme park-like transformation at Coco Cay, Bahamas, Royal Caribbean's private island that is included in all of its Caribbean cruise itineraries; the renovation *Perfect Day at CocoCay* is scheduled to be completed in 2019. "It's always a treat to be able to see all the new features Royal Caribbean comes up with."

Matt would like to experience as many Royal Caribbean cruise ships and itineraries as he can. "In order to speak to a subject you need to pull from personal experience, and repeated experience as much as possible, which helps to cement good advice that you are providing to people." In terms of his personal bucket list cruises, he knocked one off the list with his *Explorer of the Seas* Alaska cruise last summer. By far Matt notes that cruise is a new all-time favorite cruise. "Alaska was everything everybody said it would be and more," Matt adds, "Certainly Europe, Northern Europe, the Mediterranean, those are biggies. There are a lot of European itineraries we haven't done yet. Panama Canal is also a big one I would love to knock off my bucket list at some point."

Explorer of the Seas in the foreground of the beautiful
mountainous surroundings of Skagway, Alaska.

I asked Matt how the *Royal Caribbean Blog* came about. Matt recalled that his second Royal Caribbean cruise was on *Oasis of the Seas.* As alluded to earlier in *The Joy of Cruising,* almost every couple of years the world's largest cruise ship is introduced. But sometimes a new world's largest ship is so revolutionary, so spectacular, that it "changes the game" in cruising (much like Royal Caribbean's *Sovereign of the Seas* discussed in Chapter 1.) *Oasis* was that kind of ship when it was introduced. Matt said, "I remember back when *Oasis of the Seas* debuted it was a really big deal, still is, and I was really pumped to go on it. It just redefined what a cruise ship experience could be. My excitement was so great that I needed an outlet for it. I was just that kind of person that I like people to share my experience. I wanted to blog about my experience. I ended up expanding that idea beyond just blogging about my cruise on *Oasis* to actually covering Royal Caribbean in general. There were a lot of existing cruise websites, some great ones in fact. But none of them focused just on Royal Caribbean. While they did a good job, they only got, say, 10-20% deep into what Royal Caribbean is all about and there is still quite a bit left out. I felt like I'm not going to be able to compete with the major cruise websites out there and cover the whole industry, but if I do a deep dive and cover everything Royal Caribbean, then I can really stand out from other people and bring something different to the table."

Royal Caribbean Blog was born. Matt decided to cover the minutiae of Royal Caribbean: address people's personal questions and focus on specific needs; deliver news and avoid trying to be a Wikipedia of cruising. Matt pursued this niche approach casually for the first couple of years, blogging occasionally. Then he noticed that people were paying attention. Traffic was gradually going up. He started getting comments back and receiving emails about the blog posts. He got the sense that Royalcaribbeanblog.com was going somewhere, so he started investing more of his time, and the blog really started to take off.

I asked Matt about his family and their impressions of cruising. He has two daughters, Gabriella, 7, and Aubrey, 3. "They do enjoy cruising. They love, love, love Adventure Ocean (Royal Caribbean's onboard kids club) to the point where for most of the ports we go to, they don't want to get off the ship with us. They would rather go to Adventure Ocean and hang out with the new friends they have met there. I love it! You know when I was a kid none of my sisters nor I liked going to kid's clubs. I think we were too shy. Maybe because we didn't get indoctrinated when we were younger. My kids have been going to Adventure Ocean and The Royal Caribbean nursery since they were six months old. They really do love the activities there. They get something out of it and we, Marissa and I, get something out of it. We get some time alone. Get to go to dinner alone, take in one of the shows onboard. As a family we have come to appreciate cruises. It's a great way to vacation together and also stay sane at the same time!"

Matt has diversified in terms of mode of delivery information to Royal Caribbean fans; the podcast started in 2013 and now he is offering regular live events on social media platforms Facebook Live and Periscope. He wants the *Royal Caribbean Blog* to continue to grow and provide even more in-depth coverage. "Like any blogger, my long-term aspiration for the blog is to make it a full-time endeavor."

DISNEY CRUISE LINE BLOG:
SCOTT SANDERS

Scott Sanders is a USA Today/10Best Readers' Choice New Media Award winner for Best Cruise Blogger for the *Disney Cruise Line Blog*. I first became aware of Scott several years ago when I discovered his blog in advance of taking my grandkids on their first cruise, a four-day voyage on the *Disney Dream*. Two weeks before our sailing, Scott posted a video on his blog of his daughter's first time on Disney Cruise Line's *AquaDuck*, the first "water roller coaster" at sea introduced on the *Disney Dream*. So, my then 5-year old granddaughter watched Scott's daughter Isabelle screaming gleefully riding *AquaDuck*—along with the many other *AquaDuck* videos on YouTube—over and over.

Scott's blog and podcast are the go-to source for Disney Cruise fans looking for news, tips, and opinions in addition to, or instead of, official information from the company itself. It's not just Disney Cruise fans that rely on Scott's insights. Scott is extensively consulted by media such as the Orlando Sentinel and USA Today to opine on

Disney Cruise Line news and developments, and has appeared in the book, *The Unofficial Guide to Disney Cruise Line*.

Scott started the *Disney Cruise Line Blog* in 2012. He added a companion podcast April 2016. The website is more than just a blog chronicling Scott's cruises. In addition to posting daily trip reports when taking his family on a cruise, the website also offers fans a historical look at the various Disney Cruise Line itineraries and provides info about upcoming sailings. In addition, each week Scott summarizes the current special offers and blogs about the latest news surrounding Disney Cruise Line and its ports of call.

Scott lives with his wife Emily, and daughter Isabelle in Celebration, Florida, known as "The Community Disney Built." Celebration is located five miles from Walt Disney World Resort and was originally developed by The Walt Disney Company. Scott is originally from the Midwest and came south to Florida for the weather and has lived in Florida for most of his adult life. Scott and Emily were married in a Disney Wedding at Walt Disney World Resort.

Scott, Emily, and Isabelle in Alaska in front of the *Disney Wonder*.

I asked Scott to talk about how his passion for all things Disney was formed. He told me, "I did not visit the Disney Parks much when I was growing up. My passion for Disney was born out of the movies and Sunday Night TV specials. Later in life I expanded my appreciation for Disney with regular visits to the Disney Parks and cruises after I was married and our daughter was born." Scott and Emily were married at the Wedding Pavilion at The Grand Floridian Resort at Walt Disney World. Half of their honeymoon was celebrated with family at the parks at Walt Disney World, and then Scott and Emily spent the remainder of their honeymoon on a 3-night Bahamas cruise on the *Disney Wonder* from Port Canaveral. Scott and Emily's honeymoon cruise on *Wonder* was June 2005. The honeymoon cruise was short and part of a whirlwind two weeks; plus, cruising was a totally new experience. So, Scott did not immediately develop a passion for cruising.

Scott's passion for cruising originated with his and Emily's second cruise, and the first cruise with four-year old Isabelle. "The honeymoon cruise felt like it was over in a heartbeat. Our second cruise was five years later; we decided it was time to take our daughter on a vacation and she was at the right age to enjoy the youth activities on the ship. We were instantly hooked." That cruise, a 5-night sailing to the Bahamas on the *Disney Wonder* left a lasting impression on Scott and led directly to the origin of the *Disney Cruise Line Blog*. Scott's said, "I spent the next few months posting to cruise related message boards and sharing cruise photos. Then one night I was sitting on the couch with my wife and I was like, I should start a blog. I figured this way I could post all my thoughts and photos in one space." Scott spends much of his professional life behind a computer screen; he works in information technology. His blog is his primary hobby, born out of his growing interest in photography and web development, and of course his love for all things Disney.

In addition to cruising and Disney, Scott loves to travel with his family. Growing up Scott traveled a great deal with his family. Summer trips to Florida were commonplace, including a couple of visits to Walt Disney World. Every so often they would change it up and go on road trips to destinations throughout the United States. One summer in particular his family set off on a two-month road trip around the United States and Canada. Most nights were spent in campgrounds as they traveled around to many of the major National Parks, historical sites, and unique places in-between. Scott recalls it was an adventure of a lifetime and left a lasting impression him.

In total Scott has been on 25 cruises with a couple more booked for this year. All of Scott's cruises have been on the four Disney Cruise Line ships: *Disney Magic, Disney Wonder, Disney Dream, and Disney Fantasy*. Scott's cruises have covered essentially all of the Disney itineraries. Scott and his family have sailed to the Bahamas, Caribbean (Eastern, Western, and Southern), Alaska, Norway, Iceland, and the Mediterranean. He considers the highlights of his cruising have been in general all the amazing places he has been and the experiences shared with Emily and Isabelle. I asked him to talk about a couple. "That is like asking someone who their favorite child is! Over the years we've created so many wonderful family memories and celebrated life events at sea. Alaska, the Mediterranean, and our Norway and Iceland sailing all exceeded my expectations both in terms of destination and overall cruise experience. Each itinerary took us to incredible destinations that created lifelong memories."

The singular cruising experience moment that stands above any others for Scott is the Midnight Sun in Reykjavik, Iceland during Scott, Emily, and Isabelle's Norway and Iceland cruise aboard the

Disney Magic. "Originally, we booked a Disney Alaskan cruise for that summer, but once Disney released an itinerary with Iceland, I was hooked. We put the Alaskan Cruise on hold and booked the itinerary to Norway and Iceland. While researching the trip, I read about the Midnight Sun. Knowing the ship would be spending the night in Reykjavik I set my sights on capturing the moment." Midnight Sun refers to the natural phenomenon of sunset occurring around midnight and rising a couple hours later. Coupled with the breathtaking panoramas of the region, Midnight Sun results in some wondrous photo opportunities. Scott said, "Leading up to the cruise, I joked with a friend who was also aboard *Magic* that I was planning to camp out on the dock napping on a bench until the sun was right. Well, as luck would have it there was a bench and I had a tripod and remote shutter release. The weather was perfect and while most of the ship was asleep, I was out on the pier, camera on the tripod waiting for the perfect moment. Near one AM, the Icelandic sky was just right!"

Scott slept on a park bench at the pier while overnighting in Reykjavik, in order to get the perfect shot of the Midnight Sun.

Scott's perfect shot.

Over the next 5 years, Scott plans to return to most of the popular cruise destinations Disney visits as well as experiencing the three new Disney ships that are launching in the next few years. Disney Cruise Line has three ships on order with Meyer Werft shipyard in Papenburg, Germany for delivery in successive years beginning in 2021. In a report by the Orlando Sentinel last spring, Scott was quoted: "All in all, the exterior rendering fits well with the iconic ocean liner look that was selected back in the mid-90s. This new design offers a bit of a distinction from the Dream class while still fitting within the overall look of the fleet." (Dream class represents the larger 130,000 gross ton 4,000-passenger vessels *Disney Dream* and *Disney Fantasy*, which we're introduced in 2011 and 2012.)

Scott's bucket list travel aspirations include Disney Transatlantic and Panama Canal cruises, as well as travel to Hawaii, South Pacific, Baltic, the pyramids in Egypt. What about cruise lines other than Disney? Scott says, "I do want to explore other cruise lines. It is always good to have experiences outside of your core focus to help put some things into perspective and to provide honest comparisons to my readers. I am intrigued by a few cruise lines for all different reasons, but I think Royal Caribbean is at the top of the list of other lines to experience."

I asked Scott if life had changed much since earning the USA Today/10Best Readers' Choice New Media Award. "I was fortunate to be nominated for USA Today/10Best Readers' Choice New Media Award. At the time, I was still just getting started. It absolutely helped gain some exposure. From time to time, I've been asked to comment on Disney Cruise Line related news for local media outlets, which has been a fun experience."

What does the future hold for *Disney Cruise Line Blog* I ask Scott? "I am always looking for new ways to share my passion for Disney cruising. In 2019, we will have our inaugural *Disney Cruise Line Blog* group cruise which we hope will be the start of a recurring event." *Disney Cruise Line Blog* ended up planning two cruises to the Bahamas: an inaugural *Disney Cruise Line Blog* Group Cruise, June 19-23, 2019 on the *Disney Dream,* followed by a second Group Cruise, February 20, 2020 on the *Disney Magic.*

Theme Cruising:
Two Passions in One

THEME CRUISING: TWO
PASSIONS IN ONE

The essence of *The Joy of Cruising* is people's passion for cruising and the many ways in which they pursue that passion. Theme cruising fits that ethos perfectly: it's the ultimate melding of passion for cruising with passion for a hobby, interest, culture, or lifestyle, be it jazz, poker, quilting, wellness, or whatever. Or, even more esoteric pursuits: there are cruises aimed at bikers (yes, your motorcycle is loaded on the cruise ship), cruises for cat lovers (*Meow Meow Cruise*), cougars (not the cat variety!), couples seeking stronger marriages, swingers, and recovering substance abusers. Or, there are cruises for a cultural or affinity group with which you identify.

Broadly, affinity cruising involves bringing together cruisers with common interests, and theme cruises are designed to capitalize on and highlight that commonality. Sometimes the commonality is very specific, such as the *Star Trek Cruise*, or more general; that is, the cruisers' bond is not centered around a common like, hobby, or pursuit but rather the commonality is a demographic attribute such as age, culture, sexual orientation, etc. There is a staggering array of themes covered by these special interest cruises. Essentially, if a theme cruise purveyor is willing to invest money, time, and other resources necessary to design, organize and market the theme cruise—and assume the risk of the cruise failing to generate the requisite demand—it can be arranged. The nature of theme cruises I have seen marketed run the gamut. Passionate about motorcycle riding? *ETA Motorcycle Cruises* tagline is "Bring your bike with you on a cruise." (Chapter 25). Love poker? *Card Player Cruises* is run by a couple of Poker Hall of Famers (Chapter 24). How about craft beers? *The California Beer Festival at Sea.* Knitting, quilting, health and wellness? Yes, there is a cruise for you. Recovering substance abuser? Want to strengthen your marriage? Celebrate and rejuvenate your religious faith? All are covered by theme cruises. Yes, there are even clothing optional cruises—either geared more towards cruisers seeking risqué fun, or others appealing more to naturalists.

I could go on and on. The opportunity to network with other like-minded cruisers can be arranged around essentially any pastime, avocation, or interest. For the passenger, the fee structure for theme cruises is the same as for traditional cruises: a cruiser pays a set fee depending on the level of ship accommodations they select, and other than alcohol everything else like food, entertainment, and activities are included except options that are a la carte on any cruise such as spa services, casino, and specialty restaurants. The pricing will generally include a premium given the performers, speakers, celebrities, and other theme-specific costs. For instance, with *ETA Motorcycle Cruises*, storage and transport of your bike on the ship is included.

There are many formats for carrying out theme cruises ranging from the cruise line offering it directly to customers, to a theme cruise purveyor such as a travel company or a group of independent entrepreneurs chartering a cruise ship, to various iterations in between. For instance, a cruise line may choose to bring on board a performer, celebrity chef, sommelier, author, orator, thought leader, or other celebrity. Often these cruise line theme cruises are in conjunction with sponsors and feature celebrities who the sponsors are in partnership with. For instance, Celebrity Cruises partners with Fine Cooking magazine and their Emmy® Award nominated PBS series, *Moveable Feast with Fine Cooking*. Celebrity Cruises' *Moveable Feast* passengers participate in cooking classes and demonstrations, and even can opt for excursions to shop for local ingredients in preparation for a private dinner on the ship. In early 2019, Holland America Line and *O, The Oprah Magazine* are partnering on a *Girls' Getaway* cruise featuring Oprah Winfrey on Holland America's newest ship, *Nieuw Statendam* which launched in December 2018 with a transatlantic voyage. Oprah, is the *Nieuw Statendam* Godmother. The *Girls' Getaway* cruise sold out in three days after it was announced. In these instances of cruise line theme cruises, passengers may choose to partake or not in various performances, demonstrations, or presentations. Such cruises may be arranged entirely by cruise line staff or a collaboration between a cruise line and a sponsor, or with a separate theme cruise operator.

Alternatively, the theme cruise may be a music fest, or beer fest, or nudists, or whatever the theme is that takes over the entire ship; partaking is largely unavoidable and the theme and the cruise are for the most part inseparable. Generally, in these instances the theme cruise operator "rents" or charters the ship and its staff from the cruise line—at a cost of approximately $1 million to over $10 million depending on ship, season and duration of the cruise—and the cruise line is otherwise not directly involved in the theme cruise except to offer the food, ship services and amenities, and standard entertainment such as lounge acts, and activities.

For theme cruises not involving chartering the ship, an individual or organization arranges and markets a cruise centered around some common interest for a subset of passengers on a particular cruise, and only the passengers in that group have access to the theme activities—in all other ways the passengers in the group co-exist with and have the same benefits as the other passengers on the ship who are not in the group.

Music-related cruises are by far the most popular type of theme cruise. Jazz, rock, R&B, country, reggae, even classical—virtually every music genre has one or more dedicated cruises. For many well-established music artists, performing on theme cruises offers a stable source of work and a way to bring their music directly to fans at a time when radio is dramatically different as a means to get music to fans than in the past, and retail music is virtually extinct. For the fans, it is an opportunity to see artists who may no longer be regularly touring, or not accessible in a cruise passenger's home town. Music cruises can focus on a single artist who performs a couple of concerts and the remainder of the cruise activities are around meet-and-greets, DJ's and parties, and themed activities. Popular single artist cruises include the *Kiss Kruise, New Kids on The Block Cruise,* and *The Backstreet Boys Cruise.* At least one single artist cruise takes place without the actual artist! One successful theme cruise revolves around a legendary artist that has been deceased for over 40 years—the *Elvis Cruise,* an homage to Elvis Presley, celebrates his music and the musicians who performed with him. More typical is the music festival type theme cruise featuring numerous performers and accompanying comedians, celebrity hosts, and activities that are in keeping with the music genre featured by the cruise.

Particularly with music theme cruises, there is a contingent of cruisers who after experiencing a theme cruise choose never to go back to traditional cruising due to the cruise mates they meet, and more importantly, getting an intense dose of whatever it is they are passionate about. Imagine what it must feel like for a person into music of a certain period, say, the 50's and 60's, to experience that music live, performed by the original artists daily for a week! Why wouldn't someone want to keep repeating that experience without giving up any of the benefits of a traditional cruise—the ship amenities; experiencing all the joy that comes with being on the ocean; and, getting to stop at wonderful destinations? It is of little surprise that theme cruises have very high retention rates. Versus theme cruises, traditional cruises tend to be more sedate after hours. Certainly there are activities, food, and libations, but nowhere near the multitude of activities for cruises focused on a common theme, lifestyle, or culture particularly if the cruise is music oriented. The *Groove Cruise* which sails out of ports both on the West Coast and Florida and is focused on electronic dance music, or EDM, packs a couple of dozen DJ's and performers and around the clock energy into its four-day cruises; passengers do not go on the *Groove Cruise* and several other high-energy music cruises for rest and relaxation.

There are now websites that track upcoming theme cruises. So, a cruiser who is passionate about some interest could look for cruises that cater to him or her. Alternatively, some cruisers use these sites to inform themselves about cruise ships' future full or partial-ship charter plans so they can modify their own travel plans accordingly. It is possible to be "bumped" when a ship gets chartered after you book, and I have heard of passengers who wish to avoid a theme cruise that they find themselves on the same ship with, in the case of non-full ship charters. They might have had an unpleasant experience or heard about one from another cruiser. These unfortunate stories are relatively rare occurrences though. In fact, Chapter 22 Festival at Sea, tells the happy story of Ms. Dorothy, 80-something cruise passenger who experienced just the opposite: Ms. Dorothy found herself on the same ship as a theme cruise that she was not a part of, and was aimed at a very different demographic—and yet the theme cruise became an annual tradition for her.

In the next several chapters *The Joy of Cruising* examines and experiences theme cruising from the perspective of entrepreneurs with an idea, passengers, performers, and the people who help make theme cruising enjoyable.

MALT SHOP MEMORIES

Paul Anka, Frankie Avalon, Felix Cavaliere's Rascals, The Four Tops, Chubby Checker, Little Anthony and The Imperials, Darlene Love, Jay Siegel's Tokens, Gene Chandler, The Chantels, The Dixie Cups, The Coasters, Lloyd Price, Sha Na Na. All part of a line-up for a single concert event, emceed by Jerry Blavat ("The Geator with the Heater"). Sounds like an amazing music revue circa the sixties or seventies, except this was a line-up for an event being promoted in 2018. Not karaoke, but live music. Not tribute bands or impersonators. The artists listed above, backed by live bands, were all participants in this amazing music event. And these were just the headliners. The event includes a couple dozen more music artists, comedians, and DJ's, as well as parties, contests, trivia and other fun activities. So, more than just a concert—a music festival. All on a luxurious cruise ship, Holland America Line *Nieuw Amsterdam*, with ports of call in Grand Turk, San Juan, and St. Kitts. This was the most recent *Malt Shop Memories Cruise*, an annual cruise that is the flagship of StarVista LIVE's line up of seven theme cruises, which also includes: *Soul Train Cruise; The Country Music Cruise; Flower*

Power Cruise; '70s Rock & Romance Cruise; Southern Rock Cruise; and, *Ultimate Disco Cruise.* StarVista LIVE's portfolio of music events also includes the land-based *Abbey Road on the River,* the world's largest Beatles-inspired music festival, held four days annually in Jeffersonville, Indiana (right across the river from Louisville, Kentucky).

StarVista LIVE started a little over 10 years ago as an outgrowth of Time Life which sold principally pop and rock music CD and DVD box sets via television, direct sale, and brick-and-mortar retail. Time Life found that it needed to adapt to the changing dynamics in the music business as music moved increasingly to digital distribution and stores closed. "We were still selling a lot of music, but ever so gradually it was declining; people like the music but they were losing interest in what it was delivered on—discs were inconvenient. We said, let's take the music from the box sets and create a live experience so people can see the music as it is being played," stated Mike Jason, Senior Vice President, StarVista LIVE/Time Life. "Our audience had a passion for the music, and we had the ability to put it together, so we ending up switching part of our business to a live environment."

StarVista LIVE's first live presentation of the music previously sold via box sets was the *Malt Shop Memories Cruise,* music from the late 50's, early 60's which was based on a box set sold through a successful infomercial campaign; customers loved the boxed sets and accordingly a number of additional volumes had been subsequently released. *Malt Shop Memories* had built a passionate following so that was the inaugural cruise chosen.

After about a year, StarVista LIVE added the *Soul Train Cruise,* then the *Country Music Cruise* and continued to add a new cruise to their mix each subsequent year. For the most part the cruises were live versions inspired by one of the box sets. A couple of the cruises were influenced by the box sets but were not a direct iteration of the box sets. For instance, the *Southern Rock Cruise*, added in 2018 was not based on one of the Time Life box sets. "We never had a *Southern Rock* infomercial, but every time we put a southern rock song on one of our other compilations people loved it, so we knew there was an audience." As with all the StarVista LIVE theme cruises, the *Southern Rock Cruise* engendered an intensely loyal following. The next *Southern Rock Cruise* in January 2019 on the *Norwegian Pearl* will be headlined by the legendary Lynyrd Skynyrd.

In addition to those mentioned above, legendary performers abound in the talent line-ups for previous and upcoming StarVista LIVE cruises. Here are just a few for each of the theme cruises:

Malt Shop Memories Cruise: Petula Clark; The Temptations; Bobby Rydell; Little Anthony and The Imperials; Dion; Neil Sedaka; Lesley Gore; Martha Reeves & The Vandellas

Soul Train Cruise: Earth, Wind & Fire; Smokey Robinson; Isley Brothers; Patti LaBelle; The O'Jays; Gladys Knight; Frankie Beverly & Maze; Charlie Wilson; Chaka Khan; George Clinton

The Country Music Cruise: Kenny Rogers; Charley Pride; Alabama; Vince Gill; Martina McBride; The Oak Ridge Boys; Lee Greenwood; Larry Gatlin & Gatlin Brothers; Brenda Lee

Flower Power Cruise: The Beach Boys; Blood, Sweat & Tears; Jefferson Starship; Grand Funk Railroad; Chuck Negron former lead singer of Three Dog Night; Herman's Hermits starring Peter Noone; The Guess Who; Cheech & Chong

'70s Rock & Romance Cruise: Peter Frampton; Styx; Foreigner; America; Little River Band; Air Supply; War; Michael McDonald; Boz Scaggs; Christopher Cross; Ambrosia; Leo Sayer

Southern Rock Cruise (added 2018): Lynyrd Skynyrd; Dickey Betts; 38 Special; The Marshall Tucker Band; The Outlaws; Atlanta Rhythm Section

Ultimate Disco Cruise (added for 2019): KC and The Sunshine Band; Kool & The Gang; Village People; Gloria Gaynor; Evelyn "Champagne" King

Not surprisingly, given the nostalgic bent of the StarVista LIVE theme cruises, the demographics of its cruisers tend to be 50 plus; the *Malt Shop Memories Cruise* tends to draw even older cruisers, more like 60-65 plus. The StarVista LIVE constituency is relatively affluent; the cruises are premium priced given the abundance of talent for each cruise and the luxury environment. Cruisers are geographically dispersed; many come from the west coast but all of the cruises depart from Florida; the cruisers are very loyal, and are hardcore music fans. Many of the artists do not perform locally so StarVista LIVE cruises may be the only opportunity cruisers get to see them live. The cruises are all adults only. Other than kids clubs and cruise line provided entertainment, all of the normal cruise ship features and amenities such as complimentary and premium dining options, shops, spa, fitness center, casino, and exotic ports of call are available to cruisers. In addition are numerous onboard activities that are in keeping with the theme of each cruise. For instance, *Malt Shop Memories Cruise* features a Sock Hop complete with dance instructors, and a Senior Prom where patrons are encouraged to wear nostalgic prom dresses and tuxes and a Prom King and Queen are selected. Of course, the *Soul Train Cruise* features the iconic Soul Train Line, with lessons from the original Soul Train Dancers, and *The Country Music Cruise* features line dancing, Texas Swing and 2-Stepping. All of the cruises feature theme related comedy performances, cooking lessons, trivia contests, and performer events such as celebrity wine tastings, cooking exhibitions, autograph and photo sessions, songwriter workshops, artist Q&A's, etc.

Besides the scheduled artists' events, some performers choose to mingle with cruisers in unexpected ways. Impromptu poolside jam sessions, a performer joining a group of guests for a meal, or drinks at a bar, unscheduled autograph and photo sessions all are likely to take place on one of these cruises. I asked Mike what was the most memorable instance he recalled of a performer mixing with the guests. "On *The Country Music Cruise*, Charley Pride and his wife were the only artists that ever dressed up for costume night. They went as Tigger and Winnie the Pooh."

Another memorable moment was also on *The Country Music Cruise*. It was on the first *The Country Music Cruise* in 2014. George Jones, one of the greatest country music stars ever, had passed away the previous year. Nancy Sepulvado, Jones' fourth wife who Jones credited with saving his life after his long battles with substance abuse, was an honorary guest on the cruise. She went to all the events, shook hands, took pictures. Then, on the last night of the cruise, all the artists were invited up to tell their favorite George Jones story. "George was quite a character so they told their stories and got a lot of laughs out of the crowd; sang their favorite George Jones songs; and then we brought Nancy up on stage, gave her flowers, and the audience just went crazy cheering. That was pretty special."

Mike continued, "We have had some riveting musical moments. When Smokey Robinson walks on stage its just magical. The entire audience jumps to their feet; he's had one hit after another. And he's in good company. We've had Franki Valli and the Four Seasons, that was incredible; Lynyrd Skynyd was unbelievable..."

The ship is decorated throughout, not just on the music stage. The décor is converted to represent the appropriate time period. Fun touches like Lava lamps and beads for the ex-hippies (and current hippies) on the *Flower Power Cruise* make the cruisers feel a little bit at home; disco balls and dance floors that light up; AstroTurf and corn hole bean bag toss games for the *The Country Music Cruise*; a re-creation of the Soul Train club; dressing the cruise ship wait staff in uniforms that fit the time frame, such as poodle skirts for ship staff on the *Malt Shop Memories Cruise*; even down to the napkins which are emblazoned with the logo from the relevant cruise. "You want to create the environment so that when cruisers walk on that ship they leave any problems at home, and they feel like they are in a nostalgic time period. That is really special for people because they have fond memories of what they grew up listening to," Mike said. "And they're with all the other folks onboard who are similar age, similar background, and have the same interest in music. They meet new friends, reconnect with old friends; even some of the artists have become friends with the guests as they are the same age, have grandchildren, similar issues. There is not a big gap between the artists and the guests. And it is an intimate setting. Each cruise is truly a community."

The *Soul Train Cruise* is the most energetic of all of the cruises. Mike notes, "The crowd has so much energy, so much passion. They get up and do everything all day long, and then go to the disco at night, and they're in that disco until three or four in the morning. And these are not millennials; they're mature adults and then they get up and do it all again. They probably have the most fun of any guests."

Each of the StarVista LIVE cruises is an annual event. They all are sold out. When a cruiser boards the ship for the current cruise, the following years' cruise line-up, ship, and itinerary is already determined. As a testament to the loyalty each cruise engenders, Mike points out that "We probably have sold 50% of next years' cruise when we get off the ship this year."

Given that a sizable portion of the individuals profiled in *The Joy of Cruising* are from abroad, I asked Mike had StarVista LIVE ever given any consideration to departures abroad for their theme cruises. He indicated they had. However, the logistics would be daunting as their production, lighting and staging staff are all located in Florida; websites would have to accommodate multiple languages, payment in multiple currencies, transporting artists to Europe, some of whom do not stay on each cruise for the entire voyage—some fly in just for their performance, etc. "I think it would be successful; there would be a lot of challenges to it, but that doesn't mean it is not a good idea," Mike said.

I also asked Mike about possible new additions to their theme cruise portfolio, specifically cruises targeting at a different demographic. He noted that country music is so broad these days that there are probably some other areas within country they can explore. They've looked at younger R&B as there are so many great artists from the 80's and 90's. "That was 20, 25 years ago, so there is nostalgia for that time period, and I think we will look at that time period. I think we will start from our strengths, which are country and R&B; maybe rock."

As is with all the contributors I interview for *The Joy of Cruising*, I asked Mike about his personal cruising history. Similar to *The Godmother: Elizabeth Hill* in Chapter 4, prior to developing his passion for cruising, when Mike got involved with cruising he had no prior cruising experience. The inaugural *Malt Shop Memories* cruise was Mike's first. Since then he has cruised on every StarVista LIVE cruise, over 30 in all, on Celebrity, Holland America, and Norwegian cruise lines. As a music fan I envy Mike and the exposure he gets to diverse genres of music by participating on all the StarVista LIVE cruises. And as passionate cruisers, I and I'm sure the readers of *The Joy of Cruising* especially appreciate that Mike is able to do that while taking over 30 cruises in ten years' time!

FESTIVAL AT SEA

I attended my first theme cruise, *Festival at Sea 2018,* with my wife Cheryl, and granddaughter LaKi, which embarked from Miami July 21, 2018 on the *Celebrity Equinox* with ports of call in Grand Cayman; Ocho Rios, Jamaica; Labadee, Haiti; and, Nassau, Bahamas. Our first stop after boarding was the buffet, and after we got to our seats I struck up a conversation with a gentleman sitting nearby. I told him it was my first *Festival at Sea* cruise and asked him how many times he had been. "Fifteen," he told me. Immediately, I thought that I had found a potential contributor to *The Joy of Cruising*—a seasoned cruiser with dozens of past cruises. I assumed that this individual was a very experienced cruiser given how many times he had been just on *Festival at Sea.* I said, "Wow, fifteen times on *Festival at Sea*! How many cruises have you been on altogether?" He told me, "Fifteen."

Festival at Sea, www.festivalatsea.com, Patricia Nicholson Yarbrough, founder and President, is the nation's oldest and most successful African-American cultural cruise. In its 28th year, a *Festival at Sea* cruise is a celebration of African-American life and culture in all its dimensions: family, religion, education, music, dance, comedy, movies and entertainment, literature, art and more. For instance, just as one example of the foregoing, on Sunday morning after embarkation, Cheryl attended church; not a gathering of a few like-minded individuals marking the day of Sabbath but rather, a full-fledged church service replete with a pastor (who heads a church in New Jersey and has led church services for *Festival at Sea* for the last 20 years); a stunning choir comprised of passengers and formed after one evening of practice; a piano played by Fred Hamilton, *Festival at Sea*'s leader of the Gospel Committee, and other musical instruments performers. Religion was not just on the itinerary on Sunday; every morning cruisers could avail themselves of bible study, and "gospelcize." In the middle of the cruise there were two seatings of a Gospel Brunch featuring recording artist Jon Saxx and Endless Possibilities, and later in the week there was even a ceremony where couples could renew their wedding vows. And there was an actual first-time wedding ceremony—which is not uncommon on a *Festival at Sea* cruise.

Festival at Sea 2018 **group photo.**

Or, for cruisers for whom comedy is more to their liking, laughter was in abundance on *Festival at Sea*. Stand-up comedy has long been a part of African-American entertainment culture and there was plenty of it on *Festival at Sea*. Most cruise lines have stand-up comedy as an occasional part of the evening entertainment either in dedicated comedy clubs or on stage at one of the ship's other entertainment venues. *Festival at Sea* features comedy throughout the cruise, ranging from a continuous series lasting the first several nights of the cruise, *Last Comic Sailing*, which pitted up-and-coming comedians against each other, to performances from nationally known comic stars during the latter part of the cruise. We arrived a little late to the first night of *Last Comic Sailing*. Kevin Williams, a Chicago comic was on stage, as they say, "killing it." Not knowing the format of *Last Comic Sailing*, I mistakenly assumed he was one of the up-and-coming contestants. He had total command of the room and was absolutely hilarious. I whispered to Cheryl, "The other comics don't stand a chance." It turns out that Kevin Williams was the winner of the previous years' *Festival at Sea*'s *Last Comic Sailing*, and hosting the following years' contest is one of the awards for winning. Kevin's rambunctious act was just to warm up the crowd before introducing the contestants. The contestants, and Kevin, kept the capacity crowds laughing over three nights, and Chastity Washington (*HBO Def Comedy Jam, Just for Laughs Festival*) was this year's winner. Chastity, the first female winner, will host *Festival at Sea*'s 2019 *Last Comic Sailing*. The nationally-known comedians on the cruise were, Damon Williams, featured performer and cruise host from the nationally syndicated Tom Joyner Morning Show; Damon has been a featured performer and host on *Festival at Sea* since 2006. AJ Jamal, formerly of *It's Showtime at the Apollo, Def Comedy Jam, In Living Color* and more, has performed at and hosted *Festival at Sea* since

2005 (AJ is profiled in Chapter 29). The headliner was Gary Owen. Dubbed *Black America's Favorite White Comic*, and known for starring with Kevin Hart in *Think Like a Man*, Owen had the crowd in his hands with stories of his brushes with celebrity, social media, interracial marriage, biracial kids, and growing up in a Midwestern trailer park. Then Owen took questions from the audience. The highlight was his response to a question about how he met his wife. Shaquille O'Neal introduced them and that was an opportunity for Owen to do an impersonation of Shaq that was priceless.

Whether religion, comedy, spoken word and poetry, superheroes, the culture of the African Diaspora or whatever, there was programming to appeal to all, ranging from families with young children (we rarely saw our 8-year old granddaughter and she hated going to bed each night) to very senior citizens, several of whom have long and interesting histories with *Festival at Sea*. For instance, Ms. Dorothy was on board for her fifth consecutive sailing with *Festival at Sea*. Ms. Dorothy is an 89-year old white woman from Myrtle Beach, South Carolina. Her introduction to *Festival at Sea* was when in celebration of its 20th anniversary *Festival at Sea* conducted—in addition to its annual cruise—a Comedy Cruise on the *Allure of the Seas*. The Comedy Cruise was not a full ship charter; *Festival at Sea* had 500 cruisers on board for the Comedy Cruise along with *Allure's* other 5,000 passengers, one of which was Ms. Dorothy. The *Festival at Sea Comedy Cruise* group was having a dance function at one of the lounges on the ship, and Ms. Dorothy wandered by and started peeking into the lounge—all the while she was dancing along to the urban line dances taking place in the lounge. Patricia's son Kevin, one of the *Festival at Sea* staff, invited her in. "At first she was hesitant to crash what seemed like a private event. But when we are not chartering the full ship, everything is open to everybody so we convinced her to come on in. She loved it; she went to all the parties and everybody loved her too because she knew all the line dances," Patricia laughs. Ms. Dorothy asked if she could come to the *Festival at Sea* full-ship charters, was told of course she could, and has been attending *Festival at Sea* ever since. Solo!

Festival at Sea's origin was 28 years ago. Patricia Nicholson Yarbrough, founder and President, had trained and gained experience working in a San Francisco travel agency handling principally corporate travel arrangements. In 1978, she opened her own agency, Blue World Travel, continuing to focus on corporate travel but branching out into individual and entertainment travel as well. Sometimes Patricia would get groups of as many as 60 travelers that she would book on personal cruises. "We'd go on cruises and what we would find is, we would go to the clubs and they were playing very little of "our" music, or if they did, they'd play it for awhile and then they'd stop and there would be 'achy-breaky' and all these other songs, and people were just sitting around waiting for their own music to come back on. I started realizing that we're really not getting our dollars worth for the kinds of things we enjoy when we are cruising. Hairy chests contests? Maybe we'll watch it but not really want to participate. They were playing bridge, and everyone wanted to play bid whist. So, there was just a series of things including the entertainment that just wasn't designed for us." Those experiences led to the development of *Festival at Sea*.

Patricia Yarbrough, founder and President, *Festival at Sea*.

In 1991 the first *Festival at Sea* cruise took place on *Celebrity Zenith*. Patricia was influenced by her experience in going on or sending African-Americans on cruises and finding that the entertainment and overall experience tended at times to be very inconsistent and uneven. So, the notion was that *Festival at Sea* was going to be an African-American cultural event. The first *Festival at Sea* was a group cruise comprised of 250 guests. The next year the group increased to 450, and in the third year *Festival at Sea* achieved a milestone: a half-ship charter with 1200 guests! Yet another milestone was reached in *Festival at Sea's* fourth year: two cruises, a half-ship charter at 1200 guests, and then a second cruise with 600 guests after a week in between. *Festival at Sea* had clearly tapped into something and by year five did its first full ship charter, which sailed on the *Celebrity Century*. Since 1995, *Festival at Sea* has been all full-ship charters with an occasional smaller similarly-priced, similarly-themed group cruise added—but with a focus on comedy.

I asked Patricia, how has *Festival at Sea* evolved over the years—or has it stayed essentially the same? She said, "It has grown. We started off just putting some ideas together in terms of what we could do on board. Ok, electric slide competition, that'll work. It kind of evolved; it started off as mainly dancing between the entertainment and the clubs; having a DJ and being able to play *our* music. In that first year we got people who said why don't we start a committee; we've got other talents we can highlight on the *Festival at Sea* cruise. We introduced the fundraiser for the UNCF (United Negro College Fund.) We raised about $600 that first year." As has *Festival at Sea*, the UNCF Fundraiser has likewise evolved into the UNCF Bachelor Auction where ladies "bid" on bachelors in order to win a dinner date, champagne, and VIP seating at a *Festival at Sea* concert. The UNCF Bachelor Auction is a hilarious event that plays to a capacity crowd in the ship's main entertainment venue every year for the past 14, and raises well over $15,000 annually for UNCF. It is a fun means of raising money for an important cause; for the cruise I was on in 2018, *Festival at Sea* established a goal for the UNCF Bachelor Auction and accompanying UNCF Raffle to win a *Festival at Sea* cruise, at a total of $30,000.

That same year the fundraiser for the UNCF started, *Festival at Sea* started another tradition that has also spanned 26 years—an annual Book Drive to benefit children in the Caribbean. Passengers bring children's books as well as crayons, pencils and pens with them to donate. For the 27th *Festival at Sea* cruise that I sailed, the book drive was to benefit the children of Labadee, Haiti, one of the cruise ship destinations.

As *Festival at Sea* started to grow, individuals started to approach them with ideas—people with diverse talents. Patricia said, "Belinda Haywood of Cleveland, Ohio came to me with an idea about urban line dancing. It was a lot of input from people wanting to contribute; I can do this; I can do that. It was kind of wonderful to see. The *Festival at Sea* concept was growing and transforming internally with the support of passengers."

Indicative of the expansion of the programming and the evolution of *Festival at Sea* was its addition of ballroom dancing several years ago. I interviewed the instructor Calvin Sibert, known as Mr. Smooth of the dance school Mr. Smooth & Company. Mr. Smooth, from Detroit, Michigan is an international ballroom dance instructor, who appeared on the *Steve Harvey Show* last year and who has been teaching since 2001 in locations as far apart as South Africa, Sydney, Australia and Hawaii. In addition to working for *Festival at Sea* for the past 11 years, he does his own ballroom dancing-themed group cruises. For years *Festival at Sea* had featured lessons for a number of dance styles—line dance, salsa, stepping—but did not have ballroom. After the *Festival at Sea* cruise was recommended to him by a friend, he went one year and got a chance to meet Patricia, who asked him to teach *Festival at Sea* staff at a private party. Within a short period of time the *Festival at Sea* staff was on the floor ballroom dancing. "So the next year I was here as a staff member, part of the *Festival at Sea* program, and I have been coming on to instruct ballroom dance, what I refer to as 'Detroit style' versus the more traditional *Dancing With the Stars* style, ever since." I was curious about Mr. Smooth's cruising history. He told me he had cruised 26 times. He noted that none of the cruise ships are ideal for ballroom dancing—not enough floor space. "Ships are not made for dancers. You bring 700 people who want to dance. Where are they going to go?

I do my dance cruises with Carnival because they give me a lot of space I can use when many people are asleep and I can give my dancers an opportunity to dance until early am. My first cruise was in the late 80's on a vessel called the *Boblo* that cruised down the Detroit River; they had a midnight cruise with dance on all three levels. That's where I met my wife Jackie. When we cruised together for the first time, on Royal Caribbean, I proposed to her; since we met on a boat I said let me propose to her on a boat." Jackie is Mr. Smooth's dance partner, business partner, and life partner. Their business card says "We don't just sell dance; we sell romance."

As Patricia and Blue World Travel's roots are firmly implanted on the West Coast—Patricia grew up in the Bay area and attended the University of San Francisco—it was no surprise that *Festival at Sea* had a heavy representation of cruisers from California. Even though I was well aware of *Festival at Sea's* Bay Area origins from my research and conversations with Patricia prior to the cruise, I wasn't thinking about that when we walked into the Miami terminal. The Bay Area connection had somewhat slipped my mind until I noticed the terminal had a high preponderance of cruisers adorned in Golden State Warriors paraphernalia and swag. My wife was in her glory as a Warriors fanatic and her favorite player is Steph Curry whose jersey was well-represented; I on the other hand, was still lamenting the recently completed NBA Finals and the demise of my favorite player, Lebron James, at the hand of the Warriors. Over the years *Festival at Sea* has broadened its geographic reach and now attracts cruisers from throughout the nation, particularly the Chicago, Detroit, and New York areas, and increasingly *Festival at Sea* is attracting travelers out of Texas. In terms of age *Festival at Sea* cruisers fall primarily within the 40 to 60-year-old range, with of course many younger like my granddaughter, and many older like

Ms. Dorothy. I struck up a conversation with a 30-something from Tennessee at lunch who was cruising with a group of 21 to celebrate his grandmother's 79th birthday.

Interestingly, Patricia is starting to see some 20-somethings who used to cruise with their families now coming to cruise with *Festival at Sea* on their own as young adults. "To be able to attract younger cruisers represents both a challenge and an opportunity from a music standpoint; we have the DJ battles, an idea from my son Kevin who works at Blue World Travel, and this year we had DJ Kid Capri." On the cruise I attended there were 10 DJ's including Patricia's other son, Martin, aka New York City's DJ Level. Patricia notes that in terms of live music certain older performers may not be performing anymore or unfortunately begin to die off. "We filter in some of the younger entertainment; we did that this year with Avant." Other featured music entertainment this year included Grammy Award-winning R&B star Anthony Hamilton, and legendary female vocal super group En Vogue.

Although it is not primarily a music cruise, *Festival at Sea* has a rich history with a veritable who's-who of legendary R&B and gospel performers over the years: Gladys Knight; Chaka Khan; Charlie Wilson; Isley Brothers; The O'Jays; Patti Labelle; The Whispers; Kem; Jeffrey Osbourne and more from the R&B world, and gospel superstars like Fred Hammond, Yolanda Adams, and Kirk Franklin. After 27 years and dozens of performers, I asked Patricia what was the most memorable performer story she recalls, and without much hesitation she brought up the very first *Festival at Sea* cruise. The late Phyllis Hyman was the featured performer. When *Festival at Sea* approached Phyllis Hyman, she thought it would be a great idea; she had actually gotten her start as a singer on Norwegian Cruise Lines, and said she knew a lot about cruising and jumped at the opportunity to be a part of the birth of *Festival at Sea*. Phyllis Hyman was a Philadelphia R&B star and one of the most prolific female vocalists of the 80's and 90's, performing with the likes of Barry Manilow and the Four Tops, and receiving a Tony Award nomination for her Broadway role in Sophisticated Ladies, an homage to Duke Ellington. She was named the 1992 Number One Best Female Vocalist in UK beating out the likes of Whitney Houston, Aretha Franklin, and Anita Baker. In other words, Phyllis was a diva before the term was popularized, as Patricia would soon find out. "On our first *Festival at Sea*, less than an hour before sailing, there was no sign of Phyllis, and we didn't have cell phones then. Finally, Phyllis showed up 30 minutes before sail time. She had simply hijacked the limo that met her at the airport for three hours to go shopping! And we had no idea where she was. Also, she brought her musical director but didn't bring a band. The cruise line provided their show band on board, because they read music. Come to find out the band was Polish and did not speak much English. Phyllis' music director apparently had a partially Polish background and was able to communicate with the band, and along with Phyllis Hyman they put on an amazing show!" Later Blue World Travel received a bill from the limousine company for the extra time. In those days, Patricia said, "Blue World Travel didn't know much about performer contracts; however, it was worth every penny and we will never forget what Phyllis did for us. She performed for much less than her normal price just because she believed in the concept of cruising with an African-American twist."

Patricia noted they did not have a whole lot of money, but Phyllis Hyman agreed to perform for the first two years of *Festival at Sea*. "We ended up also just looking at the trades from the entertainment industry. We learned from a magazine that Sinbad was going to be in St. Croix at the same time our ship was going to be stopping in St. Thomas, so we called up and found out we could have a matinee performance. Lennie Williams of Tower of Power was on Sinbad's show; Lennie was from the Bay Area, and a good friend of his from the *Festival at Sea* cruise contacted him and joked "Hey Lennie you want to sing for your supper?" so *Festival at Sea* ended up having Lennie Williams, Phyllis Hyman, and Sinbad on the first *Festival at Sea*!

In 1998, *Festival at Sea* launched a second annual cruise targeted at a much smaller, more affluent, more adventurous clientele: *Friends of Festival at Sea*. The first cruise of *Friends of Festival at Sea* was a group cruise of 500 people on the Royal Caribbean *Legend of the Seas* with a European itinerary departing from Barcelona, Spain. They brought their own DJ's for parties during limited specified times in *Legend's* lounges. Due to an injury, Royal Caribbean's DJ ended up being out of commission for the cruise and those limited specified times became unlimited on that first *Friends of Festival at Sea* cruise, as their DJ became the DJ for the entire ship's passengers. *Friends of Festival at Sea* has gone to a number of destinations more esoteric than those visited by the regular *Festival at Sea* cruise, including Africa, Brazil during Carnival, Sydney, Singapore, China, Athens and Dubai. "*Friends of Festival at Sea* is just for people who like to explore. The group sizes vary. A couple of years ago we took 200 to China. While *Friends of Festival at Sea* cruises are not full ship charters, we have a number of private activities and when touring will have our own busses. For *Friends of Festival at Sea*, we use the more luxury brands. Like this year we are on Regent. They are all-inclusive and people like that. The *Friends of Festival at Sea* clientele is a more mature group as the pricing can be pretty expensive." The 2018 *Friends of Festival at Sea* took 67 cruisers on the *Regent Seven*

Seas Explorer, one of the most luxurious cruise ships ever built, for a 12-day "Wonders of the North" Baltic Sea itinerary leaving from Copenhagen, Denmark with stops in St. Petersburg, Russia, Finland, Sweden, The Netherlands and more.

I asked Patricia if besides being more mature and affluent the cruisers who go on *Friends of Festival at Sea* are a different market altogether or a subset of regular *Festival at Sea* cruisers? She told me there is a lot of crossover between the two annual cruises. Those who attend *Friends of Festival at Sea* are more focused on exploring the destinations rather than shipboard activities. They do bring a DJ and dance instructors but do not have parties every night, and do not feature any guest performers, because most people spend a lot of time touring the magnificent ports of call during the day. Dr. Mary Bacon, whom we sat with in the main dining room all week, typifies the type of cruiser who over the years has been a regular attendee on both the *Friends of Festival at Sea,* and the regular *Festival at Sea* cruise. Mary, who lives in Hillsborough, California is the CEO of Images of a Culture, a human resources, education, and family con-sultancy, and is also the owner of a fine art gallery. Mary has attended over 15 *Festival at Sea* cruises and for a while displayed art from her gallery as part of the cruises but stopped due to the prohibitive ship-ping cost. She has been on several *Friends of Festival at Sea* cruises. Mary is the ideal target customer for *Friends of Festival at Sea.* While she enjoys the music, comedy and other the non-stop activities of *Festival at Sea,* Mary is a seasoned cruiser, having done dozens of cruises, including exotic destinations, and is inclined more towards high-end itineraries and luxury cruise ships. The week right after the *Festival at Sea,* Mary flew to Paris to embark on a river cruise.

Friends of Festival at Sea truly embodies "Luxury Cruising with an African American Twist" and continues to grow like its sister cruise, *Festival at Sea*. In fact, in 2020 in response to the top requested destinations for the next *Friends of Festival at Sea* adventure, there will be two *Friends of Festival at Sea* cruises: Southeast Asia on the *Crystal Symphony* in March, and Southern Africa on the *Regent Seven Seas Voyager* in December.

An unofficial motto of *Festival at Sea*, is "Once you go, then you know." I recall Patricia casually dropping it in her conversation during one of our interviews before the cruise, and I heard it throughout the week during the cruise. The more I experienced *Festival at Sea*, and spoke to other cruisers, beginning with the gentleman at lunch on the first day who told me he had never gone on another cruise other than *Festival at Sea*, the more I could appreciate "Once you go, then you know." From the time we walked into the cruise terminal, there was a feeling of familiarity—not unusual with theme cruises—and family. It brought to mind the first time visiting my daughter Shornay's college; it was North Carolina A&T State University, an historically black college and universities (HBCU), on freshman move-in day. After a great deal of apprehension about leaving my baby daughter, once I got there it felt very welcoming and reassuring, and I felt like a member of the family. Similarly, with *Festival at Sea* I kept hearing the word family from other cruisers, both first time and seasoned *Festival at Sea* passengers in the first couple of days. *Festival at Sea* also reminded me of *Essence Music Festival*, the premiere land-based African-American cultural event held annually over several days in New Orleans and drawing several hundred thousand tourists. Like *Essence Music Festival*, pride, family, and empowerment were in the air. Of course *Festival at Sea* is much more intimate than Essence, even at close to 3000 passengers. It had a giant family reunion vibe.

We found we were able to participate in as little or as much of the "family reunion" as we wanted, and otherwise *Festival at Sea* offered all of the serenity, rest, and relaxation of any cruise. We got to enjoy the spoken word performances, the fraternity and sorority "Step Show," the fashion shows, and the talent show modeled after *American Idol*. I even entered the chess tournament (and got destroyed). We did not dress up for Superheroes night or Africa night but observed superhero costumes and majestic African garb that you would have to see to believe—think Eddie Murphy's *Coming to America* wedding scene. *Black Panther*, which got a featured screening during the cruise, spanned the themes of both Superheroes night and Africa night, so Wakanda was well-represented in the impressive outfits. We did dress up for the Kid Capri White Party though!

Cheryl at the Kid Capri White Party.

I also enjoyed my first cruise experience with Celebrity. The real grass lawn on the *Equinox* top deck is as stunning a departure from convention as say, bumper cars on *Anthem*; just appeals to different senses and sensibilities. The *Equinox* was a gorgeous ship and that was before the multi-million-dollar refurbishment due Spring 2019, just in time for *Festival at Sea* 2019, which will also be held on *Equinox*. And its spirits shop sold both Hennessy Pure White Cognac and Sheridan's Coffee Layered Liqueur, with its novel two-compartment bottle. These spirits are popular in cruise lore as neither is available in the United States for some reason and are common cruise ship purchases. I stocked up on both and the shop sold out.

Festival at Sea continues to improve on a successful formula. It ushered in African-American cultural cruising, creating a market niche and owning it for the last 28 years. There are numerous theme cruises that specialize in aspects of what *Festival at Sea* does: R&B music cruises, hip-hop cruises, gospel cruises, comedy cruises, and they all compete, along with other theme cruises and of course regular cruises for the passengers that *Festival at Sea* appeals to, but no cruise offers the full-spectrum of the African-American cultural experience like *Festival at Sea*.

On the next to the last day of the cruise, a line snaked out from the *Festival at Sea* hospitality lounge into the ship promenade. I thought perhaps it was cruisers lined up to buy the ubiquitous *Festival at Sea* tee shirts I saw throughout the cruise, deeply discounted at the end of the cruise like the two-for-one *Celebrity Equinox* tee shirts I had seen at one of the promenade shops earlier that day. The line actually was to book cabins on *Festival at Sea* 2019. Lacking itinerary and line-up of performers for next years' cruise, nonetheless, a significant percentage of the ensuing *Festival at Sea 2019* cruise, and all the least expensive cabins sold out that day. (While writing this chapter, I received a notification on August 31, 2018–a month after returning from *Festival at Sea*—that *Festival at Sea 2019* is sold out!)

Festival at Sea from that 250-person group cruise in 1991, to now, over 50,000 passionate cruisers later. "Once you go, then you know."

MUSIC ON THE OCEAN:
CRUISE PRODUCTION, INC.

In the summer of 1989, to celebrate his high school graduation, 17-year old Tim Cabral boarded a plane with his parents and sister to fly from his home outside of Boston to Miami to embark on his first cruise, a three-day voyage to the Caribbean on Carnival Cruise Lines' now retired *Carnivale*. Tim had already been working as a DJ and once on board was enthralled by the festive atmosphere of the *Carnivale*, especially observing the ship DJ in the nightclub. It was love at first experience for Tim, and he knew right away what he wanted to do with his life; specifically, work on Carnival cruise ships in the area of entertainment. At the time, Carnival only had eight ships, with only one DJ per ship. Within a couple of weeks of returning home from the cruise, Tim started college at New England School of Communications in Bangor, Maine to study radio in preparation for his long-term goal to become an on-air personality, but found time to call Carnival a couple of times each week to see when the next opening for a DJ would be. His persistence paid off. Soon after Tim graduated from the one-year radio broadcasting program at college, the opportunity presented itself and after only two weeks home, he headed to Miami and was onboard the *Carnival Holiday*. A year and a day after that life changing high school graduation cruise, Tim was hired to work as a DJ on *Holiday* (still in service today for the British cruise line Cruise & Maritime Voyages as the *Magellan)*.

Tim (left) with part of the Cruise Production, Inc. crew.

Today Tim Cabral is the entrepreneur behind Cruise Production, Inc., a Fort Lauderdale, Florida company that handles the technical and logistical aspects of connecting the performers with the audience on music theme cruises. This includes matters such as concert lighting and custom stages; sound equipment; backline (generally, the amplification equipment and speakers behind the band that you see on a stage at concerts and are used by all the acts performing at a venue); and on-and off-stage artist requirements associated with their performance. Essentially all the logistics that are involved in music concerts at land-based venues are required for music theme cruises except it is exacerbated by a number of unique dynamics: customs, which means everything is opened and closely scrutinized; lack of permanently situated source of power; a condensed set-up time—from when a cruise ship arrives from its previous sailing and departure later on that same day. And oh, by the way, after all equipment is loaded—seven trucks worth—the venue starts moving, which means some unique requirements in terms of safety and securing the equipment.

From that start as DJ on the *Holiday*, Tim worked in a variety of capacities related to entertainment, working his way up from on board cruise ships to working in the Carnival corporate offices in Miami, ascending to Entertainment Manager of Special Projects. He retired from Carnival in 2012 to found Cruise Production, Inc. At Carnival and continuing on to Cruise Production, Tim was responsible for all aspects of cruises related to music and entertainment. For each theme cruise, Tim had to coordinate between the theme cruise production management, the cruise line, and the contractual stipulations of the performers to ensure the efficient deployment of all required equipment and staffing needs in order to execute a successful theme cruise. Between his time at Carnival and then at the helm of Cruise Production, Inc., Tim has worked on the production of well over 400 theme cruises—more than anyone else in the business.

I asked Tim for his most memorable experience of those over 400 theme cruises. "One of the most unique experiences I ever had was when Precious Moments, the figurines company sailed on Carnival." (Precious Moments is a giftware company known most for its collectible porcelain figurines.) "They were doing a show in the main theater and they had life-sized Precious Moments dolls that performed on stage, and the costumes were too heavy for the entertainers to carry and move in, so that made for a very enter-taining but awkward experience with seven–feet tall figurines trying to dance across the stage. So, to see larger-than-life-sized Precious Moments dolls was the most unique. One of the most exciting was when I produced my first cruise as Cruise Productions, Inc., for Blake Shelton, country superstar. That was one of the most exciting moments for me because I was able to produce it as my own company."

In the several years since venturing out on his own, Tim and Cruise Productions has worked with a very diverse mix of music theme cruises: *Welcome to Jamrock Reggae Cruise; Glamorous Life Latin Cruise; Shiprocked; Soul Train Cruise; Ship-Hop, I Love the 90's, Country Music Cruise,* and so on. I asked Tim what it is like to work with such diverse genres of music. He told me, "My back-ground when I was younger was I was DJ'ing quite a bit, and my education in college, my original career path was to be in radio and radio broadcasting. So, we learned at a very early time that you can have your favorite type of music but you have to be prepared to work with every type of music. And every type of music for me has its own qualities whether it be rock or reggae or country. What's most exciting about all of this is it doesn't matter what type of music that I listen to; it's a matter of the energy that comes from the guests that are sailing. These guests onboard, whether it's a hard rock cruise with *Shiprocked* or it's a classic country cruise with the *Country Music Cruise,* is that people are there to bring themselves back to a time in their lives when this music impacted them the most. And to be a part of that energy and a part of that experience is one of the best aspects of what we do."

I was able to relate to what Tim said about the guests on theme cruises. I told him that I had just returned from my first theme cruise, *Festival at Sea,* which, while not a music cruise per se, does feature a number of major music and comedy performances. Tim told me, "*Festival at Sea* is run by some great people. We helped them out recently. They had a situation with power, and we have some unique power transformers that work exclusively on cruise ships, and we were able to send them out to the ship." I told Tim how impressed I was with the theme cruise experience and how I ran into so many who doubted they would ever be able to go back to a regular cruise. Tim was not surprised. He told me, "I have gone on hundreds of cruises, regular and theme cruises, and one of the things that I have always observed, one of the best parts of theme cruising is that on a normal everyday cruise people say hello to each other and exchange pleasantries like 'hey, where are you from, and what do you do?' If you don't really have anything in common after those two first questions you kind of chit-chat and you move on and go about your vacation until you find somebody else to talk to. But with a theme cruise, literally the minute people get off the plane, or get in the embarkation terminal and get on board, they already have something that's extremely important to them in common. Whether it's a corporate charter and they work for the same organization, or it's something they have in common whether it's sewing or cooking or poker and now the big one is music. Everybody already has this energy about them because they can share that energy with others who can relate. 'Oh you went to Woodstock too? Oh I remember when I saw this band. I remember growing up listening to this artist. Smokey is my all-time favorite singer too, etc.' All these kinds of things, everybody has commonality as soon as they start their vacation. So I think that has always been the thing for me; people already have this connection and it sets the cruise at a whole 'nother level."

Tim with Kenny Rogers backstage at the Country Music Cruise 2016.

Tim with Barry Williams (Greg Brady of *The Brady Bunch*) at the Rock & Romance Cruise 2017.

In looking at some of the theme cruises listed on the Cruise Production, Inc. website, I saw several I was intrigued about; they sounded interesting and I hadn't heard about them in my research on theme cruises. I asked Tim about a few. One was the *Glamorous Life Latin Cruise*. "That's a program we worked on with Sheila E (Grammy-nominated percussionist best known for her collaborations with Prince) and a travel partner called Flying Dutchmen Travel. That was extremely exciting for us because I grew up listening to her music and she is such a remarkable woman. That was her cruise and it exposed a lot of first time cruisers to theme cruising especially in the Latin music genre."

Two cruises I was unfamiliar with that I saw among the Cruise Productions portfolio were both branded around one superstar group, respectively, a *New Kids On the Block* themed cruise, and a *Back Street Boys* themed cruise. "Both of those cruises started when I was still with Carnival. I worked with them when I was with Carnival, and they hired Cruise Production once we left Carnival. *New Kids On the Block* is going on their tenth cruise and is one of the longest running single artist cruises, if not the longest. And *Back Street Boys* followed suit and started their own cruise as well. Those are both very successful programs, run really well and fans of those cruises walk away with an experience of a lifetime and have a really high return rate of repeat guests. Similar to the reggae cruise we work with, they have a very diverse audience. *New Kids On the Block* is more US-based but diverse with every state in the country representation, and *Back Street Boys* is more internationally diverse with folks from all over the world." Surprised, I ask Tim if these single star themed cruises are full ship charters. "They are full ship charters, and *New Kids On the Block* has always been one of the fastest selling charters in theme cruising history." I ask Tim what happens when *New Kids*

On the Block is not performing. "It's all about the fan experience. So those guys are some of the hardest working performers in the business because they'll be up at nine o'clock in the morning doing meet and greets and photo sessions, and then they'll be at the pool at 2:00 for games and activities, and then they'll do an 8:00 show, and then they'll be back at the pool deck at 10 for a massive deck party every single night, sometimes until the sun comes up." Fascinated, I ask Tim if there are other performers. "They have DJ's that perform but the fans are about that particular band and that's what the fans are there to see. Just like with the nostalgic music theme cruises like *Flower Power Cruise* to see the music of the 60's and experience that vibe, a lot of the fans on these *New Kids On the Block* and *Back Street Boys* cruises are there to relive the interaction they had with the band growing up. It is really a fan-based type of cruise where it's all about the artist having a direct connection with their fans."

Conversely, I had uncovered in my research on theme cruises the *Welcome to Jamrock Reggae Cruise* and when I saw it on the Cruise Productions website was interested to hear about it from someone closely involved. I love reggae music; perhaps it is cliché but anytime I am in or headed to the Caribbean I always play reggae music on my portable speaker. I told Tim I would love to experience an entire reggae cruise. "The *Welcome to Jamrock Reggae Cruise* is one of our largest productions that we put on every year; our biggest stages, our biggest systems, and the largest line-up in reggae cruising. It was the first of its kind; it's the largest and most successful reggae cruise. It's run by some great people. What's most exciting about the *Welcome to Jamrock Reggae Cruise* is it is so internationally diverse; there is no other cruise like it. We know because we order individual flags for each country represented by the guests. Even if there were just a couple from a country, we would make sure we had their flag represented on the *Jamrock* cruise. People come from everywhere; sometimes there would be over 40 countries represented on the *Jamrock* cruise. People come from every corner of the planet to be a part of that and it is an incredible music experience. And the cruise is hosted by Damian Marley (youngest son of reggae legend Bob Marley) who we have had the great pleasure of working with over all their cruises and he's a remarkable person as well, and that is one of the driving forces that makes that cruise so successful."

I asked Tim if Cruise Production ever does non-music themed cruises. Tim mentioned he was actually en route to Tampa where Barbizon USA, which operates the Barbizon Modeling and Acting School is headquartered. I recalled Barbizon from my youth, appealing to aspiring young models who wanted to pursue a modeling career. "One of the non-music cruises we do is for Barbizon USA. A fantastic modeling company for kids and young adults, the Barbizon cruises are very interesting because their cruises give kids the opportunity to walk the runway, take acting classes and do the acting auditions on the cruise. Normally if a parent has to take a child to do auditions, they have to travel all over the place whether New York, Chicago, LA, Miami, Orlando and so on. But what happens on this cruise is that they invite all of their students, and when they walk the runway, or do the acting or voice-over or comedy auditions they're basically in front of 120-plus booking agents. Sometimes these kids get call-backs right away and at the end of the cruise some of these kids walk away with jobs before the cruise is even over. Barbizon has been doing this for nine years and they do it every fall." I asked Tim what Cruise Productions' role is on non-music cruises. "We do a lot of video production, lighting, staging, and we do a lot of special effects for their awards ceremonies and runway competitions. We only do a couple of non-music cruises a year. It keeps us on top of the other areas of the production business."

I asked Tim if Cruise Productions does non-cruise work. "We do some non-cruise stuff but it is largely related to cruise work, cross-over with the cruise work. We do some private islands experiences—the cruise lines own private islands. We've done some private exclusive events for other clients. A lot of these cruises are branching out into the islands for these performances. We have been asked by some non-cruise companies and small arenas in the Florida area to do some work. It's something that we've been looking into, but we want to stick to what we know, which is the cruise business. We obviously want to grow just like any other small business, but the core of our business is the cruise business." Clearly Cruise Productions has been growing in the area that they know. Their first year they did production on four theme cruises, and they now do about 30 cruises per year. "We have been very fortunate with all our travel partners. Flying Dutchmen, who was our very first client as Cruise Productions, who produce *Country Cruising, Powerball, Sheila E, Melissa Etheridge, Fan2Sea*, and many others; Rose Tours who produce *New Kids on the Block, Backstreet Boys, Invicta* and the *Jamrock Cruise*; Ask4 who produce the extremely popular *Ship Rocked, Motorhead* and *I Love the 90's Cruises*. These past few years we have had the great pleasure of joining up with Star Vista LIVE who have become one of our largest clients with over seven cruises per year: *Soul Train, Flower Power, Rock & Romance, Southern Rock, Country Music Cruise, Malt Shop Memories* and the newly added *Disco Cruise*."

During the weekend of my interview with Tim I was visiting with my daughter Shornay. I had already prepared my questions, but right before I called Tim, I asked Shornay if she could think of anything I should ask him. I had explained to her that Tim had done performances by hundreds of artists including a number of super-stars on all kinds of music-oriented theme cruises from genres rang-ing from rock, to country, to R&B, to reggae. "Ask him," Shornay said, "If he was stuck on a theme cruise indefinitely, which one would it be and why?" So, I thought I would close the interview with Tim with Shornay's question. Tim said, "I can tell you that I really was stuck on a theme cruise; we were stuck on board for three days." In 2008, Carnival hosted the *Elvis Cruise* onboard the *Carnival Fantasy.* It was a full ship charter celebrating the music and the life of Elvis Presley, and featured artists who performed with Elvis and was led by his music director. The *Elvis Cruise* was scheduled to be four-days, leaving from New Orleans and sailing to Cozumel, Mexico, but Hurricane Gustav got in the way. "What ended up happening is we had to stay on the ship for three more days. Through a series of events, I had to change several hats during this cruise and take on a much bigger role and work directly with the artists and come up with and help develop a few more shows because all the artists were still on board, and all the guests were still on board. What became of that cruise is probably one of the most amazing experiences that I have ever had. All the entertainers had worked with Elvis Presley. These are legends of music who worked by his side, helped write his music and helped get him to where he was. It was a Sunday and they all wanted to put together a gospel show for the guests. And I tell you we put together the most amazing gospel show, the most amazing show I have ever been a part of. The thought was, if the storm wasn't there the show would have never happened and nobody would have had this life experience. So, it's a great question, to ask if I was stuck; when I was actually stuck, this is what happened. All the artists pulled together, all the musicians pulled together, and we did this amazing gospel show, and then did two more nights of rock shows that were created as we went. So that was really a stuck-on-board experience."

A whole new way of thinking about the Scorpion's anthem, "*Rock Me Like a Hurricane.*" (I couldn't resist.)

CARD PLAYER CRUISES

When I first heard of *Card Player Cruises*, I thought about many years ago when in the Army we would play spades through the night sometimes until the sun started to rise. I wondered, is this a cruise where between cavorting in the pools, hairy chest contests, bingo, and attending shows, that groups of cruisers congregate in various ship lounges to engage in games of pinochle, bridge, bid whist and other popular card games? My somewhat uninspiring view of what *Card Player Cruises* was all about was somewhat off the mark. Once I learned more about what *Card Player Cruises* entails, and the story behind its origin, I knew that I had to try to reach out to *Card Player Cruises* in the hopes that the story could be shared with the readers of *The Joy of Cruising*.

Card Player Cruises offers poker cruises in conjunction with major cruise lines such as Royal Caribbean, Celebrity Cruises, and Holland America. A poker cruise is essentially the same as a standard cruise but converts each cruise ship's conference space into a professionally run Las Vegas style poker room replete with all the trappings: top dealers in the poker world, cashiers, chips, poker tables, shift bosses, cocktail service, buffet, and of course gambling, from low-limit games to tournaments with buy-ins of upwards of $1000. Unlike the Las Vegas poker rooms of days gone by however, the poker rooms on *Card Players Cruises* are smoke free. In actuality, in the last decade virtually all Las Vegas poker rooms became smoke free, but *Card Player Cruises* was ahead of its time. "The first non-smoking card room in the world," Linda Johnson, one of the founders of *Card Player Cruises* told me. Cruisers choose to play as much or as little poker as they desire—as long as their budget permits—and get to partake in all the other shipboard activities, entertainment, food, and ports of call available on traditional cruises. While there are also traditional cruisers onboard most of the time, *Card Player Cruises* has done several cruises where they charter the entire cruise ship. Individuals that book their cruise through *Card Player Cruises* receive—in addition to exclusive access to the poker room—invites to private parties, events, *Card Player Cruises*-only excursions, and poker lessons and seminars taught by the partners of *Card Player Cruises*, Linda Johnson and Jan Fisher, renowned poker players, authors, and inductees in the Women's Poker Hall of Fame.

Women in Poker Hall of Famers, Jan Fisher and Linda Johnson.

Jan and Linda in the Poker Room on *Brilliance of the Seas*.

The vast majority of *Card Player Cruises* passengers are rec-reational poker players. Family members and friends who are not poker players can avail themselves of lessons and beginners' games. Poker players often bring their entire family, although there is an age minimum of 18 to enter the poker room; young children can be entertained at the cruise ship's kids camp. *Card Player Cruises* has even hosted family reunions. *Card Player Cruises* booked one family of four generations; in total they had 26 family members on board. They also hosted a wedding for two of their guests along with their wedding party of 20 cruisers. As is often the case with theme cruises, customer loyalty is high and numerous cruisers take multiple *Card Player Cruises* each year.

From time-to-time renown poker players such as Daniel Negreanu, Mike Sexton, Scotty Nguyen, Kathy Liebert, Maria Ho, Robert Williamson, Kenna James travel with *Card Player Cruises*, and *Card Player Cruises* hosts televised, high-payout events. For those who are not poker aficionados, the foregoing are all major poker stars, Poker Hall of Famers, and Negreanu is the biggest live tournament poker winner of all time with $40 million in prize money. In addition to these poker stars, other celebrities famous from others walks of life have been been on *Card Player Cruises*. Orel Hershiser, Major League Baseball star, played poker on *Card Player Cruises*. After a stellar baseball career highlighted by leading the Los Angeles Dodgers to a World Series win in 1988 and awarded the World Series Most Valuable Player award and National League Cy Young award that same year, Hershiser became a competitive poker player. Academy Award nominated actor James Woods, an avid poker player who has played in numerous major tournaments also has sailed with *Card Player Cruises*. Over the years, *Card Players Cruises* has hosted a number of national and international poker tour events and hosted the first $1,000,000 guaranteed limit hold'em tournament. In January, *Card Player Cruises* hosted the televised Heartland Poker Tour on the current title holder of largest ship in the world, Royal Caribbean *Symphony of the Seas*.

Linda Johnson is a founding partner of *Card Player Cruises*, which began in 1992 and has taken over 50,000 cruisers along on 200 poker cruises. The formation of *Card Player Cruises* was the result of combining two of Linda's passions: travel and poker. She certainly had plenty of experience and insight from both passions to draw upon. She has been to nearly 100 countries. Her favorite travel involves African safaris, and she has been to Kenya twice. Currently Linda travels six months of the year, mostly on cruises, but she also travels throughout the United States hosting poker tournaments and charity events.

With respect to cruising, Linda has been on almost 350 cruises, mostly with Royal Caribbean, but she has also on cruised with Carnival, Holland America, Norwegian, and Princess. *Card Player Cruises* does 7-8 cruises each year, at least one of which is to an exotic locale. Past *Card Player Cruises*, in addition to the Caribbean and Bahamas, have been to the Norwegian Fjords, Russia, The Greek Islands, Scandinavia, Australia, Hawaii, Panama Canal, Dubai, Egypt, Morocco, India, United Kingdom, Greek Isles, Italy and Asia. *Card Player Cruises* celebrated their 25th anniversary in 2017 by featuring a $25,000 poker tournament on, at the time, the world's largest ship, Royal Caribbean *Harmony of the Seas*.

Jean Plante (Linda's mom) and Linda on Royal Caribbean *Allure of the Seas.*

I typically ask passionate cruisers for the highlights of cruises they have taken. I felt a little sheepish asking that of someone with 350 cruises. I am glad I did with Linda though, because with that many cruises if you can pick out a few highlights, they must really stand out. Linda's response did not disappoint: how about getting a massage from an elephant in Thailand; scuba diving with the seals in Mexico; seeing the biggest and best architectural structures in

Dubai; river rafting in Costa Rica; and seeing the Northern Lights in Iceland.

In 2019, *Card Player Cruises* will be doing a South America *Celebrity Eclipse* cruise departing from Buenos Aires, Argentina including three days in Rio de Janeiro during Carnival; in the fall they depart from Seattle, Washington on Royal Caribbean *Ovation of the Seas* for an Alaska Glacier Cruise. Accordingly, there is not much on Linda's bucket list. When I first met her, Linda mentioned Cuba, but she just checked that one off at the end of 2018. Her other bucket list cruise is Antarctica, and that one is booked!

Linda Johnson's other passion, of course, is poker. Nicknamed the First Lady of Poker, Linda's résumé in the world of competitive poker is long and in-depth both as a player and in allied roles. As a poker player, Linda's career highlights include winning the coveted World Series of Poker gold bracelet and being elected to the Poker Hall of Fame and the Women in Poker Hall of Fame. Among her influential roles in the poker world, Linda was the owner and publisher of CardPlayer Magazine and founder of the Tournament Directors Association. In 2017, Linda was the inaugural honoree of the World Poker Tour, WPT Honors Program for her contributions to the poker community.

Despite having given so much of her life to the world of competitive poker, it was a relatively easy transition to theme cruising for Linda, as she was not walking away from poker. "I had so much fun in brick and mortar card rooms that I thought playing poker and getting to enjoy cruising would be even more fun. We have found the perfect staff and we all work together to make sure our customers have the most fun possible on their cruises. I still play poker in Las Vegas."

Linda is originally from Long Island, New York. I learned during my discussions with Linda that I am from the same town as she, Huntington, and we grew up there around the same time. (Speaking of coincidences, turns out I was born on the same date in the same year as Jan. So much in common with *Card Player Cruises*; I can't play poker though!) When not on the ocean, Linda lives in Las Vegas. Other than tending to her two passions of travel and poker, Linda enjoys theater and dancing. "I am so fortunate to be able to combine my two passions...poker and cruising. I get to travel all over the world and play poker with very nice people, many of whom are like family to me. It's truly lucky when you can look forward to going to work!"

ETA MOTORCYCLE CRUISES

The more I researched the various aspects of theme cruises, the more it became clear to me just how diverse theme cruising is. *ETA Motorcycle Cruises* is as unique as a theme cruising concept can be and is virtually impossible to compete against. There are a number of factors supporting that statement: regulatory and logistical barriers for sure, but the biggest is because *ETA Motorcycle Cruises* has as its founder and President, Steve Wallach, whose career inside the cruise entertainment industry runs wide and deep, and externally his stints in law enforcement, as a musician, and then in international entertainment management and promotion provide him with a blend of skills, experience, and perspective that is difficult to match. Steve began his career in the entertainment cruise industry in the 70's, working his way up from musician to an Entertainment and Cruise Director for Carnival, Costa, Holland America, Home Lines, Italian Lines, Norwegian, Royal Caribbean, and Sitmar. Steve has also worked in a promotional capacity on world tours for a number of music superstars including Stevie Wonder, Billy Ray Cyrus, Lou

Rawls, Michael Jackson and The Jacksons, Pat Benatar, Pink Floyd, Barry Manilow and more.

That unique blend of entertainment industry and cruise industry skills and experiences enabled Steve to gain a foothold as a purveyor of entertainment and theme cruising. He was one of the pioneers in music theme cruises and collaborated with Norwegian Cruise Lines to whom he gives a lot of the credit for the music theme cruise industry flourishing. I recall when I started cruising in the late 80's being envious of friends who would cruise on the NCL jazz cruises on the SS Norway. Steve started the company as Entertainment Travel Alternatives (ETA), focusing on corporate group cruises and event planning. But it was keen entrepreneurial foresight that pushed Steve to conceptualize the idea of *ETA Motorcycle Cruises*, which is centered around simultaneously a very simple, yet ingenuous notion, captured in the *ETA Motorcycle Cruises* tagline: *Imagine taking your bike with you on a cruise!*

Steve Wallach (orange shirt) posing with crew on the *Celebrity Eclipse* on its way in 2018 to the Southern Caribbean for 14 days.

Steve's first experience on a cruise ship was with Home Lines out of New York. Home Lines, an Italian company that operated both ocean liners and cruise ships was the leading cruise line out of New York in the 60's and 70; it was merged into Holland America Line in 1988. "They had ships like the *Homeric*, the *Oceanic*, the *Doric*, and the *Atlantic*. My parents took me on a cruise on the *Homeric* when I was in the fifth grade. We wore a suit all the time. Even if visitors came to the pier to visit you on the ship—they could do that back then—they had to be dressed appropriately. I can remember walking around and thinking 'oh man.' It nailed me right away, in the fifth grade." I said, "You knew right away what you wanted to do?" Steve told me he knew. "Yeah, I knew right away. I didn't get into the cruise industry right away upon reaching adulthood. I had other professions well before that, but I knew I would be involved with ships in some way, shape, manner or form." He says he was driven by a favorite saying of his dad: "You don't know unless you try."

Steve's opportunity to get involved with the cruise industry happened when he was working as a police officer with the Port Authority of New York and New Jersey. During that time, he got married and for his wedding he went on a cruise on *Home Lines Oceanic*. While on the cruise Steve noticed an idle piano in a lounge, so he sat at the piano and started playing. Playing from the age of 5, Steve was primarily self-taught and continues to play by ear. His erstwhile piano teacher pronounced that Steve lacked the patience to learn the piano, and would likely never learn to play. "I was blessed to have parents that took me to many Broadway shows in New York City. Upon arriving back home, I would go directly to the piano and within minutes I would play the songs from those plays and shows." Steve has gone on to write, produce and publish his own music.

Steve said, "This guy came over to me and said I'm Eddie Dawson, the cruise director; you're incredible. Ever think about working on a ship?" The cruise director gave Steve the name of a booking agent in New York City, and he went to see him, in uniform. "Pulled the squad car in front of the address, double parked, went inside and played the piano and got hired. That's what started my cruise career in the early 70's." Steve worked part-time on board the *Home Lines Doric* and *Oceanic*. The *Doric* subsequently became Royal Caribbean *Royal Odyssey*, and then for Regency Cruises became *Regent Sun* before sinking in 2001 en route to being scrapped; the *Oceanic* eventually became *The Big Red Boat* for Premier Cruise Line, then the official line of Walt Disney World. Steve worked several years for Home Lines, progressing from cruise staff to assistant cruise director to cruise director before moving to Sitmar Cruises, and then stints at Holland America, Royal Caribbean and Carnival. Steve worked for cruise lines for 11 years. He left to go into popular music full-time, touring in a management and promotions capacity with major acts. After retiring from the high pressure music business in 1995, Steve tried to figure out what he would do next with his life.

In 1996, Steve was talking with his son, who said, "You're bored. You have to find something to do. I'm going to give you an ultimatum. You have to find something to do." Steve said, "Well that's actually not an ultimatum." The son said in a joking manner, "Actually it is. Because if you don't find something to do, the dogs and I are going to kill you. You're making us crazy. Please dad, you're bored!"

Steve told me, "Paul, that night I went to bed and I had a dream. Now mind you I was already doing other various things that had to do with ships; my music, consulting with Norwegian Cruise Lines and things of that nature, but that night I dreamt I rode my personal bike up on a ship and rode off onto the islands. I went 'whoa can't be'. But again, thinking back to my father, you don't know unless you try." So, the next day Steve made a call to a friend, Captain Howard Newhoff, Royal Caribbean Manager, Terminal & Port Security, former Coast Guard Commander, and, Harley rider! After Steve shared his epiphany with Captain Newhoff, at first Captain Newhoff laughed, and then he told Steve, there was no way. He said that these are passenger ships not ferries. But Steve kept pushing back, saying "what if?" Finally, Captain Newhoff proposed a deal to Steve. He told Steve to get all the approvals that would enable him to do what he proposed to do as far as transporting motorcycles on a cruise ship is concerned and then to come back and see him. Two-and-a-half years later Steve called Captain Newhoff and told him he was coming to Florida and wanted to come by and see him. When Steve arrived in Captain Newhoff's office he brought with him all the approvals the Captain had challenged him to obtain. "From every port, every government, every motor vehicle office, insurance, from every island I wanted to do this on; even correspondence from the Coast Guard."

It took several years to operationalize *ETA Motorcycle Cruises;* for instance, it took Steve years to convince Bermuda officials alone to waive their maximum 150 cc restriction regarding motor scooter displacement (the smallest Harley Davidson engines on the bikes used for *ETA Motorcycle Cruises* are six times that.) "This is not just a regular group cruise where you call the cruise line and say 'hey I would like to book some space'. There are lots of legalities that are involved; safety; following SOLAS (The International Convention for the Safety of Life at Sea, which sets minimum safety standards in the operation of merchant ships); there's the Coast Guard; and of course individual cruise line policies." Having done all the legwork, Steve was ready to realize his dream, although it was with Costa not Royal Caribbean. So in 1998 ETA did their first motorcycle cruise on *Costa Atlantica*. They were allotted space for 25 bikes. They did two one-week motorcycle cruises—the space for 25 bikes on both sold out. This year, their 19th year of doing motorcycle cruises, what started as two-weeks out of the year is up to 27-weeks, and ETA is sold out through early 2020.

Bikes in en route to Bermuda on *Celebrity Summit*.

Each *ETA Motorcycle Cruise* is limited to approximately 28 bikes—2-wheeled variety or 3-wheeled trikes—so full capacity on ETA charters is approximately 60 cruisers. Steve says, "We do have people who come as part of our group but do not have a bike; family members who don't ride but want to come with us. They book right through us; they participate in group activities, have the private dining with us, and they get all the advantages that *ETA Motorcycle Cruise* gives all of its guests. We also give them the opportunity to rent vehicles on the island and follow the motorcycle tour."

Most ETA cruises allow a mix of bikes and trikes, but there are some specialty cruises that focus on one or the other. The cruise fee works similarly to other group cruises: it enables passengers to take advantage of any ETA charter-specific events plus enables access to all the other cruise ship amenities and activities that non-group passengers have available to them. There is a per-bike premium that covers transport and storage of the cruiser's bike on the cruise ship and covers fees associated with the island tours, all of which are escorted either by law-enforcement or a local riding group. *ETA Motorcycle Cruises* does not rent bikes; its competitive advantage is that it is the only company that allows cruisers to bring their own bikes.

I asked Steve about the demographic make-up of his cruises. He told me riders have ranged between 19-years old to 82-years old. I was intrigued about an 82-year old riding a motorcycle in the roads of the islands. (I once made the mistake of renting a bicycle in Bermuda, not realizing I had to ride in traffic with cars that were oblivious to the fact that you were a tourist; I thought I was going to die!) Steve said, "They called him Grumpy. A very determined man with an attitude and mouth of a sailor but the heart of a gentle giant. Riding a custom trike, he was quick to let everyone know that his real love was his 119' yacht and his 86' play toy cruiser. He did a great job riding the islands and his stories were journeys of his life." Riders are from all walks of life—some blue collar, some white collar. *ETA Motorcycle Cruises* attracts a lot of law enforcement and firemen as well as judges, executives, and physicians. A regular cruiser every couple of years is a software company owner from Germany worth billions. Steve adds, "we've had some notable passengers including country music stars, comedians and celebrity bike enthusiasts." In terms of gender, *ETA Motorcycle Cruises* has attracted clubs of all women riders; and the group of riders for every cruise is diverse in terms of gender. In fact, Steve told me that the majority of the riders are couples, either husband and wife, or significant others, along with a few men and women who ride solo. About 65% of *ETA*

Motorcycle Cruises customers are from the United States, with 30% coming from Canada and the remaining 5% coming from abroad. Every three years a group from Budapest Hungary comes; they rent all 28 of their bikes—from a third party, not from *ETA Motorcycle Cruises*—and the bikes are waiting for them when they arrive at their hotel. Conversely, over 80% of riders ride their bikes to the port with the rest using trailers or motorcycle transports, although that number fluctuates depending on the time of the year due to climate. "Riders want to ride. In the winter months they often will use a transport, but the rest of the time riders want to ride. Most of the cruisers from Canada like to ride their bikes down. We have customers from California who ride cross-country to get on the ship."

A combination ETA bike cruise from both *Celebrity Silhouette* and *Celebrity Eclipse* in St Maarten.

Steve says one of *ETA Motorcycle Cruises* best selling points is, "You know so many guys will say to their wives 'I'm not going on a cruise.' Here's the kicker: the woman says, 'you can take your motorcycle with you!' 'I'm there,' the guy responds. This kind of conversation is illustrated or repeated at every cruise at the first stop. ETA riders always get priority disembarkation at ports: "When we take the bikes off at the first port of call, we tell the riders to look up at the balcony and you see all these other cruisers watching us. You sometimes see a husband mouth to the wife, 'you never told me I could bring my bike!' We get calls at our main office all the time that goes something like this: Hi I am sitting on my balcony on *Celebrity Equinox* in St. Lucia and I see motorcycles coming off the ship. I want to know how I go about booking a future motorcycle cruise."

Riding through an outside mall after their lunch and beach stop at the Green House, Curacao.

After that first ride, when *ETA*'s riders return to the ship and get back on board they get treated by other passengers as celebrities. "Passengers are stopping them and wanting to know all the details about who they are and the circumstances behind how they arranged to bring a bike with them and be able to get off the ship on a priority basis." The riders also get looked upon like celebrities on their island motorcycle riding tours. Locals come out of their homes and businesses to see the riders in formation with Steve leading the way in a jeep, a couple of ETA Road Captains on bikes, and sometimes lights flashing on the vehicles of police escorts. (When Steve rode for 37 years, his bikes of choice were a Harley-Davidson Heritage Classic, and then a Harley-Davidson Muscle V-Rod.)

Imagine a relaxing couple of sea days and then climbing Timothy's Hill in St Kitts.

Steve relishes the way the *ETA* riders are received by the other passengers, especially given that over the years he has been exposed to occasional misconceptions about bikers, for instance, being gang members—including sometimes from other cruisers. "This is nonsense and stereotype that they are gangs; there's a camaraderie among riders. There are so many wonderful people who ride bikes," Steve says. Prior to every ride. Steve takes the time to offer a prayer for the entire group, their families and friends, "It's a great feeling, a warm feeling Steve says, having people come over to me and thank me for offering a prayer before we ride." He proudly cites that motorcycle groups are among the leading contributors to charitable causes; as a cancer survivor himself, Steve and the *ETA Motorcycle Cruises* include fundraisers for St. Jude's Children's Research Hospital and the American Cancer Society. Steve notes that bikers spend more money on the ships than regular cruisers, and they are very loyal customers for *ETA* with eight in ten returning to *ETA Motorcycle Cruises* within a two-year period.

ETA Motorcycle Cruises' flagship is the *Celebrity Equinox*, which does Caribbean cruises from Miami. *ETA* departs from Fort

Lauderdale on *Celebrity Reflection, Celebrity Silhouette, and Celebrity Eclipse.* In March 2019, *ETA* will sail an Eastern Caribbean itinerary from Fort Lauderdale on the amazing new *Celebrity Edge. ETA Motorcycle Cruises* regularly departs from Port Liberty in Bayonne, New Jersey on the *Celebrity Summit.* All of the bike space for the aforementioned cruise ships are sold out for 2019. But if a motorcycle cruise is now on your bucket list—and Steve hears that from first time *ETA* cruisers all the time—you can tick-off that bucket list aspiration beginning in 2020.

It started with a dream 19 years ago, and became a dream fulfilled. Just as *ETA Motorcycle Cruises* enables motorcycle riders to realize once-in-a-lifetime memories—or over and over memories given *ETA*'s repeat rate—Steve has many, many memories including some very poignant ones. Steve says the one thing that surpasses everything in the world to him is when a rider tells him, "Steve, this was on my bucket list," and then a few months later that rider is gone. Or, on a happier note, someone experiencing a bucket list goal, and on the same cruise gets married. Steve has officiated dozens of weddings on *ETA Motorcycle Cruises.*

Sint Maarten French Side.

Steve closed with what really is the essence of theme cruising. "With *ETA Motorcycle Cruises,* it's two birds with one stone; people who love to cruise, and, they get to bring their bike."

Performing On the Ocean

THE CRUISE DIRECTOR: ALONZO BODDEN

O kay, I admit it. I am a huge fan of comedian Alonzo Bodden. If he wanted to be quoted in *The Joy of Cruising* reading a passage from the dictionary, I would have found a way to weave that into the context of cruising. Fortunately, I did not have to ask him to read the dictionary, as Alonzo has a fairly significant connection with the world of cruising. I first became aware of his involvement with cruising as a long time listener of his podcast, *Who's Paying Attention*, where he reflects on social issues, sports, music and popular culture in a thoughtful yet humorous way. At certain times of the year Alonzo would mention that he is recording his podcast from a cruise ship, or explain that the reason he has not posted a new podcast for awhile was because he had been away on a cruise and had just returned. Alonzo did not spend a lot of time during his podcast talking about his activities on the cruise ship so I wasn't entirely aware of his role, but since every cruise I have been on has had comedians as part of the ship's entertainment, I assumed Alonzo was one of the ship comedians on regular cruises.

Alonzo Bodden, Cruise Director, *Smooth Jazz Cruise 2018*, *Celebrity Summit*.

It turns out that Alonzo exclusively works on theme cruises. He serves regularly on several Entertainment Cruise Productions theme cruises. He is the Cruise Director on *The Smooth Jazz Cruise*, and is the featured comedian on *Blue Note at Sea*, and *The Ultimate 80's Cruise*. Having learned of Alonzo's involvement with theme cruising, I now was driven to make contact with him given that theme cruising was going to be an integral part of *The Joy of Cruising*. As alluded to earlier, *The Joy of Cruising* is all about passion, and I view theme cruising as the ultimate blending of a couple of passions: cruising, and passion for something else; in Alonzo's case music—principally, jazz. It was not easy making contact with a comedy star and actor, especially when you are, as I referred to myself earlier, "just some guy on the internet." To get Alonzo's attention I tried to strike the right balance between being a professional, a serious writer, which I try to be, and a "fan boy," which I am! I tried pointing Alonzo to my previous writing, which was a serious treatment about a very sobering subject (brain surgery and recovering from trauma). On the other hand, I let him know we are both from New York City (Alonzo from Queens, me from Brooklyn); have the same taste in music (contemporary jazz); that he is my favorite comedian (he really is, saw him live here in Southwest Florida). No response! I even resorted to repeating catchphrases from his podcasts in my messages to him. Again nothing. I was beginning to feel self-conscious. Was I coming across like a stalker? Persistence paid off though, and eventually Alonzo responded and agreed to talk to me about theme cruises.

Alonzo Bodden has been in the entertainment business for 25 years. Although he is identified as a comedian—and most of the year he performs stand-up in venues ranging from tiny clubs to sizable arenas around the country, as well as internationally—he is incredibly diverse as an entertainer. Alonzo has a number of television acting credits, including several appearances in the final season of the Showtime series *Californication*, and voice acting in the Power Rangers animated series; in movies including parts in *Scary Movie 4, The Girl Next Door,* and *Bringing Down the House*; writing and producing credits for numerous television comedy episodes; and dozens of television guest appearances as himself such as *The Tonight Show with Jay Leno,* and *Last Comic Standing*, which he won in 2005. He hosts the aforementioned critically acclaimed podcast *Who's Paying Attention*, and is a regular on National Public Radio's *Wait Wait... Don't Tell Me!* a weekly news-based radio show.

I suspect that most people interviewing a star comedian would be inclined to ask him or her to tell them a joke. I am familiar enough with Alonzo's work to know that would be futile. I have listened to every one of well over 200 of his podcasts and he never tells jokes; but when I am listening alone in my car—my preferred listening environment—it is not unusual for a car to pull up next to me at a traffic light and stare at me having trouble holding it together and sometimes just laughing deliriously. And often the subject that Alonzo is riffing on is not what you would normally think of as a laughing matter, like racism, or senseless gun killings, or politicians or team owners or celebrities saying and doing things beyond stupid. So I just asked Alonzo about cruising.

Prior to performing on cruise ships, had you cruised? When was your first cruise, what ship was it, and did it have any lasting impression on you?

My only prior cruise experience was a 3-day cruise out of Long Beach with a girlfriend back in the 80's; just a quick fun getaway. It left no lasting impression. I know that because I can't remember the name of the ship.

First time performing on a cruise ship: When, what cruise line; any anxiety about the sailing?

My first time performing on a ship was a Royal Caribbean cruise from Florida; Miami I believe. I just remember the cruise director saying it was nice to see a comedian onboard who was on the way up, not the way down. I appreciated that. I really didn't have any anxiety about sailing. It was just a new experience.

Did the cruise director say that because you had won *Last Comic Standing*? What would have made him/her make the observation that you were on the way up?

No, I had not done *Last Comic Standing* at that point. I think the cruise director said I was on the way up because at that time I was probably in my 30's and younger than most cruise comics.

Contrast performing on cruise ship versus performing in a club?

The biggest difference is every show on a given cruise is for the same audience, so I have to change the material I do; it involves more improv. In a club it's a different crowd every night so I can lean on the set-list a bit more.

What's the difference between performing on cruise ships like on that first cruise above, and the work you are doing now with theme cruises?

Well my cruise gigs are different than most cruise ship comedians in that I work charter cruises. I don't work for the cruise lines; I work for Entertainment Cruise Productions. They do predominantly jazz cruises. I've also done theme cruises in different genres of music such as *The Soul Train Cruise, The 80's Cruise,* even *The Gospel Cruise.* My most memorable experiences have been the artists I've met such as the late George Duke, Marcus Miller, Dave Sanborn, Dave Koz, Earth, Wind and Fire, Patti Labelle. The list goes on and on.

What cruise lines have you worked with? What was your most memorable experience?

Royal Caribbean, Holland America, and Celebrity. My favorite cruise experience travel-wise was a Mediterranean cruise because I got to bring my mother and she got to see Europe. That was a great trip and great way for us to see Italy and Greece.

What is your motivation to perform on cruise ships? Is it a passion that you have for cruising, or is it more of just a job?

The cruise isn't the motivation for me as much as the music and artists; but if I have to work, the Caribbean isn't a bad place to do it. As a performer I get to see so many beautiful places but I don't get the time off to enjoy them all. Not complaining though. Cruising is still a magnificent environment.

I see you are the host on some theme cruises; how did that come about?

I only recently moved up to hosting on *The Smooth Jazz Cruise* after being resident comic for years and learning how it all works. How it came about is that I had been working with these crowds, musicians, and shows for 10 years, so when the prior *Smooth Jazz Cruise* director left Michael Lazaroff, the CEO of Entertainment Cruise Productions asked me if I'd like to take over as Cruise Director. It's fun hosting the cruise; mingling with the passengers and introducing the artists. We definitely have a fun, family atmosphere on the *The Smooth Jazz Cruises*.

Alonzo in the Caribbean, *Smooth Jazz Cruise 2018, Celebrity Summit*.

What's hosting like versus being a resident performer?

Well, a friend of mine who performs on ships says it's just a gig. I think the biggest difference is that my comedian friends tell me they can't socialize with the passengers. On *The Smooth Jazz Cruise* a big part of my job is socializing with the passengers. I also host excursions. Oh, and I get a nice verandah cabin! The regular cruise performers are often in the below decks. I guess I'm a bit spoiled.

Are there any aspects of cruising that you haven't experienced but you would like to? Bucket list cruises?

Maybe cruising Australia would be nice; I haven't done that.

Alonzo with jazz great Chick Corea on *Celebrity Summit.*

Closing thoughts? Any theme cruise advice you can share?

I would say what I've learned from the passengers is do some research before you book. You would hate to be a more mature adult on a young persons' booze cruise; or 22 years old on a seniors' cruise. Passengers tell me they love themed cruises because all the cruisers share a common love of music or sports or whatever the theme may be. I think that is the way to go. Oh, and if you think you might get seasick remember to start treatment/preventative measures before the ship starts moving. Nothing worse than being on vacation and unable to leave your room—that's no vacation. Go with an open mind and have fun!

If you want to find out why I am such a fan of Alonzo Bodden, check out *Man Overboard*, a CD Alonzo recorded in 2018 on the *Smooth Jazz Cruise*. After an introduction as "one of the most talented comedians in the world" by legendary bassist Marcus Miller, Alonzo gets into his first bit, "Lifeboat Drill." He welcomes the audience but then lets them know: "…this ain't Alonzo the cruise host…" For the next hour or so hilarity on the ocean ensues.

JAZZ ON THE OCEAN: THE LEGENDARY MANNY KELLOUGH

Settling into the plush leather armchairs in the intimate, purple-tinged walnut paneled Jazz On 4 lounge on Royal Caribbean's *Symphony of the Seas*, my friends Lonnie and Jodi of Oakland, California were enjoying the straight ahead jazz stylings of the Manny Kellough Jazz Experience. As soon as he boarded the world's largest ship, Lonnie had checked to see if there was any jazz entertainment he could partake in and was happy to hear *Symphony* had a club for live jazz. Lonnie is a jazz aficionado; his favorite artist is Long Tall Dexter (Dexter Gordon) and he has over 2000 jazz albums, yes vinyl in this digital age. As he sat grooving to the Manny Kellough Jazz Experience renditions of familiar jazz standards such as Duke Ellington's "Satin Doll," Louis Armstrong's "What A Wonderful World," Frank Sinatra's "World On a String," and the stunning versions by the female lead vocalist of Billie Holiday's "All of Me," and Ella Fitzgerald's "Don't Get Around Much Any More," Lonnie recalls thinking "These guys are good," even though he was unfamiliar with Manny Kellough and his band. Though the band was drummer

Manny Kellough's namesake, Manny did no talking, instead letting his sticks speak for him. The female lead singer did all the talking. After a stirring rendition of Dinah Washington's "What a Difference a Day Makes," she took time out to introduce the members of the band. Saving the leader for last, she emphatically referred to him as the legendary Manny Kellough. After the show, as Lonnie and Jodi were walking out of Jazz On 4 they talked about how the jazz was "smoking" and how enjoyable of an evening they had. Lonnie was a little perplexed though that given his long history of following jazz he was unfamiliar with someone introduced as the "legendary" Manny Kellough....

The legendary Manny Kellough.

.... Over 40 years prior to the above scene, I settled into my front row seat of the sold out Municipal Auditorium in Columbus, Georgia where I lived while in the Army stationed at Fort Benning. We were there to see bass player extraordinaire Larry Graham's funk super group Graham Central Station, Grammy nominated for Best New Artist and riding high on one of the hottest soul albums of the year, *Ain't No 'Bout-A-Doubt It*. Graham Central Station launched into "The Jam" the lead song on *Ain't No 'Bout-A-Doubt It*, an eight-minute tour de force which really was an extended introduction of the band members of Graham Central Station, where each one would sing or rap a verse and then tear off an extended solo riff on their instrument.

I am Manuel... Graham Central Station's drummer exclaimed. He did a clever little rap and then Manny Kellough ripped into a torrid drum solo. 1975's "The Jam" is widely considered one of the funkiest and most iconic anthems of funk and R&B music ever.

Graham Central Station. **Manny is on the far left and Larry Graham is on the far right.**

Prior to playing drums for Graham Central Station, Manny was the drummer for Grammy Award-winner Billy Preston (the "Fifth Beatle"), playing on hit songs "Outa-Space," "Space Race," "Nothing from Nothing," "Will It Go Around in Circles," "You Are So Beautiful," and more. Manny won a Grammy Award for Best Pop Instrumental Performance for "Outa-Space." Billy Preston was the first music performer on *Saturday Night Live;* Manny also appeared with Billy Preston on The Midnight Special, Soul Train, Johnny Carson Tonight Show, Dick Clark American Bandstand, and numerous television shows in England and other parts of Europe. Playing with Billy Preston enabled Manny to perform live with the Rolling Stones. (Search YouTube for the video, Billy Preston, The Midnight Special, Will It Go Round in Circles, 1973. Manny is the guy with the Afro bigger than Billy Preston's!)

Already drawn to cruising, Manny (left) and Billy Preston cruising the canals in Amsterdam.

"I first met Billy Preston at a local LA club, when he came in to hear the group I was playing with. One evening I followed him out as he was leaving and introduced myself. I told him I loved his music, and I would like to be his drummer. He said that he had been checking out the band every week and told me he would love to have me as his drummer. From that evening on, I spent the next twenty-five years as Billy's drummer, live and in the studio. We received four gold singles and two Grammys."

Manny segued from one music legend to another. "Around the end of 1973, Billy decided he needed a break from touring. At that same time, another member of Billy's band, Robert "Butch" Sam, mentioned that he heard bass player Larry Graham, formerly of Sly and the Family Stone was looking to put together a group. After getting in contact with Larry, I was invited to Oakland for an audition. I got the gig with what became Graham Central Station, featuring Larry Graham on bass and vocals. We recorded the well-known album *Ain't No 'Bout-a-Doubt It*, which immediately went gold."

In addition to the numerous television appearances with Billy Preston and Graham Central Station, Manny attained several other film and television credits. He recorded with Quincy Jones on the theme song of the hit television show *Sanford and Son*; and movie credits with Little Richard for the movie *Down and Out in Beverly Hills*; and with Billy Preston in the movies *The Bus is Coming*, and Jim Brown's *Slaughter*.

In the years following the establishment of his legendary status as the drummer for funk rock icons Billy Preston and Larry Graham's Graham Central Station, Manny worked with Barry White, and toured with top soul group The Main Ingredient ("Everybody Plays the Fool"), serving as the music director for their South Africa tour in 1976, returning home prematurely due to apartheid-related issues. Manny then started working with jazz trumpeter Freddie Hubbard, a welcome return to his jazz roots from which he never looked back. After a stint with jazz singer Carmen McCrae, Manny formed his own group, Manny Kellough Jazz Experience. Jazz music really represented Manny's music career coming full circle. He started playing the drums at the age of eight at Pleasant Hill Baptist Church in Los Angeles, California where he was born and raised. Manny started playing the drums professionally at the age of thirteen with gigs featuring diverse styles of music but jazz was truly Manny's forte. At 17, Manny was fortunate to play with the Ray Charles band. He earned his Bachelor's Degree in Jazz Studies from the University of Southern California.

If you've cruised on Celebrity or Royal Caribbean—subsidiaries of the same parent company—and you appreciate listening to live jazz, then you very likely have experienced Manny performing as part of the Manny Kellough Jazz Experience, Manny Kellough All Stars, Manny Kellough Jazz Quartet, or Manny Kellough Trio. Like my friend Lonnie, you may not have had any inkling of Manny's funk, rock, pop legendary status until you just read about it. Why would you? Manny told me he never talks about himself when performing. His passion is the music he is playing now, jazz.

Manny does have a couple of other passions. He told me he is passionate about cruising. Another passion is his wife Jan. Manny didn't tell me that expressly but he didn't have to. What he did say was, "I met my wife Jan on board the *Allure of the Seas* December 5th, 2013. She is my #1 supporter, fan, and manager. I have the best wife in the world, and I 'm very blessed to have Jan as my wife." And Jan also loves to cruise, having been on 20 cruises.

Manny's entrée into cruise ship performing was in 1994 with Princess Cruise Lines. In 2008, he was contracted to work for Celebrity Cruises, and was tasked with setting set up a jazz program for Celebrity. He loves to cruise and it has allowed him to see the world from a different perspective than when he traveled extensively during his stints with Billy Preston, Graham Central Station and others. However, Manny's introduction to cruising was not a pleasant one.

His first cruise was in 1967 on the Italian Lines *SS Cristoforo Colombo*. Despite the *Cristoforo Colombo's* glamorous legacy—it appeared in a couple of movies and was prominently featured in *Rome Adventure*, starring Suzanne Pleshette and Troy Donahue— Manny's maiden voyage was anything but glamorous. "My first experience on the high seas was not a good experience for me. The seas were so rough and I got so sick I turned green out there on the ship, and we still had to play. I had a little high school band called the Rhythm Rebellion." And, he was not on the *Cristoforo Colombo* by choice. The circumstances of teenager Manny cruising from France to New York was tantamount to indentured servitude. Unaware of the backstory I said to Manny, "So, it was just a job." He told me, "We had to play in order to get back home, and we did not get paid. The only compensation we got was food and a place to sleep."

Perplexed, I asked Manny how he found himself in a situation where he thought he was not going to get paid. Manny said, "Well, let me see if I can explain it. Rhythm Rebellion's manager sent us to France; to south France, Saint-Tropez, at a jazz club called Byblos. I think Bridgette Bardot owned it." Hotel Byblos is an iconic French Riviera hotel inspired by Saint-Tropez' most famous resident, Brigitte Bardot. Manny continued, "We had a vocalist, bless his heart, who would go to the boutiques, and we thought he was buying all these nice clothes. Well he was stealing the clothes. So rather than putting him in jail, Rhythm Rebellion got kicked out of the country. We had no clue what was going on, where we were and how we were going to get back to the states. So we ended up having to work our way home on the *Cristoforo Colombo!*" So, on his first cruise rather than young Manny getting to marvel at the magic of cruising, he and his band were confined to playing and then retreating to their rather austere quarters.

Besides the *Cristoforo Colombo,* Manny's entrée to cruise ship performing was in 1994 with Princess Cruise Lines. The ship he worked on initially was the *Crown Princess.* Manny played drums as part of another musician's trio comprised of bass and keyboards, mainly on Alaska itineraries. Consequently, Manny loves cruising to Alaska to this day, and has been on about 30 Alaska cruises. "It was real nice. We would play in the ballroom; they had ballroom dance instruction so we would play swing music, cha-cha. We had to learn how to play all kinds of music for them to dance to; that's what our job was—to play for the ballroom dance instructors and the passengers that wanted to learn ballroom dancing." After working with the trio to support Princess ballroom dancing for over a year, Manny left to form his own group. He eventually returned to Princess, this time leading his own group and played in a club called the Wheelhouse, a performance and dance venue across the Princess fleet. "My agent, he sent me back to Princess; again that was a dance environment where we were playing for the dancers as opposed to a showroom where people were sitting down enjoying what you are doing. It was strictly playing cha-chas, rumbas; I think I had to learn to play just about every type of rhythm that I could think of which I had learned in school anyway. Nonetheless, I was able to learn some things playing out on the cruise ship."

In 2008, Manny was contracted to work for Celebrity Cruises, and was tasked with setting up a jazz program for the *Celebrity Solstice* which launched that year. *Solstice* was the first of Celebrity's new Solstice-class and boasted industry firsts, such as The Lawn Club on the top deck featuring a half-acre of real grass, and the Hot Glass Show offered in conjunction with the Corning Museum of Glass. Nevertheless, *Solstice* wasn't quite ready to properly present live jazz. "When I started, they didn't even have a place for me to play. They had us playing underneath a staircase in the Atrium. Eventually they move us to the Ensemble Lounge, where people would have cocktails before or after dinner. We did that on just about every Celebrity ship. I fussed and fussed so much. I said, "I need to have some lights, we are in the dark; we need to be seen. We need a stage. I guess Celebrity got tired of me fussing because they finally constructed a proper stage for us. Ever since then its gotten better and better from there."

Manny moved to Royal Caribbean, Celebrity's sister cruise line brand which has a live jazz club on each of the Oasis-class ships called Jazz On 4. "Which is strictly my lounge; I'm in charge of the jazz lounge. It's a mini show room. I do three shows each night. This is what I am all about; the guests are on vacation and they come out looking to be entertained and not have to worry about anything. They come to the jazz lounge and I give them what they came to hear—strictly jazz, nothing but jazz. Pure music, no computers, no soundtracks, no nothing. We are playing real live jazz." Manny has been the resident jazz artist on each of the successive Oasis-class ships that get launched as the largest cruise ship in the world. The reigning size champ and the newest in Royal Caribbean's fleet, *Symphony of the Seas,* is Manny's home ship (until Royal Caribbean launches their 5th Oasis-class ship in 2021 joining respectively, *Oasis, Harmony, Allure,* and *Symphony of the Seas.*)

Manny Kellough Jazz Experience on *Symphony of the Seas*: Ross Nixon, Piano; Justin Peterson, Bass; Janine Gilbert-Carter, Vocals; Manny Kellough, Drummer and Bandleader.

In total, Manny has sailed over 80 cruises. I asked him to recap the cruise lines he has been on. Manny laughed, "Other than the slave ship?" (Referring to that ill-fated trip to France with the Rhythm Rebellion and having to work his way back home!) "Seriously, just Princess, Celebrity, and Royal Caribbean." Manny loves to cruise, especially to Alaska. Manny said, "I love cruising myself; I get a chance to visit the lounges and be incognito and not have to let anyone know I am there and sit down and have a cocktail and not have to worry about anything and be entertained for a change. I especially love cruising to Alaska; between taking the cruise and then in Alaska taking the train trips is what I like to do. I say to those that have never cruised: there's nothing like it. Everything is just there for you, they wait on you hand and foot. The service is impeccable, it's the only way to go."

In addition to his many cruises to Alaska, Manny has been to Greece, Israel, Panama, Egypt and other countries in Africa. What's on your bucket list I ask Manny. "A cruise that I have not done, which Royal Caribbean is now offering is a cruise to Dubai. That is one I really would like to do."

When I conducted the interview with Manny in September 2018 he had just returned from yet another cruise to Alaska. This one was a personal vacation; it was on the Royal Caribbean *Explorer of the Seas* where Manny and Jan were celebrating Manny's 70th birthday, and 57th year behind the drum set. Happy 70th birthday to truly a legendary musician and a passionate cruiser!

"Having cruise ship passengers leave my lounge with a smile on your face, makes me feel good knowing that you are digging what I'm giving you."

LECTURES AND LUXURY

The auditorium of the *Crystal Serenity* full of affluent, mostly senior passengers of the ultra-luxury 980-passenger cruise ship was abuzz with anticipation for the featured guest speaker, Ruth Westheimer, the German-born Jew who escaped the Holocaust (her parents perished at Auschwitz) and who immigrated to the United States to become the internationally known sexologist and media personality known as Dr. Ruth. The diminutive, octogenarian Dr. Ruth bounded onto the stage. "I want everybody to stand up. I want everybody to repeat after me: o-rrr-gasm," Dr. Ruth said with her distinctive accent and trademark rolling of her r's. Then she said "I want everybody to say, E-rrr-ection." If you are blushing as you read this, then you probably have never seen Dr. Ruth on television! By the way, Dr. Ruth was not the only well-known octogenarian onboard that day. *Crystal Serenity* is the ship that Lee Wachtstetter, also know as Mama Lee, has famously lived on for the past ten years—at a cost of approximately $170,000 a year.

Dr. Ruth was onboard the *Serenity* as part of the Crystal Visions enrichment lecture and seminar program which brings guest lecturers onboard. Crystal Visions speakers have included Hugh Downs, Marlin Fitzwater, Johnny Bench, James Carville and Mary Matalin, Jack Hanna and other media stars, athletes, diplomats, military leaders, scientists, authors, and subject-matter-experts like Thomas Eastwood of Estero, Florida. Tom was in the audience when Dr. Ruth spoke. He was onboard the 14 day Christmas/New Years cruise to give talks of his own during the cruise about, respectively, Spies and Espionage, WWII Codebreaking, and Interrogations and Polygraphs. Tom lectures regularly for cruise lines that offer enrichment programming like Crystal Visions.

Tom told me, "I always aspire to be the most memorable speaker on the ship, which is quite an ambitious objective because some of the speakers are fairly renown. There are usually two to six speakers depending on the length of the cruise. The speakers might be comprised of an accomplished dignitary or cultural or corporate leader, a scientist of repute, and a celebrity like Dr. Ruth. I knew on this cruise I was not going to be the most memorable."

My daughter Shornay learning how to make sushi on the *Anthem of the Seas*.

Cruise passengers have ample opportunities to satisfy their physical needs and wants ranging from the relaxing—the serenity of the gentle rocking on the ocean and the many opportunities a cruise presents for chilling and pampering, to the frenetic—zip lines, water-slides, go karts, surfing and skydiving simulators, fitness centers and more on the ship, and off the ship, shore excursions where a traveler can hike, ride scooters, snorkel, scuba dive and swim with dolphins. Less apparent is that cruising offers passengers enrichment opportunities to nourish the mind and soul. Virtually all cruise lines provide some kind of enrichment opportunities from sushi making classes, and computer and internet classes; to lectures about Cuban culture on Cuba itineraries and seminars about the history, construction, and operations of the Panama Canal on Panama Canal itineraries.

The more upscale the cruise line is the more extensive the enrichment opportunities are, and the ultimate in enrichment offerings are on the six-star cruise lines such as the aforementioned Crystal Cruises along with Azamara Club Cruises, Hapag-Lloyd Cruises, Oceania Cruises, Regent Seven Seas Cruises, Seabourn Cruise Line, Silversea Cruises, and Viking Ocean Cruises. The six-star ultra luxury cruise lines feature smaller ships, capacity for 100 to 1250 cruisers, and exemplary service with a staff to passenger ratio of less than two-to-one. Six-star cruises are virtually completely all-inclusive—sometimes airfare, and always exotic itineraries, excursions, and onboard dining, alcohol and activities, and appeal to a more affluent, slightly older demographic than mainstream cruising, and children onboard are a relative rarity. Six-star cruise prices can start in the low five figures and go into six figures for a world cruise—not including optional helicopter rides, or the private jet for up to 44 cruisers offered by Hapag-Lloyd!

Tom lectures almost exclusively on "six-star" or ultra-luxury cruise lines; essentially every six-star cruise line that sails from the United States. In addition to lecturing frequently on Crystal, Tom has spoken often on Azamara; he has done most of his lecturing on Regent Seven Seas; Seabourn, and in January 2019 Tom will accomplish one of his professional bucket list items by lecturing on Silversea Cruises. Tom and his significant other, Elaine Cawley, will do a 10-day Western Caribbean cruise on the intimate 296-passenger Silversea *Silver Wind* where Tom will deliver five lectures including "Churchill's Secret Army" and "Presidential Assassinations." Tom has also lectured many times on Celebrity Cruises and got his first opportunity to lecture on a cruise ship in 2002 on the Norwegian Cruise Lines *Sun*.

Tom has "performed"—contracts refer to lecturers as performers—dozens of times, presenting on topics relating to espionage and counterintelligence, interrogations, and US and Allied intelligence operations during WWII, drawing on his extensive background as a retired special agent and managerial employee with the United States Treasury Department (Bureau of Alcohol, Tobacco and Firearms; and, Internal Revenue Service) and as an executive with the Department of Defense. Tom, who calls himself a "retired T man," delivers over 150 lectures yearly. Most are on land where he is engaged by clubs, libraries, up-scale communities in Southwest Florida, and a university. However, Tom describes his lectures at sea as "my most enjoyable gigs."

Tom's cruise history began in 1990 with a cruise for leisure on Norwegian Cruise Lines. Tom says it was not an ideal experience. Among other things it was on one of NCL oldest ships that has since been retired. Nevertheless, cruising immediately had a particular appeal to the government agent. Tom says the main reason he took to cruising is because it was the one place he could not be reached. "When I was a special agent, I was on call 24 hour a day. There was no place I could go where the government could not reach me—with one exception, and that is on a cruise. In those days there were no cell phones. You did have ship-to-shore radio, but it was tremendously expensive. Even the government is not going to call me on a ship unless it is a dire emergency. So cruising gave me the opportunity to unplug completely." In addition, Tom had met Elaine, who had cruised extensively in her past life as a model. With cruising's appeal to them both, coupled with their mutual love of dance which was regularly available to them on cruise ships, cruising developed into a passion for Tom.

Tom and Elaine boarding the *Seabourn Pride*.

In total, Tom has sailed on 130 cruises all over the world— 100 of the cruises were as a performer. He has sailed on 10 cruise lines besides the aforementioned six-star lines: Celebrity, Royal

Caribbean, NCL, Holland American, Majesty Cruise Line and more. Currently, Tom and Elaine cruise about three times a year, mostly in the Caribbean. "Our favorite ships are on Regent Seven Seas: the *Voyager*, and the *Navigator*." They are also fond of the *Crystal Symphony* and *Serenity*. Tom and Elaine closed out their cruising in 2018 with a leisure cruise to the Western Caribbean on *Celebrity Infinity* in November.

Besides the higher end furnishings and decor, all-inclusive nature of most amenities, and the relatively smaller size, Tom pointed out one contrasting feature of the six-star lines versus the mainstream lines that was somewhat surprising to me, having never experienced six-star cruising. "One of the unique things about the six-star cruise lines is that they employ gentlemen dance hosts. Usually four to six are hired to dance with women on the ship. They are sophisticated, often retired, and good social dancers. Their "job" is to dance with single women on the ship, or married women whose husbands don't want to dance. They also host social functions such as dinners and shore excursions. For every one of the six-star cruise lines, dance is a very significant component because you will have 60 or 70 single people onboard, mostly single women who want to dance. Dance is a major enjoyment for many guests on these lines. Dozens of passengers dance before and after dinner. Ballroom dances are the norm: rhumbas, foxtrots, waltzes, tangos, cha cha, etc. "Elaine and I love ballroom dancing, so when I go on the six-star lines I get to combine two joys—dance and work. We are not professional dancers, but it is one of the many things we enjoy about cruising."

Tom's first opportunity to lecture on a cruise ship was in 2002. Tom recalls his entree into cruise ship lecturing. He had been giving some thought to what he was going to do after he retired from the government. As he had developed a passion for cruising with Elaine in the 1990's, Tom gave some consideration into getting into cruise ship security, perhaps becoming a director of security for one of the cruise lines. Tom pursued cruise ship lecturing after being a passenger on *Celebrity Century*. "One of the speakers was a gentleman who was a self-made millionaire and was talking about the way that he made his money. We were about five minutes into the lecture and I turned to Elaine and said 'I can do better than this with no preparation.' The speaker was well-informed; he just did not know how to present material well. He was not a speaker. I was a senior executive so I did a lot of public speaking. So that's what put the thought in my head that maybe when I retire one of the things I want to do is be a speaker on cruise ships, and I began researching how you do that. When I retired I got an agent, and NCL hired me for the *Sun* to talk about criminal investigation and interrogations."

Tom points out that getting the first cruise gig is hard, because if the cruise lines don't know you, of course they would be reluctant to hire you. Once you develop a reputation it is easier to get additional work—though many do not—as long as your evaluations are good. "The passengers rate you as does the Cruise Director—you are working for the Cruise Director. Perhaps half of the lecturers don't get invited back. They are all very knowledgeable about their content but are too professorial; that style doesn't work too well on a cruise ship. What you want on a cruise ship is the ability to engage with the audience. You want the ability to not only educate but to entertain. To put that in perspective, a good example is Dr. Ruth. She not only knows her subject matter; she presents it in an entertaining way. There's lots of experts who know sex education but only one Dr. Ruth."

Once you are established as a cruise ship lecturer, a talent agent usually makes the arrangements. They coordinate with the cruise

lines to fill their needs—usually a year in advance. The agent pro-
poses dates and suggested lecture topics which are approved by the
lines. New lecturers must submit sample videos. For known, experienced cruise lecturers like Tom, the process is truncated. He provides his agent with a "wish list." She does the rest.

Typically, lectures are held on sea days, one in the morning and
one in the afternoon, and a lecturer will speak several times on different topics during the cruise. As a lecturer, Tom has departed out
of ports from all over the world. Today he and Elaine tend to have
Florida departures as they don't particularly like to fly.

I asked Tom who are some of the other "performers" that have
been guest lecturers on ships with him. Tom told me two come to
mind immediately: Robert Levy (Chairman, CATO Institute) and
Ambassador Marc Ginsberg. "Ranked golfers, politicians, ambassa-
dors, Apollo astronauts. By the way, the astronauts easily have the
best slides. They show NASA-produced photos."

Tom notes that patrons on the six-star cruise lines are a perfect demographic for his type of topics; older Americans, mostly
Europeans, many Canadians. "Interestingly a lot of the subjects I
teach deal with British intelligence: Special Operations Executive
(SOE), MI5, MI6, and the Brits love this, especially to come on an
American-type cruise line and hear Americans speak about British
subjects that most Americans know very little about. Same thing
with the Canadians. I mention quite a bit about the Canadian efforts
during World War II that related to intelligence—things like Camp
X which was their spy school where they trained Americans; their
code breaking program which most Americans have never heard
of. WWII intelligence, espionage, and codebreaking specific to what
the Brits and other allies did like Bletchley Park and breaking the
German Enigma code. I also get into the Double Cross System—the

World War II British counter-intelligence program. I also will cover interrogations. And then I segue into a more modern day perspective, contemporary topics like how we catch spies, what motivates people to commit espionage, particularly Americans. Those are topics that are tremendously relevant and that the older passengers just love."

Accordingly, Tom attracts sizable audiences and receives positive passenger feedback, important because the only way for a performer—be it a lecturer, lounge singer, or comedian—to get contracted to be invited back by the cruise lines is to get positive evaluations. I asked Tom if he ever tailors his talk because of a particular audience, or are the passengers of these ships always a general cross-section of Americans, Europeans and Canadians. Tom told me he will definitely focus based on his audience. Even though Tom has to submit a synopsis of his talks in advance of the cruise, he will customize his talks based on the audience; so, on the first night of the cruise Tom asks the cruise director to break down the demographics of the passengers. "If I know my audience is principally Brits, I will gear toward the British. I teach a course called Operation Underworld about the cooperation of Italian and Jewish organized crime figures like Lucky Luciano and Meyer Lansky during World War II, which assisted the United States Navy in protecting our docks, and assisting in Operation Husky, the allied invasion of Sicily. So, that course that I teach, the Italians in the audience love because I get into the role the mob played in assisting us in invading Sicily."

Coming up in 2019 after the Silversea *Silver Wind* in January, Tom and Elaine are going on *Celebrity Infinity* again in March 2019 for a family cruise. Then, in November they cruise for 10 days on *Crystal Symphony* where Tom will give a number of lectures. Long-term, Tom aspires to speak on *The World*, an ultra-luxury residential ship of 165 shipboard condominium units. In terms of bucket list destinations Tom would like to go to Alaska, to the Polynesian Islands, and to Australia.

"When I consider some of my passions in life—we enjoy cruising, we enjoy fine dining, we enjoy dancing, and I also enjoy speaking. Doing what I do allows us to combine passions, and we have met some wonderful people over the years."

LAUGHTER ON THE
OCEAN: AJ JAMAL

AJ Jamal is fixture on the *Festival at Sea* African-American Cultural Cruise, having performed on it for the last 10 years. When I attended *Festival at Sea* on the *Celebrity Equinox* in July 2018, I was able to interview AJ in person. It was somewhat difficult to do the interview because I was laughing so hard. He was not necessarily trying to make me laugh; it's just that everything he said, at least the way my mind processed it, was funny to me. His first comment after I explained the premise of *The Joy of Cruising* and noted that it was approximately 60% done, was to ask me how long I had been working on the book. I told him, "Since early this year." He replied, "Wow, that ain't bad. I been trying to write a book for 15 years. I haven't even started."

Because AJ is just naturally funny, at times it wasn't clear to me when he was being serious and when he was being funny. For instance, my first question to him was: "Who is AJ Jamal?" He responded, "I'm AJ Jamal. I am a comedian by nature. Born and raised in Cleveland, Ohio. I have a Masters in Electrical Engineering…." My immediate reaction was, get the $@#* out of here! A master's degree? Of course, I didn't say that out loud. I don't know AJ like that; responding in that way would have been rude and crude. Besides I was familiar enough with AJ to know that he is a clean comedian and had I verbalized my instant reaction that could very well have been insulting to him and made the rest of the interview awkward or even cut short. In the ensuing split second I'm thinking maybe he is messing with me—I just didn't know if he was being serious. Let me be clear, there is nothing that says comedians can't be very accomplished academically and I have heard about some who are. It's just that in the few hours from when I first met AJ and requested to chat with him and the time we had set for the interview, in the little research I was able to do I had not learned of his degree. And I recalled nothing in his act over the years, as well as the couple of times I had seen him perform on this cruise that hinted at him having such an impressive academic background. AJ continued, ".... I was a computer engineer with IBM. IBM told me I need to be in comedy. I honestly asked them 'we got a comedy division?' They said no. So I said, are you trying to tell me I need to leave the company? They said yeah. So that's what happened, and I started doing comedy."

AJ's very first open microphone opportunity at a comedy club happened to be hosted by fellow Cleveland native Drew Carrey, then an up-and-coming comedian on his way to becoming a superstar actor, comedian and game show host. "I won that competition; $50 and get to come back and host the next one. That was in 1986." In 1987 *It's Showtime at the Apollo* premiered, and AJ began appearing frequently on the weekly show broadcast from Harlem, New York's famous Apollo Theater featuring performances from stars as well as up-and-coming music and comedy artists. After *It's Showtime at the Apollo*, AJ made a number of television appearances in the early nineties including the groundbreaking HBO comedy series *Def Comedy Jam.* AJ became a featured performer on the short-lived but iconic sketch comedy series, *In Living Color*, in 1993, the fourth season of its five season run. That same year AJ hosted and co-wrote the ACE Award-nominated *Comic Justice* series on the Comedy Central Network. AJ's rich body of work in the nineties led to a couple of decades of steady appearances on television such as *The Tonight Show with Jay Leno*, and *The Arsenio Hall Show*, and live performances ranging from small venues, even churches, to Radio City Hall. AJ has acted in films, and through his own animation company, Green Machine Films, has created and been writer, producer and done voice-over work in animated programming. In 2000 AJ wrote and directed a movie, *The Cheapest Movie Ever Made.* Yet, despite garnering a reputation of one of the hardest working comedians around, AJ has found a performing niche usually thought of as relaxing, slow-moving, and tranquil: cruising.

Initially, AJ just occasionally performed on theme cruises. Then one day, someone he knew who had left Royal Caribbean to go to work for an agency that books talent for cruise ships called him and asked if he had ever considered performing on cruise ships. He told them that he already had performed from time-to-time on specialty cruises. The booking agency told him they were not talking about those occasional cruises where you are hired by the theme cruise company, but rather regular cruises that sail each week and you work for the cruise line. AJ responded that he hadn't thought about doing that. The booking agency suggested he try a week and see how he liked it. AJ tried a week and found it to be a nice experience. So the booking agency asked AJ if they could send him some more weeks to pick from. AJ agreed that the booking agency could send him some weeks for him to consider. "So they sent over a whole year—52 weeks of work. A calendar with different ships for 52 weeks! And I must have picked about 40 of them!" I said to AJ, "Wow, all that good eating; how do you maintain your weight?" AJ replied, "Weight? Look at this stomach. Man I had an ultrasound last week!" (Once again I had no idea whether AJ was being serious or not.)

AJ Jamal. After chatting with him for an hour I can't
look at this photo without laughing!

So, AJ started performing on cruise ships, almost exclusively. "People in Hollywood said 'AJ, you need to come back. People are wondering where you at.' I told them, man, these ships…there's something about them…." He seemed momentarily lost for words in his amazement at his surroundings as he looked around the area of the *Equinox* where we were sitting with its scenic view of the ocean. I interjected, "This is the life." AJ exclaimed, "Man, this is the life! There's things about these ships…that go with things about AJ Jamal: I'm not a Hollywood person. I like peace, tranquility, and I like the ocean…I like that vibe. So when you get on the ship, there's a lot of things that I love. And it takes you places that your mind can take you…but a ship can take you places physically. So I started doing ship gigs, and it became so secure. One month became a year, and then four years, and now six years. I'm away from the house 300 days a year, either traveling to a ship, getting off a ship, or on the ocean. So now I do the ships and it's an amazing getaway. For one thing, it's safe. There's no guns on the ship."

AJ then turned his discussion specifically to the *Festival at Sea* African-American cultural cruise we were on. "It is such a family environment. To some people this is their extended family. I mean they may not have another family." I agreed with AJ, telling him, this was my first *Festival at Sea* experience and when I got on the cruise, the word that quickly came to mind was family. I told him it reminds me of Essence Music Festival. The feeling of family and cultural celebration reminds me of Essence Music Festival. Held annually in New Orleans on the weekend closest to the 4th of July, Essence is the nation's premier R&B music festival featuring dozens of concert performances at night, and African-American empowerment events during the daytime. I said to AJ, *Festival at Sea* is like Essence on the ocean. He responded, "That's a good concept—Essence on the ocean. I love Essence. Four times I hosted Essence. You walk out on the stage… all my life I have been doing comedy; when I walk out on a stage, I am in a zone. It's like I am talking to you in a living room. Essence was the first time in my comedy career my mind snapped out of that zone and went into…AJ Jamal where are you at? Comedians can talk to the audience and be thinking about a different subject: what bit I didn't do; what am I going to do next; it is like they are on autopilot. For the first time in my life I looked around and I go AJ, there's 65,000 people in front of you. What are you doing? And then I snapped back into my thing and when I walked off stage I said 'that was deep.' I never felt like I was performing for 65,000 people. When I go out on stage it's like I am performing for you in my living room. Essence loved me. For one thing I always stayed clean. That's why I do the cruise ships. I can do family. I like family. I can do churches. What you saw me do last night (at *Festival at Sea*), that was my so-called dirty show and I don't even curse for that. On cruise ships, there are kids at most of the shows…and they love me for that on the ships. Essence was the same way."

"Another thing about cruise ships, I am still one of the youngest things on a ship. So, as I am doing comedy the cruisers on the ship are older than me. I use to do a lot of college shows. I've outgrown college and the millennials. Same with some of the other venues. The crowds are getting younger and I am getting older. But the ships, people are 'in my ballpark.' The people appreciate me. You know I used to do the Catskills; all older, mainly Jewish people. And they were so nervous. They would say you're not like Eddie Murphy or Richard Pryor are you? I would say no—I am a cross-over comedian. Well the ships are the same way. They provide my audience without them being in fear of me alienating them—just like those folks in the Catskills. Cruising people are my audience. They are sophisticated, got a little money, they don't like cursing, and they don't like that crazy stuff. The ship audience appreciates me so much, so it's hard for me to leave. Even though I may not be making the money…the gratitude is tremendous. I probably could make double the money on land, but I won't be doubly as happy."

I asked AJ if he does any performing on land anymore. He told me just a few engagements. "I don't miss Hollywood. I was in Hollywood for 20 years, and I never was a Hollywood person. I just did that because that was the progression of the way you go," AJ said. I asked AJ if he does clubs anymore, or anything on land. Just a few, he told me. He said even when he regularly worked on land, he rarely did comedy clubs. He opened up for a lot of major music stars in concert appearances. So much so that the book he was considering writing was to be called *Opening Act.* "I opened up for Ray Charles, Aretha Franklin, the Temptations. Cher's biggest tour was called the Hearts of Stone Tour. I was the opening act. The reason being because I was clean, and they knew I wouldn't offend the audience. Diana Ross fired her comedian on the first night. They called me up in Atlanta and said 'AJ you have to fly here right away, Diana Ross fired her comedian. He went out on stage making fun of the audience. She needs a comic and she needs him tomorrow.' I came up on stage and they loved me. I became friends with Diana's kids and everything."

I asked AJ, outside of *Festival at Sea*, what cruise lines is he currently working with. "I do Princess; I was nominated as Entertainer of the Year on Princess Cruises." Annually, Princess Cruises does a sort of theme cruise called *The Entertainer of the Year Cruise*, where cruisers choose the winner of Princess Entertainer of the Year from among the singers, comedians, magicians, tribute bands and other specialty acts selected by Princess as finalists for Entertainer of the Year. AJ performed as a 2015 finalist on the March, 2016 *The Entertainer of the Year Cruise* on the *Caribbean Princess* cruise to the Western Caribbean. "I do Royal Caribbean; I perform on Celebrity." Besides being a featured performer on regular cruises, AJ occasionally does other theme cruises like *Festival at Sea*. In 2019 AJ will be a featured comedian on the *Soul Train Cruise.*

I told AJ I originally planned to get a quote or two from him to include in *The Joy of Cruising's* chapter on *Festival at Sea* given his role as its comedian on this cruise. However, as a result of our engaging conversation, I learned of his passion for cruising and that the cruising life is so much a part of him, and that's what *The Joy of Cruising* is really all about. I told AJ, "I did not know you cruise this much. You're pretty much just doing cruises now." AJ told me, "300 days a year. I know because I counted them. You know how I know? I told Jessica (his wife) I didn't get my check this week. I looked at my calendar. I worked 28 days in July, so that means there was only three days I was off. I do a week where I may perform two days. So the rest of the week I am cruising. I can't even do a land gig. I don't want to cancel a cruise gig, because it is such steady work. And, to top things off, I'm booked to 2020." For the little time that he is home AJ lives in Rancho Cucamonga, California with Jessica, his wife of 12 years.

I ask AJ what he has coming up in the remainder of 2018 and 2019. He said, "I really don't even know what's coming up until the day before we get off a ship and I check my calendar. It's so funny because I do so many ships, I don't know where we going. Tomorrow I become a regular cruiser. I will get off in Grand Cayman, fly to Vegas to be on a show with George Wallace, and then I fly right back to get on Royal Caribbean *Harmony of the Seas*. And then we fly to Barcelona to get on another ship."

I close by pointing out to AJ that since *The Joy of Cruising* is about passion for cruising, I want to tell readers a little about his cruising history. He obviously has been on far more cruises than most, even most of the avid cruisers profiled in *The Joy of Cruising*. I asked him to tell me a little about his personal cruising history— when was his first cruise, before he ever got involved with performing on cruise ships. "I have never been on a cruise I paid for," AJ told me. "My first cruise was to perform, about 15 years ago, on the Tom Joyner cruise." Tom Joyner is a renown nationally syndicated radio personality and his annual *Tom Joyner Fantastic Voyage Cruise* featuring dozens of R&B, hip-hop, and comedy performers is one of the world's leading theme cruises. In total, in only 15 years' time AJ has cruised somewhere between 300-400 times.

Wow. Doing what you want to do, comedy, for people who appreciate you immensely, and oh by the way, getting to see the world all while on the world's grandest cruise ships!

The Joy of Cruising Reprise

THE HOLIDAYS

A number of contributors to *The Joy of Cruising* are from Europe, and I have learned that for them "holiday" is synonymous with "vacation" in the United States. In this instance, I am using "holidays" in a US context, specifically my Christmas 2018 family cruise including my wife Cheryl, daughters Kina and Shornay, Kina's husband Lance, and my grandchildren 14-year old Kalen and 9-year old LaKi. Booking that cruise was ultimately the impetus for *The Joy of Cruising*. It was during the research process for the Christmas 2018 family cruise that the idea of writing a book about cruising was crystallized.

In a lot of ways, the addiction to cruising many feel after just one or two cruises is similar to what many grandparents experience upon being blessed with grandkids. Much of what Cheryl and I do is with the grandkids in mind, and that is particularly true when it comes to cruising. I booked the Christmas 2018 cruise on *Anthem of the Seas*, immediately following Christmas 2017, the first time Cheryl and I got to spend Christmas with our grandchildren since relocating from the northeast for a career opportunity in Southwest

Florida. It was a surprise for my grandchildren when we knocked on their door Christmas morning 2017. The sentiment we felt and that my grandchildren expressed as my daughters and son-in-law watched was one of sheer joy, and we immediately began pondering how we could replicate that feeling in Christmas 2018.

I booked *Anthem* some 360 days prior to embarkation; on Christmas Day 2018 we would be frolicking on the beach in Coco Cay, Bahamas. Besides being one of the best ways a cruise enthusiast might choose to celebrate the holidays, this was going to allow me to fulfill another longtime nostalgic aspiration of mine. 30 years ago Cheryl and I had taken my preteen daughters, Kina and Shornay, to Disney World in Orlando, Florida one Christmas. We took a photo of Kina and Shornay in the pool in the 85-degree weather at our Disney resort on Christmas Day. It was a fun photo to show off to friends and relatives up north where we were used to a white Christmas, or at least frigid temperatures. When Cheryl and I moved to Florida, I vowed to do the next generation version of that photo with my grandkids on Christmas Day at Disney World but have not been able to get the grandkids to Florida for Christmas yet. A photo of Christmas Day in the ocean in the Bahamas was going to be even better!

The moment after I booked the Christmas 2018 cruise I started planning. I wanted the cruise to be a perfect, once-in-a-lifetime Christmas gift for the family, so I researched kids' clubs, activities, excursions, food and drink, etc. Moreover, the cruise was going to be a surprise for my grandchildren, so I spent a little time seemingly everyday working on the logistics of air and ground transportation, and hotels involving three states—Florida, Delaware, New Jersey—without divulging the surprise. For the next 360 days I got to daydream about the look on the grandkids' faces when they got in the car with their parents, not knowing where they were headed, and then receiving two surprises. First, finding out they are going on a cruise for Christmas, and then learning that Cheryl and I were up from Florida to join them on *Anthem of the Seas.* You know, grandparents stuff!

We first got the idea of a cruise with the grandkids for Christmas a couple years earlier. In 2016, just a few days before Christmas Day, Cheryl and I were feeling a bit sorry for ourselves for having an empty house again at Christmas and decided on an impulse to go on a short Caribbean cruise leaving a couple of days before Christmas. The cruise was on *Norwegian Sky,* which had a decidedly funky, anything goes vibe because it had ushered in open-bar all the time to mainstream cruising, and it had no dress code other than the requirement you had to wear some. It sounded like Hedonism in Jamaica, which first attracted me to the all-inclusive resorts I used to frequent. While *Norwegian Sky* was often a booze-cruise more adult-oriented party atmosphere when kids are in school, I learned that wasn't the case for Christmas. I was surprised at how many families with children were on the *Sky.* And the décor, staff, and special events were festive with Christmas decorations and events. To see all those kids and families and the Christmas spirit throughout the ship, we began to acutely miss our grandkids while on the cruise. The good thing is, the idea of a Christmas cruise was planted.

Another very significant thing happened during those months leading up to the *Anthem* cruise. Planning for the family cruise closely parallels the genesis of *The Joy of Cruising.* In my research for our cruises in previous years I voraciously browsed every information source I knew of in anticipation of booking; once booked, my browsing was motivated by fantasizing and escapism, plus a search for validation of my decision. So I scoured my sources often, sometimes multiple times a day. The days following Christmas 2017 when

I booked *Anthem*, I commenced my regular visits to cruise-related social media, blogs, internet discussion forums, YouTube and wherever else I could soak up information. I couldn't help but notice—particularly as a casual cruiser—just how passionate many were about cruising. By March 2018, I was moved to write the first words of *The Joy of Cruising*.

By December 2018 *The Joy of Cruising* was virtually complete and I planned to write the final chapter during the cruise. Friday December 21, embarkation day finally arrived. My grandkids couldn't understand why they were not going to school. With a ruse of driving from their home in Delaware to New York to my mom's house, the grandkids and my oldest daughter and son-in-law drove up to my younger daughter's office in New Jersey ostensibly to pick her up en route. In the lobby of the office building my grandkids were given a giant Christmas card which announced the cruise and contained photos of all the Anthem fun activities—bumper cars, surfing and skydiving simulators, rock climbing wall, and so on. My wife and I could see all of the high fives and jumping up and down through the dark tinted windows from a limo parked outside the lobby as the grandkids got the first surprise. The second surprise was when they came out to the limo and my wife and I were sitting inside.

The Christmas vacation was everything I had fantasized it would be. After experiencing cruising vicariously through the stories of 32 other passionate cruisers as I wrote the book, I received my own ultimate realization of *The Joy of Cruising*.

ABOUT THE AUTHOR

Paul C. Thornton is originally from Brooklyn and Long Island, New York. *The Joy of Cruising* is Paul's second book, a stark departure from his first: *White Man's Disease*, a memoir described as "gripping and inspiring" in the press release announcing it as the winner of the North Street Book Prize, about Paul's harrowing brush with death, journey of recovery from trauma, resilience and ultimately transformation. *White Man's Disease* is at once poignant, sad, tragic and funny. Despite their very different subjects, at the heart of both *White Man's Disease* and *The Joy of Cruising* is passion and how passionate people do wondrous things.

Paul lives in Fort Myers, Florida with his wife Cheryl and considers cruising with their grandchildren life's ultimate escape. Paul longs to cruise as much as the people he writes about in *The Joy of Cruising*.